The Adversaries

Also by Michael Balfour
Propaganda in War

Michael Balfour

The Adversaries

America, Russia and the Open World 1941–62

Routledge & Kegan Paul
London, Boston and Henley

First published in 1981
by Routledge & Kegan Paul Ltd
39 Store Street,
London WC1E 7DD,
9 Park Street,
Boston, Mass. 02108, USA, and
Broadway House,
Newtown Road,
Henley-on-Thames,
Oxon RG9 1EN
Set in 11 on 12pt Plantin by
Computacomp (UK) Ltd
Fort William, Scotland
and printed in Great Britain by
Redwood Burn Ltd
Trowbridge & Esher
© Michael Balfour 1981

British Library Cataloguing in Publication Data

Balfour, Michael, b. 1908
The adversaries.
1. History, Modern − 20th century
I. Title
909.82'4   D842.5   80−41559

ISBN 0 7100 0687 X

The great mistakes of history tend to be made not through ignoring the lessons of the past but through retaining habits of thought which under changed conditions are disastrous and the difficulty lies, not only in preserving the required elasticity of mind to cope with new conditions but in realizing when in fact conditions are new.

Michael Howard

Contents

Contents

Preface

Jakob Burckhardt stands for me in the front rank of historians. He saw the importance of power in society without being awed into admiring all its results. I realise also why he warned us against the terrifying simplifiers. Yet I believe that there is a stage in writing history when simplification has its uses. As the present recedes into the past, there is at first too much to take in; one cannot tell what is going to prove of real significance and what is not. But as soon as one can begin to assess past events in perspective, the first step towards understanding is to arrange them in some sort of overall framework. As time goes on, many modifications and qualifications will be necessary but, if the arranger is dispassionate and alert, there is a chance that his simplification will continue for some time to be accepted as illuminating.

The present book seeks to provide such an interpretative framework for the period from the early 1940s to the early 1960s, in the belief that a pattern is beginning to be visible in that period which it is still too early to look for with any confidence in later years. The starting-point is the moment at which it became reasonable to think that Germany was not after all going to win the war, thus justifying the serious preparation of plans for the post-war world. In the framing of these plans, the United States played the dominant role, as the possessor of dominant power. They sought to restore, with only minor changes, the open world of which the Enlightenment had dreamed in the eighteenth century and the Liberals in the nineteenth. Though the British had by 1939 become somewhat disillusioned about the practicability of such a world, many of us still used it as a model and in any case we were in no position to oppose the country on which our existence in freedom and prosperity depended.

The Americans made two big mistakes; they underestimated the size of the task and they overestimated the readiness of the Russians to work with them. By 1947 they seemed to be on the verge of failure. But a second attempt was more successful and by 1960 they had established a wide degree of political and economic freedom over half the world. Their faith in the system had been justified by the unprecedented affluence of that half-world. But they had only succeeded at the cost of clashing with the other half of the world which rejected their aims and proved too strong to be forced into compliance. This antagonism made the United Nations ineffective as the organ of world government for which it was intended, even though it retained value as a meeting-place. Was the clash of views bound to end in nuclear war or could the two halves learn to co-exist? By the end of 1962, after the Berlin and Cuba crises, there were reasonable, if tentative, grounds for answering that question optimistically. Accordingly it is at this climacteric that the narrative part of the book ends.

I have added a final chapter in which I have tried to discuss, or at any rate list, some questions which its predecessors seem to me to raise, including that of the extent to which economic growth is a desirable aim. This has inevitably taken me beyond my time-limits; it can be regarded as the synopsis of a book which I do not intend to write. Some may think such a conclusion inappropriate, others wrong-headed. But though the first seven chapters make an intelligible whole by themselves, they are open to the criticism of neglecting the wider issues.

I have tried throughout to avoid using the words 'capitalist' and 'Capitalism' (except where I was reproducing Marxist standpoints) because they seem to me to obscure a vital point. All states and economies are 'capitalist' in the sense that they all save some part of their current spending power and devote it, not to current consumption, but to providing the means of producing more for future consumption. This is after all how the world has advanced to its current standards of life. In this sense the Soviet Union is more capitalist than the United States, in that it saves a higher proportion of its income for use as capital. The crucial difference between systems lies in who owns the savings, who determines how they are used, and who receives any profit resulting from their use. Most writers who use the term 'Capitalism' mean of course the system of private rather than communal or collective or public ownership.

This is more than a matter of semantics. For in the campaign to get private ownership and private aggrandisement superseded, 'capitalism' has become a dirty word while 'profits', which are such an important source of saving, have come to be regarded as something disreputable which should be kept at a low level. But, on my reading of history, the prosperity of the world and its inhabitants is closely bound up with the maintenance of a high level of investment, which calls for both capital and profits. I realise that a number of qualifications have to be made to this broad principle and I have mentioned some of them in the final chapter. But if the world is to prosper, then in my view one of our most urgent tasks is to rethink our attitude towards these terms and realise that the activities which they describe are not bad in themselves but depend on the use to which they are put.

In another direction, I am aware of the thesis that the system in which capital is owned privately is not entitled to describe itself as a 'free' society because, although its members may be politically independent, a large proportion of them are dependent economically. To discuss this thesis adequately, however, would involve considering how far anyone can be said to be 'free' and what kinds of freedom are most important. But my book is not a treatise on political science or ethics or theology and I have employed the terms 'free', 'free enterprise' and 'the Free World' as convenient labels whose application is generally understood.

As the book's aim is to indicate how the events described in it can be seen as hanging together, it makes no attempt to include all the things which a well-informed person should know about the period. Throughout my life chance circumstances have led me (like most people!) to interest myself in certain subjects rather than others and it is usually prudent to avoid discussing matters about which one is ignorant. During the period covered by this book, there were many things going on outside the fields surveyed in it which were likely to have important influences on the fate of mankind. But, with certain exceptions like the Korean war, I feel that they still had not developed to the point at which they exerted an immediate major influence on world events.

It is notoriously difficult to tell an ongoing story in which a number of things are happening concurrently; as a result, no way of arranging the material can be wholly satisfactory. As will be seen from the list of Contents, I have adopted a system of sub-sections devoted to individual topics within a general chronological framework. But I have not hesitated to go outside the dates of any chapter if I considered that by so doing I could make comprehension easier.

It occurred to me that I might lighten a text which, in the interests of brevity, is rather closely packed if I illustrated it not by pictures but by a variety of quotations and anecdotes. They have been printed in a distinctive type so as to make clear that they are not part of the text.

It may be of interest to say that, of the persons mentioned in this book, I encountered, in the role of cat looking at king, Khrushchev, Mikoyan, Adenauer, Erhard, Attlee, Bevin, Macmillan, Butler, Churchill and Franks. During the period covered by the book, I spent a considerable time in Germany and visited briefly the United States, Canada, the Soviet Union, Finland, Sweden, Denmark, Yugoslavia, Austria, Italy, Switzerland, Holland, Belgium, France, Spain, Portugal, Algeria, Syria, the Lebanon and India. I was throughout the period employed by the British Government but not in positions where I had access to any particularly confidential information. Of course I did not at the time of the events have all the information or hold all the views which I do now.

The book was read in draft by Sir Alec Cairncross and Miss Elisabeth Barker, while Miss Marie Rossi played the part of guinea-pig student. The final result has been much improved by their suggestions but I am alone responsible for the mistakes, misjudgments and misapprehensions in which it undoubtedly abounds especially as I did not always see my way to acting on their advice. Professor James Meade and Mr Redvers Opie advised me about the expectations held during the war as to Soviet readiness for international economic co-operation after it. Professor H. G. Nicholas and Mr J. C. Furnas advised me about the United States. Sir Duncan Wilson was kind enough to let me read his book *Tito's Yugoslavia* in proof. Mr K. A. D. Inglis of British Petroleum helpfully provided the information on which the table on p. 116 is based. I am very much indebted to my wife and Mrs Janet Caldwell for typing my drafts.

Burford   M.L.G.B.
5 November 1979

Abbreviations

BRD	Bundesrepublik Deutschland = Federal Republic of Germany
CDU	Christlich-Demokratische Union = Christian Democratic Union
Comecon	Council for Mutual Economic Assistance (English title)
CSU	Christlich-Soziale Union = Christian Social Union (Bavarian counterpart of CDU)
DDR	Deutsche Demokratische Republik = German Democratic Republic
ECA	Economic Co-operation Administration
ECSC	European Coal and Steel Community
EDC	European Defence Community
EEC	European Economic Community
EFTA	European Free Trade Association
EPU	European Payments Union
Euratom	European Atomic Energy Community
FDP	Freie Demokratische Partei = Free Democratic Party
FNL	Front National de la Libération (of Algeria)
GATT	General Agreement on Tariffs and Trade
IMF	International Monetary Fund
ITO	International Trade Organisation
MRP	Mouvement Républicain Populaire
NATO	North Atlantic Treaty Organisation
OECD	Organisation for Economic Co-operation and Development
OEEC	Organisation for European Economic Co-operation
SED	Sozialistische Einheitspartei = Socialist Unity Party
SPD	Sozialdemokratische Partei Deutschlands = German Social Democratic Party
UN	United Nations
UNRRA	United Nations Relief and Rehabilitation Administration
WEU	Western European Union

N.B. $1 billion = $1,000,000,000

My creed is the American creed. ... I believe in freedom of religion, freedom of speech, freedom of thought, freedom of the press, freedom of criticism and freedom of movement. I believe in the goal of equality of opportunity and the right of each individual to follow the calling of his or her own choice, and the right of every individual to develop his or her capacity to the fullest. ... I am opposed to arbitrary and unwarranted use of power or authority from whatever source or against any individual or group.

I believe in a government of law, not of men, where the law is above any man and not any man above the law.

> Part of the statement made on 13 August 1948 to the House of Representatives Committee on Un-American Activities by Harry Dexter White, in answer to the charge that he had passed confidential information to a Russian spy ring

I would not be frank with you if I did not say that America believes in free enterprise. We believe neither in monopolies nor in cartels in restraint of trade. We are convinced that we have attained a high standard of living for our people through a system of free enterprise. Nevertheless, as strongly as my country believes in free enterprise, it believes even more strongly in democracy.

> General Lucius D. Clay, US Military Governor in Germany, to the Council of the *Länder* in the US Zone, 9 September 1947

CHAPTER 1

1941-5

1 The signing of the Atlantic Charter

Cynics declared that Roosevelt and Churchill only published the Atlantic Charter on 14 August 1941 because they had to say something to the world about the four days which they had spent together in the foggy recesses of Newfoundland but could not talk about the military plans which they had really discussed without revealing secrets to the enemy and getting into political hot water at home. Such criticism was however as imperceptive as it was uncharitable. Both statesmen had good reasons for wanting to produce a scrap of paper; each was concerned to deny full satisfaction to the other. Churchill hoped to commit the United States to entering the war; he had to rest content with a document which took 'the final destruction of the Nazi tyranny' for granted and thus by implication committed the President to ensuring that it occurred. Roosevelt wanted to prevent Britain from once again complicating the process of making peace by concluding 'secret and selfish Treaties' with any of her Allies and in particular from satisfying the Soviet Union's lust for acquiring territories in Eastern Europe inhabited by non-Russians; he had to be content with a statement that Churchill desired no territorial changes out of accord with the freely expressed wishes of the countries concerned and respected the rights of all people to choose the form of government under which they would live. He had even less luck with an attempt to get Britain to abandon the tariff system of Imperial Preference set up in 1932 because Churchill insisted on inserting the weasel words 'with due regard for their existing obligations' into a clause committing him to further the enjoyment by all states of access on equal terms to trade and raw materials.

Naturally enough the Charter had a bad reception in Germany, even though the fact that its terms did not apply to that country 'as of right' was not to emerge for another two-and-a-half years. It also had a bad reception in Britain from those who thought it might have gone further and in the United States from those who thought it had gone too far, the former being oblivious and the latter all too conscious of the limitations placed by the Constitution on the lengths to which a President may go. But the document came under more sophisticated fire in Britain from others who were familiar with the complexities of American politics but also familiar with the difficulties of putting ideals into practice. As one critic said, 'The principles are admirable but nobody knows who is going to see that they are carried out.' To such observers, as to the Germans, the Charter was uncomfortably reminiscent of Wilson's Fourteen Points – 'all the old clichés of the League of Nations period' (Oliver Harvey). Roosevelt had indeed been Assistant Secretary of the Navy in Wilson's Administration, when his Secretary of State, Cordell Hull, had been a junior Congressman. Yet nobody can deny that FDR, that superb political operator, had his feet firmly planted on the ground, while Hull's youth in the mountains of Tennessee must have afforded ample insight into life's realities. Moreover Roosevelt had adroitly passed the job of making the first draft of the Charter to Churchill who in turn delegated it to Cadogan, the Permanent Under-Secretary of the Foreign Office, whose *Diaries* show him to have been anything but a dreamer.

Why then had such practical men produced such verbiage? The explanation is three-fold. Without Congressional approval (which he had no intention of seeking), Roosevelt could commit nobody but himself. At that stage in the war, with America not a belligerent, precise terms would have involved making promises which might not prove capable of fulfilment, so that the only course was resort to broad principles, no matter how much their vagueness might disappoint. And when it came to principles, British and American leaders could only talk in terms made familiar by political thinkers like Locke and Jefferson, since it was in these that they had been nurtured. There was all the same a clear prospect that, if only the war could be won, the United States would emerge with greater power than any nation had ever possessed, thus obtaining an unprecedented opportunity to get principles put into practice. Consequently the Charter had greater significance than contemporary opinion was inclined to give it and the points which caused later debate deserve to be scrutinised since they were to plague statesmen for many subsequent years.

2   Roosevelt rejects a compromise peace

Cordell Hull, reflecting on the approach to war and on the reasons for
its outbreak, had found them predominantly in two directions. The first
was the failure of his countrymen to ratify the Treaty of Versailles and
their subsequent withdrawal into isolation. In retrospect we can see that
the combination of power needed to achieve Germany's collapse in
1918, without which a Treaty on the lines of Versailles could never
have been imposed, did not remain available to uphold its terms.
Awareness of this spurred the Germanophobes, particularly in France,
to press for its strict observance, and the Germanophiles to press for its
revision. In the event it was not maintained enough to intimidate the
losers nor moderated enough to placate them. Showing the
determination to learn from history which was a marked feature of the
Second World War, Hull set out to ensure that his country should not
again turn back from any plough to which it set its hand. The
establishment of some international political organisation, and US
membership of it, became two of his guiding purposes. But the form
which he expected the organisation to take was dependent on his
conviction that it would be little good without the membership. He
showed scant sympathy with the enthusiasts for supranationalism
because he believed that they would wreck the prospects of
internationalism. When in 1943 four Senators (of whom Harry Truman
of Missouri was nearly one) proposed a permanent United Nations with
a police force to suppress aggression, Hull counselled extreme caution
in following up so ambitious an idea. The caution was rewarded on the
next Guy Fawkes Day, when the Senate passed a resolution which was
admittedly less far-reaching but which as a result gained the
overwhelming majority of 85 votes to 5; it favoured US participation in
machinery with adequate power to establish and maintain a just and
lasting peace among the nations.

Roosevelt had blocked the insertion into the Atlantic Charter of any
reference to an international organisation, partly for the same reasons as
Hull but also out of disillusion over the record of the League of Nations.
He thought that power was a more effective means of getting peace kept
than promises and wanted the United States and Britain to act as world
policemen, at any rate in the early post-war years. Later he extended
membership to the Soviet Union, whose First Party Secretary, Stalin,
thought in much the same way. A negative version of this concept was
to pass into the UN Charter in the shape of the Great Powers' veto in

the Security Council. Certainly little can be achieved unless the Great Powers agree to it but this does not make the lesser ones any happier at decisions being taken over their heads. Hull genuinely believed that, once an effective world organisation had been set up, there would no longer be any need for 'spheres of influence, for alliances, for balance of power, or any other of the special arrangements through which, in the unhappy past, the nations strove to safeguard their security or to promote their interests'. In his determination to make the future happy, he refused to consider whether agreement among the Great Powers might prove unattainable or a revival of spheres of influence and balances of power consequently inevitable. 'Make-believe in diplomacy' has been defined as hoping 'that the reality of agreement may gradually grow up under the shelter of an identity of verbal formulae'. A good deal of such make-believe went into the drafting of the UN Charter, since only by taking chances about Russian good faith could the US secure agreement on its verbal formulae.

When however Churchill and Roosevelt had come together in 1941, the war had still to be won. To achieve that end, not only did the US have to be brought in but the USSR had to be kept in. The first was achieved not only by Japan's calculated risk at Pearl Harbor but also by Hitler's precipitate declaration of war on America four days later. But those who had been so anxious to bring America to accept the need to fight had soon to bring themselves to accept that America had views as to how the war should be fought. Prominent among these views was the doctrine of Unconditional Surrender, which Roosevelt announced in a press conference during the Anglo-American Summit meeting at Casablanca on 24 January 1943, seeking later to pass off as a sudden but happy thought what the archives have shown to be a premeditated plan.

To it he stuck through thick and thin until, by the time of his death, the arguments for abandoning it had lost their force; there was no need to induce the Germans to stop fighting since they were on the point of being compelled to do so anyway. The arguments for maintaining it were in any case strong. To make no commitments was an obvious way to avoid repeating the recriminations about whether the 1919 Peace Settlement had or had not departed from the commitments made in Wilson's Fourteen Points. Complete defeat in the field afforded the best hope of convincing the Germans that they had lost the war militarily, as a result of overestimating their strength, and not politically, as a result of one half of their nation being induced by enemy intrigues to stab the other in the back. Allied hands needed to be kept free if they were to make the thorough overhaul of German society which many thought to be essential. For Germans to overthrow totalitarianism, the essential step towards establishing the sort of government with which a conditional surrender could be negotiated, they would have to have arms in their hands and thus belong to the 'militarists' whose eradication was a declared war aim. In any case they could not be expected to agree to the extinction, even if only temporarily, of Germany as a power factor in world politics. Yet unless German power was so extinguished, Allied purposes might be hard to carry out. A compromise peace which failed to produce radical shifts in power, though it might shorten the present war, might merely hasten the start of a further one.

Admittedly complete victory could only be achieved with Russian help. But that was a further reason against premature discussion of peace conditions, which might result in the Allies disagreeing and the Russians in consequence making terms on their own. Against that possibility had of course to be set the danger that the victorious Russian armies would reach Central Europe, would there create a power vacuum and proceed to fill it. But although most Americans (in contrast to most British) had preferred Fascism to Communism, Roosevelt had consistently taken the line that the Soviet Union was less dangerous to American interests than Hitler's Germany. He wrote in 1941 that 'Russia is in no sense the aggressor nation: Germany is'. In 1944 he said that he thought that the Russians were perfectly friendly:

They aren't trying to gobble up all the rest of Europe or the world. They didn't know us, that's really the fundamental difference. They are friendly people. ... They haven't got any crazy ideas of conquest and so forth. ... They have got a large enough 'hunk of bread' right in Russia to keep them busy for a great many years to come without taking on any more headaches.

A little later he told the Polish Prime Minister 'Of one thing I'm certain ... Stalin is not an imperialist.' He was however quite capable of talking like this to bring about a state of affairs which he desired rather than to describe the one which he actually believed to exist.

3 Articles 2 and 3 of the Charter and political freedom

The second and third articles of the Atlantic Charter declared that Roosevelt and Churchill desired to see no territorial changes resulting from the war which did not accord with the freely expressed wishes of the people concerned and respected the right of all peoples to choose the form of government under which they would live. The last seventeen words had been in Cadogan's original draft. Yet they were not strictly true. Churchill was soon to make clear that they were not intended to apply to the British Commonwealth, over whose dissolution he had not become the King's First Minister in order to preside. But opposition to 'imperialism', 'colonialism' and all that went with them was a lively sentiment among Americans, from the President downwards. They suspected that one of Britain's principal war aims was to preserve the Commonwealth with a minimum of change.

They also suspected that Britain had made, or might be thinking of making, promises inconsistent with the Charter principles in order to enlist or retain allies. In fact no occasion to do so had at that stage arisen. But those who looked ahead could see a danger which steadily became more obvious. A persistent Russian aim was to maximise the amount of Russian-held territory which any future invader from the West would have to conquer before reaching Moscow. British negotiations for an alliance with Russia against Germany in 1939 had been held up by (amongst other things) the Russian desire to absorb the three Baltic states of Estonia, Latvia, and Lithuania, in whose extinction Britain was not prepared to connive. Another obstacle had been the reluctance of the Poles to admit Russian troops into their country to fight the Germans, for fear of not being able to get them out again. Hitler had been less squeamish and the Russo–German Agreement of August 1939 contained a secret clause, activated a month later, allowing the USSR to take the Baltic States and Eastern Poland.

When Eden went to Moscow in December 1941 for the first high-level political discussions since the German attack had made Russia into an involuntary ally, Stalin, even though Hitler's troops were at his capital's gates, demanded British agreement as to what he could do when he had beaten them and made clear that he intended at the very least to recover what he had gained in 1939, with acquisitions from Rumania into the bargain. The question of how to reconcile such forcible acquisitions with the Charter was got round by the very ambiguous words with which in September 1941 the Soviet

The USSR and the Atlantic Charter

In common with other belligerent Governments, the USSR 'made known its adherence to the common principles of policy set out [in the Atlantic Charter] and its intention to co-operate to the best of its ability in giving effect to them' but added the following rider:

> Considering that the practical application of these principles will necessarily adapt itself to the circumstances, needs and historic peculiarities of particular countries, the Soviet Government can state that a consistent application of these principles will secure the most energetic support of the Government and peoples of the Soviet Union.

At a meeting of Allied Governments in London, 24 September 1941

The two Presidents

Trying to follow [Roosevelt's] thinking was like chasing a vagrant beam of sunshine.

Stimson

It was a wonderful relief to preceding conferences with our former chief [Roosevelt] to see the promptness and snappiness with which Truman took up each matter and decided it. There were no long-drawn-out soliloquies from the President and the whole Conference was thoroughly business-like so that we actually covered two or three more matters than we had expected to discuss.

Stimson, Diary, 18 April 1945

Stalin is as near like Tom Pendergast as any man I know. He is very fond of classical music. He can see right through a question quickly

Truman, in a letter written after Potsdam

Government had acceded to that document, as well as the claim that the areas concerned had traditionally been Russian (and indeed the 1939 line with Poland had been suggested in 1920 by the British Foreign Secretary Lord Curzon as the ethnic frontier). When Eden, on prompting from both Churchill and Washington, objected that Stalin's demands were incompatible with the Charter, he got the reply that that document was supposed to have been directed against those who sought world domination but was now beginning to look as if it had been directed against the Soviet Union. Eden contented himself with saying that Britain could make no promises without consulting the United States.

Consultation took various forms, including a letter in which Churchill told Roosevelt that the increasing gravity of the war had led him to doubt whether the principles of the Charter should be so construed as to deny Russia the frontiers which she had occupied when Germany attacked her. Hull objected with typical tenacity, arguing that such a concession would compromise not only the principle of self-determination but also that of making no agreements about peace terms before war ended. He brushed aside the danger that Russia, if refused satisfaction, might make a separate peace with Germany. When Molotov arrived in London in May 1942 to negotiate a Treaty with Britain and pressed the frontier demands remorselessly, Hull stood firm and persuaded a distinctly less convinced President to do the same. The Treaty was signed without containing any reference to frontiers. Moscow was encouraged to desist from demanding such a thing by a promise from Roosevelt of a Second Front that very year. These tactics proved unfortunate when it became clear that such a venture was only possible in North Africa. In January 1943 the Soviet Government announced that it considered the 1939–41 frontier with Poland to be the operative one. This set off a long diplomatic wrangle.

After the German victory over Poland which Britain had ostensibly gone to war to prevent, a government-in-exile had been set up in London. This was almost as anti-Russian as anti-German, the tragedy of the Poles being that, having been oppressed in the past by both Russians and Germans, they found it hard to agree on which to hate most and did not see that they were too weak to afford the luxury of hating both. The London Poles refused to consider striking a bargain with the Russians to compensate for the loss of Eastern Poland, even when it became clear that this would soon be an accomplished fact. When the Germans in April 1943 discovered at Katyn the graves of 4,000 Polish officers presumably killed by the Russians two years earlier, the London Poles on their own initiative asked the International Red Cross to investigate, whereupon the Soviet Government broke off relations with them. The British were torn between a guilty conscience towards the Poles and their desire to keep the co-operation of the Russians. At the Teheran summit meeting in November 1943 Churchill suggested compensating Poland in the west for losses of territory to Russia in the east. As this meant giving Poland areas which had for long been German, it also meant that future Polish governments would fear German revenge and look to Russia for protection; Stalin accepted the idea eagerly. If the British thought that their concession would make the Russians more ready to accept the London Polish Government, they were to be disappointed.

Roosevelt could not have been blind to the threat which an over-powerful Russia would present to the practicability of an Open World. In August 1944 his Chiefs of Staff put on record their view that

> the defeat of Germany will leave Russia in a position of assured military dominance in Eastern Europe and the Middle East and Japan's defeat will leave Russia in a dominant position in continental north-east Asia as far as military power is concerned. ... The end of the war will produce a change in the pattern of military strength more comparable ... with that occasioned by the fall of Rome than with any other change during the succeeding fifteen hundred years. ... The United States and Russia will emerge as the strongest military Powers in the world and ... the relative strength and geographic positions of these two Powers are such as to preclude the military defeat of one ... by the other, even if that Power were allied with the British Empire.

Roosevelt, however, although admitting that it might be wishful thinking, hoped that the Russian intervention in Europe would not be too harsh. He said to Cardinal Spellman in September 1943 that

> European countries will have to undergo tremendous changes in order to adapt to Russia, but he hoped that in ten or twenty years the European influences would bring the Russians to become less barbarian. Be that as it may ... the US and Britain cannot fight the Russians. ... He hopes that out of a forced friendship may soon come a real and lasting friendship. The European people will simply have to endure the Russian domination, in the hope that in ten or twenty years they will be able to live well with the Russians.

The Europeans could not, in the President's view, expect the United States to rescue them from Russian as well as from German domination. His fellow-countrymen seemed prepared to renounce isolation to the extent of taking an active part in the new world organisation of the United Nations. But to prevent relative national strengths in Europe from having their natural effect, the United States would have to maintain a permanent armed presence in that continent in peace as well as in war, and to achieve such a step was something which he believed to be beyond the power of any President. 'Do please don't,' he said to Churchill 'ask me to keep any American forces in France after the war. I just cannot do it. I would have to bring them all back home.'

Accordingly he sought all the more to exercise a moderating influence on Russian policy by building up a relation of personal trust with Stalin and by paying sympathetic attention to Russia's need for security. The second aim was one of the reasons why the military power of Germany had to be unmistakably broken. It also explains the overriding priority which he gave during the war to Russian requests for supplies. At Teheran he told Stalin privately that he agreed with the proposal to move Poland's frontiers to the west and had no intention of going to war over a Russian seizure of the Baltic States. He merely explained that there were six or seven million people of Polish origin in the United States and, with an election due in the following year, he could not afford to alienate them by openly siding against the Polish Government in exile. As a result that Government went on thinking for fifteen months that they had American backing when they did not.

People of Polish origin were not Roosevelt's only difficulty. There was also his Secretary of State who, in his own words, was 'grounded to the tap-roots in the iniquitous consequences of spheres of influence' and thought that an adequate international organisation would render them unnecessary. There were a considerable number of people who believed that Russia was bent on world revolution and were not prepared, like the President, to accept her domination of the Eurasian landmass as inevitable. There was a large body of opinion which took as axiomatic the right of men to choose their own government. This belief was of course enshrined in the Declaration of Independence, but its prevalence was hardly due to theory alone. Behind it lay the expectation that people, if left to choose their form of government, will choose one in which they themselves can participate; the example of Germany prior to 1939 should have shown that this is an over-simplification. There is in addition the widespread conviction that democracies are not bellicose so that a democratic world would be a world without war. The history of the word 'Jingo' shows that there have been limits to this, but the average person today certainly shrinks from the sufferings and privations which modern war entails. The acts of democracy which contribute to war tend to be ones of omission rather than commission. Many consider that free nations will be more inclined to free trade. Those writers who have found in the Open Door the dominating influence behind American policy (below, p. 15) have seen the American emphasis on self-determination in Eastern Europe as motivated ultimately by the American desire to trade there; what is undeniable is that Communist states do not keep their doors open. To treat democracy as a general panacea for the world's political ills overlooks the need for a widespread willingness to sink internal differences if a society which is open is to be successful. Such a

---

The snags in Soviet negotiation

There is no doubt that the Soviet Government has tremendous ambitions with regard to Europe and that at some time or other the US and Great Britain will be forced to state that they cannot agree, at least in advance, to all its demands.

Hull to Roosevelt, 4 February 1942

Matters are rapidly approaching the point where the Soviet Government will have to choose between the development and extension of the foundation of international co-operation as the guiding principle of the post-war world as against the continuance of a unilateral and arbitrary method of dealing with its special problems. ... The American people will be unable to reconcile the contradiction between the two and will not be disposed to favour American participation in a scheme of world organization which will merely be regarded as a cover for another great power to continue to pursue a course of unilateral action in the international sphere based on superior force.

Hull to Harriman (US Ambassador in Moscow), 9 February 1944

What frightens me is that when a country begins to extend its influence by strong-arm methods beyond its borders under the guise of security, it is difficult to see how a line can be drawn. If the policy is accepted that the Soviet Union has a right to penetrate her immediate neighbours, penetration of the next immediate neighbour becomes at a certain time equally logical.

Harriman to State Department, 20 September 1944

Gratitude cannot be banked in the Soviet Union. Each transaction is complete in itself without regard for past favours. The party of the second part is either a shrewd trader to be admired or a sucker to be despised.

General Deane (of US Military Mission in Moscow)
to General Marshall, 2 December 1944

---

willingness requires a high level of conditioning by history and ideology or of self-discipline. To impose democratic procedures where such conditions do not exist is apt to result in governments which are weak or corrupt or otherwise inadequate.

Roosevelt, who has been described as a 'renegade Wilsonian' – that is, one whose liberal convictions had been tempered by realisation of the powerlessness of justice unsupported by force – might have been expected to take the line that, since Russia could not be prevented from interfering in the countries on her borders, wisdom lay in securing firm concessions from her in return. But to have said so openly would have produced a storm of criticism imperilling his own position, while his technique of government was always to leave questions open and hope that the progress of events would play into his hands (as it so conspicuously did at Pearl Harbor). In May 1944 the British Government asked the American how it would view an arrangement by which Britain was allowed a free hand in Greece in return for Russia being allowed one in Rumania. Hull was flatly opposed and, on his prompting, Roosevelt replied that the US would prefer to see consultative machinery set up for the Balkans as a whole. When Churchill pointed out the impossibility of deferring action until such machinery had been established and produced agreement (which, as we can now see, would have involved a very long wait), the President consented to the scheme being applied for three months – but omitted to tell the State Department that he had done so. Four months later the Prime Minister, on a visit to Moscow and without warning the Americans, proposed to Stalin an extension of the bargain to give Russia 75 per cent influence in Bulgaria, while Hungary and Yugoslavia would be split fifty–fifty. Although this was only to be 'for immediate war-time purposes' (and nothing was said about Poland), he deprecated describing the deal as 'dividing into spheres' for fear such language might shock the Americans. How delicate the situation was is shown by the fact that Britain's subsequent action in preventing (without Soviet interference) a Communist take-over in Greece is said to have excited the American public more than Russian action to assist such a take-over in Poland.

By the time that Roosevelt, Stalin and Churchill met at Yalta in February 1945, the Soviet Government had recognised as the Provisional Government of Poland a Committee of Polish Communists which had been formed from exiles in Moscow and which accepted Russia's wishes as to frontiers but with which as a result the London

Poles refused to deal. At Yalta Stalin agreed to sign an American 'Declaration on Liberated Europe' by which the three Powers promised to bring about by joint action 'the establishment through free elections of governments responsive to the will of the people' in all the liberated countries. He also agreed that the Provisional Polish Government should be 'reorganised on a broader democratic basis with the inclusion of democratic leaders from Poland itself and from Poles abroad'. This new Government would then be called 'the Provisional Polish Government of National Unity'; it was pledged to hold 'free and unfettered elections as soon as possible'. Churchill, whose readiness to indulge in political bargains was being increasingly restrained by his fear of Bolshevism, fought for wording which would place clearer limits on Communist freedom of action. But although the obduracy of the Russians indicated that the wording was not imprecise by accident, Roosevelt was not prepared to make Poland a breaking-point – nor would he necessarily have helped the Poles by doing so. He told his wife that he was 'a bit exhausted' and did not want to be delayed by a deadlock from getting home. There was nobody in the American delegation to challenge him, for the health of Hull (who probably would not have attended in any case) had collapsed in the previous autumn, and he had been succeeded by Stettinius, known to his staff as 'big brother Ed', who was more of a co-ordinator and communicator than a man of principle.

After the conference was over, the Russians insisted on leaving to their Poles the question of what other Poles should be brought into the Government and it became clearer than ever that the Communists would keep a majority. There were no signs of elections (which were not in practice to be held for nearly two years). Sixteen leaders of the underground army attached to the London Government were induced to come out of hiding and then arrested for 'terrorism and spying'. Although Stalin had once said that Communism did not suit Poland and the Western leaders admitted Russia's right to insist on having a friendly government in that country, the proportion of Poles hostile to Russia made it doubtful whether such a government could be strictly representative, while a regime in which communists were predominant would be unlikely to satisfy Western interpretations of 'democratic'. Significantly the Finns, who had shown greater awareness of the need to reassure Russia (and were less important strategically), were allowed more freedom of choice. In Rumania and Bulgaria, and to a lesser extent in Hungary, the Russians put their friends in charge and gave the

13

British and American representatives as little say as they had themselves been allowed in Greece. After the First World War they had bitterly resented the action of Western Europe in setting up on their western frontier a *cordon sanitaire* of anti-communist countries to keep the infection of Bolshevism out; after the Second World War they were bent on having their own *cordon* to prevent the infection of liberalism from getting in.

This was the stage which affairs had reached when on 12 April 1945 Roosevelt died.

4   Article 4 of the Charter and economic freedom

Economic nationalism was the second evil which Cordell Hull blamed for the war: 'Unhampered trade dovetails with peace; high tariffs, trade barriers and unfair economic competition with war.' He accepted the view of the eighteenth-century Enlightenment that a system which allowed economic resources (i.e. manpower, materials, machinery, money and skills) to go where they could be used most productively (as measured in cash terms) was the one most likely to bring the greatest possible prosperity to the greatest possible number. For a government to interfere with this free flow would mean, if it was done effectively, making its own people richer in the short term and the people of other countries poorer than they would have been otherwise. The temptation to other governments to interfere in retaliation and indeed the popular pressure on them to do so would be more than many of them could resist. Thus clashes between governments would replace the rivalry of the market place. A businessman would no longer try to outbid his competitors by efficiency but by getting his government to hinder or bar them. The next step would be peaceful pressure by one government to prevent another from interfering in a way damaging to its businessmen and, if peaceful pressure failed, the temptation to replace it by threats and then by violence would grow.

> Though realising that many other factors were involved, I reasoned that, if we could get a freer flow of trade – freer in the sense of fewer discriminations and obstructions – so that one country would not be deadly jealous of another and the living standards of all countries might rise, thereby eliminating the economic dissatisfaction that breeds war, we might have a reasonable chance for lasting peace.

Hull realised however that government interference had already gone too far for the situation to be remediable by simply ignoring economic issues in political negotiations but that instead politicians must be brought to agree on a conscious positive policy of deliberate restraint.

Other Americans, as Hull knew, saw a more immediate need for freeing trade. They could not forget the Depression – we should always remember that there were still seven million Americans out of work in 1938 and even three million in December 1941; only the turnover to full war production had really ended unemployment. How could the conveyor-belts be kept running once the free world had ceased to need an arsenal? The most obvious answer was 'by increased exports'. The fact that exports had hitherto been marginal to the US economy might explain what had been wrong with that economy; the incomparable industrial machine produced more that its own population needed. By no means all who reasoned like this remembered that imports had also been marginal to a United States which, unlike Britain or Belgium, was largely self-supporting. They did not therefore stop to ask how the recipients of the extra exports were to pay for them. But that question did admit of the orthodox answer that the more efficient distribution of resources brought about by unimpeded trade would raise productivity all round and thus increase everybody's purchasing power.

Some writers have gone so far as to see in the policy of the 'Open Door' for trade, traders and information the ultimate motive behind American policy as a whole. Most of them are people who claim that, in the last resort, all human actions are inspired by material considerations. But by no means everybody is keenly interested in or well-informed about economics. Roosevelt was a typical case; he looked for solutions in terms of political possibilities rather than of economic theories. One of the many things about him which upset Hull was his reluctance to invest trade liberation with moral fervour. The Secretary of State was 'keenly disappointed' by the President's acquiescence in Churchill's watering down of the clause in the Atlantic Charter about international trade. He redoubled his efforts to get something more satisfactory put into the agreement still being negotiated about the terms on which the US were to aid their allies.

Roosevelt for his part deplored Hull's stiffness of mind which he thought to be aggravated by the 'striped pants boys' in the State Department. Although the Southern Democrat's years in Congress had given him such prestige on Capitol Hill that the President retained him as Secretary of State for over eleven years, he was not kept properly informed of what was going on internationally or taken to 'Summit' meetings. As a result it fell to the Assistant Secretary Sumner Welles, a much smoother figure, to argue the case against British tariffs at the Atlantic meeting. He was countered by Churchill who recalled

the British experience in adhering to Free Trade for eighty years [1846–1932] in the face of ever-mounting American tariffs. We had allowed the fullest importation into all our colonies. Even our coast-wise traffic round Great Britain was open to the competition of the world. All we had got in reciprocation was successive doses of American protection.

Welles 'seemed to be a little taken aback'. Hull would have agreed that his own country's record was far from blameless but would have urged that, under his leadership, it had mended its ways and set a new example for others to follow. He had worked against protection from the moment of taking office in 1933 and had in 1934 persuaded Congress to pass the Reciprocal Trade Agreements Act, authorising him to negotiate reductions of tariffs with individual countries in return for balancing concessions by them; the most notable result had been the Anglo–US Trade Agreement of 1937. For Hull, however, deals with individual countries about individual commodities were not enough; his ideals could only be achieved by something broader. Indeed his chief bugbear was 'discrimination', any agreement by which the goods of a particular country entered another country on terms more favourable to those accorded to the rest of the world in general and the United States in particular. Such bilateral discrimination had been the essence of the trade network set up by Dr Schacht (as Hitler's Minister of Economics from 1934 to 1937) which had prevented the US from concluding with Germany an Agreement similar to that with Britain. To Hull the British system giving entry on preferential terms to goods from and to the Commonwealth (the effects of which in deflecting trade were considerably overestimated in America, as in Britain) was another form of bilateralism all the more significant because the British Government was more vulnerable to pressure than the German. Having failed to exert that pressure over the Atlantic Charter, Hull saw an even better opportunity for doing so in the negotiations over Lend-Lease.

Even before the war began, it had been clear that Britain and the Commonwealth could not by themselves provide all the men needed to fight it and all the arms needed for them to fight with. Extra supplies had to be obtained and the obvious source was America. By 1940 it had become clear that these supplies must be on a scale which could not be paid for by normal exports from a Britain concentrating its output on arms, or even by selling all the investments accumulated by Britons in North America. 'At the present rate of loss', wrote HM Treasury in December 1940, 'our reserves will only last till about Tuesday next.' The Churchill Government faced a choice between making a compromise peace and finding a new source of finance. Roosevelt, determined to prevent the first and aware from experience between 1915 and 1932 that big loans of cash could not be paid back, obtained power from Congress to lend or lease to any country whose defence he considered essential to US safety such equipment or installations as seemed to him appropriate. When it came to working out the small print of the consequential agreement with Britain, the question arose of what *quid pro quo* should be required. There was no prospect of the beneficiary ever being able to repay in cash, whilst repayment in kind would be complex and often undesired. Thus the idea arose of Britain

---

Pros and cons of discrimination

The [provision against discrimination in Article VII of the Lease-Lend Treaty] calls up, and must call up ... all the old lumber, most-favoured-nation clause and the rest, which was a notorious failure and made such a hash of the old world. We know also that it won't work. It is the clutch of the dead, or at least the moribund, hand. If it was accepted, it would be cover behind which all the unconstructive and truly reactionary people of both our countries would shelter. We must be free to work out new and better arrangements.

J. M. Keynes to Dean Acheson, 1941

What Mr Keynes has completely failed to see and understand is that the idea of non-discrimination ... is not a philosophical concept but rather a matter involving considerations of practical politics and economics. The imposition of high, though non-discriminatory, trade barriers for the protection of its own products does and has aroused resentment but this resentment is mitigated by the fact that a certain degree of preference by a government for its nationals is understandable and tolerable. But discrimination in favour of other foreigners is not so regarded. And above all he fails wholly to see that, after the sacrifices the American people are called on to make to help Great Britain in the present emergency (even though we are thereby helping ourselves), our public opinion simply would not tolerate discriminations against our products in Great Britain or, at Great Britain's instance, in other countries.

Harry Hawkins of the State Department, 1941

---

wiping out her debt by committing herself to join after the war was over in a world free from impediments to and discriminations in trade.

At this point however they encountered the scathing opposition of Keynes who was acting as the British Government's chief economic adviser and who once described Hull's proposals (behind his back) as 'lunatic'. Keynes was not at heart a protectionist any more than most of his countrymen. His point of departure was that which Churchill had adopted towards Welles; experience had shown the impracticability of Britain pursuing a free-trade policy in a protectionist world. During the 1930s America's high tariffs had prevented other countries from paying for the goods they imported from her by exporting enough of their own goods in return; as a result they had paid to such an extent in gold that she had amassed three-quarters of the world's stock – only to lock it up in the middle of Kentucky. But Keynes was also and with good reason obsessed about the crisis which would confront Britain at the end of the war, with her export trade run down, her overseas investments sold, her machinery worn out, her people tired. He did not believe that she dare take the risk of throwing her markets open in the benevolent hope that other countries would buy from her enough to pay for all she needed to get from them. Imports did not automatically breed exports. If she could not afford all the imports she would like, a system of priorities would have to be worked out which would involve bilateral deals and discrimination. Hull's intentions were admirable but depended for their execution on the co-operation of Congress which had a bad record for yielding to protectionist lobbies.

Another British objection to the US approach concerned tariffs. The lower a tariff gets, the less effect it has. Thus cutting back by half a tariff with an average rate of 20 per cent will have more effect than halving one of 10 per cent. Keynes and the other Britons who negotiated with America during and after the war sought to establish the principle that high-tariff countries like the US could fairly be expected to do more than low-tariff ones. But they sought a further assurance. Easy access to the US market would be of little value if demand in that market was so weak as to stimulate not imports but calls for protection against imports. They knew that the Americans feared a return of the Depression. But Keynes had found (or thought he had found) a way for governments to avoid depressions by consciously stimulating growth and full employment. The British sought, and in Article VII of the Lend-Lease Agreement obtained, an assurance that the US Government would, in agreement with Britain, take 'action directed to the expansion of production, employment and the exchange and consumption of goods', and only in return for this did they allow their own Government to become committed to 'action directed to the elimination of all forms of discriminatory treatment in international commerce, and to the reduction of tariffs and other trade barriers'. To quite how much these words committed either side remained a matter of argument. In any case, later years have underlined the difficulty of agreeing how much action to liberate trade is a fair equivalent to action to stimulate growth. And, as it has become clear how hard it is to stimulate growth without thereby fuelling inflation, the question has emerged of how far a country can be justified in losing control over its money supply in order to keep the world open to trade. If moreover the US Government were to succeed in stimulating growth and full employment, so much American output might be consumed at home as to make an increase in exports unimportant, especially as they were not needed to pay for indispensable imports.

There were further worms in the buds of Hull's ideals. The world is far from uniform, differing in such things as climate, location of raw materials, energy resources, accumulated wealth, the willingness to show initiative, labour supply, the skills of workers and their readiness to work. Certain areas can produce more efficiently than others. If trade were left absolutely free, there are some things of which, given modern methods of manufacturing, a few countries could supply the whole world, rendering their production elsewhere unnecessary. The classical doctrine postulates that countries which can no longer make them competitively should shift their resources to making other things, on the argument that, until every Hottentot has a Rolls-Royce, there will be enough needs to keep everyone at work satisfying them, provided only that unsatisfied needs can be converted into effective purchasing power. Even though things have not been carried to such lengths, the basic resources of all countries are continually changing in relation to one another and adjustments to these changes are in the long run inescapable. An open free world has the advantage that it forces adjustment as a continual process of small changes whereas, if change is resisted, it may end by arriving on a large scale with violence. But no matter how small a change may be, there will usually be somebody who suffers from it, even if only temporarily. Moreover it is not today always easy to find alternative uses for resources which have become uncompetitive. Thus an open world favours those countries which by reason of their resources, their skills, their low level of costs, their social mobility or some other advantage, find it easy to be competitive. Elsewhere it will produce poverty, unemployment, stagnant or falling standards of life, and once these discomforts reach a certain level, the public demand for protection against them will generate strong political pressures. These are the sources of the barriers and interferences which Hull so much deplored, and to say that free trade will eliminate them is to oversimplify the problem.

What Article VII of the Lend-Lease Agreement unquestionably did was to commit the American and British Governments to discuss how their aims could best be realised. As far as trade was concerned, informal talks began in 1943 but were then held up by political objections in Britain. They started again in 1945 when a decision to set up an International Trade Organisation was soon reached. But decisions were also taken to adopt a complicated method of negotiating tariff cuts and to include in the ITO Charter comprehensive and detailed provisions covering the whole range of commercial policy. These were matters which could not be settled quickly, so the United Nations Committee to draft the Charter did not meet until October 1946. In the interval much more progress had been made on the financial front where American leadership was taken over by the Secretary of the Treasury, Henry Morgenthau Jr.

During the nineteenth century and until the First World War, the world's currencies had been linked together by being freely interchangeable into gold; if the value of a country's currency in gold changed, corrective banking measures were at once taken to remedy the situation. After 1919 the system was re-established to the extent that governments undertook to change their currencies in gold with other governments. But in 1931 this system broke down in face of the Depression and, until 1939, currencies floated up and down without any fixed norms. This made it impossible for traders to tell how much their own money would be worth in terms of others in a few months' time, and, as most trade involves making commitments about prices several months (or even years) ahead, the uncertainty had an inhibiting effect on international business. Any plan for reviving international trade was therefore expected to include proposals for putting exchange rates on a stable basis. In 1942 a British plan was devised by Keynes and an American one by Harry Dexter White, a member of Morgenthau's staff. These led on to a Joint Statement of Principles which in the summer of 1944 was discussed by a conference of forty-four nations at Bretton Woods in New Hampshire. There it was decided to set up an International Monetary Fund (IMF) and an International Bank. These two institutions, along with the ITO, were to be the key economic pillars of the American Open World.

In order to belong to the IMF a country was required to set a fixed value on its currency and promise to make that currency freely convertible into those of the other members. The value was actually set in terms of gold but members were not necessarily expected to offer gold in exchange for it. They were however required to offer dollars, and as thirty-five dollars had since 1934 been exchangeable in the US for an ounce of gold, currencies were in effect being linked to gold through the dollar. Member countries were required to keep the exchange rate of their money within one per cent of its gold value by buying or selling dollars; they could alter the gold value but only in agreement with the Fund (though the Fund was bound to accept changes of up to 10 per cent). Moreover each member was required, on joining, to pay to the Fund a 'quota' proportionate to its size, a quarter in gold and three-quarters in its own currency. Out of the pool of money thus created, the Fund was intended to make loans to countries whose exchange rate was falling, so as to enable them to support it at its fixed level. But in return for the loan the country would be expected to make changes in its policy so as to remove the downwards pressure and render the support no longer necessary; the Fund's Executive Board, on which the various member countries have voices proportionate to their quotas and the US (since its quota is over 20 per cent of the total) has a veto, can lay down conditions as to those changes. Keynes's plan had proposed to base the system not on the dollar but on a special international currency called the 'bancor' and he wanted the Fund to have much more money to lend than was ultimately provided. But the Americans saw no prospect of persuading Congress to accept such proposals. (In 1968 the Fund introduced a scheme of Special Drawing Rights ('Paper Gold') intended to serve somewhat the same purpose as the 'bancor'.)

Underlying the system was the assumption that the rates at which countries exchange their currencies are on the whole stable in the long term and that most of the fluctuations up and down are either temporary or remediable by changes in government policy. The loans from the Fund were therefore intended to enable a government to ride out a transient disturbance or give time for corrective measures to take effect. But exchange-rates are not plucked out of the air or devised by faceless men with green eye-shades in Wall Street, Lombard Street or Zürich's

Bahnhofstrasse. They reflect a country's competitiveness in world markets and such competitiveness depends on the rate at which its economy is growing. Growth rates vary; exactly why they do is hard to say and differs from case to case but in general they are the outcome of all the factors which go to give each economy its character. Thus while some of the fluctuations in exchange rates will be temporary, others will reflect lasting trends as one country gets relatively poorer or another relatively richer. This is particularly likely to be the case after a disturbance like a war when the desire to win (or to avoid defeat) drives countries into policies which they would not otherwise adopt or else adopt more slowly. Thus the immediate aftermath of a war is a bad moment for setting up a new system of rates since there has not been enough opportunity to see what, in the light of changes brought by the war, the peacetime relationships are going to be. Yet is is notoriously easier to get international agreement on such things during the emergency of war than it is once that emergency is over. Accordingly the Fund agreement contained an article allowing members to retain restrictions on the convertibility of their currencies for five years after it came into operation (i.e. until 1952).

The articles of the IMF do also, as has been said, allow for lasting adjustments in the fixed values of currencies, once it has become clear that the downward (or upward) pressure on that currency is a lasting trend and not a temporary fluctuation. But when such pressure begins, there may be little to show which of the two it is, and as governments (and their critics) usually regard devaluations as badges of shame, they have tended to put off accepting the inevitable as long as possible. During the interval their producers have found it hard to sell abroad, because their prices are relatively too high, while speculators do well, selling the currency at its existing rate confident that they will be able to buy it back later at a lower one.

Devaluation becomes necessary when one country fails to keep up with the others, making its costs unduly high. But a country can get ahead of the others, making its costs unduly low so that it sells more than it buys and takes in large quantities of money, which are added to by the desire of foreigners to hold funds in what they regard as a 'safe' currency. For all other countries to adjust by devaluing downwards involves them in numerous complications. For the country which has got ahead to adjust by revaluing upwards is simpler. The idea developed that a country which has a persistent surplus has just as much of an obligation to the international community to adjust as has one which runs a consistent deficit. In the wartime discussions leading to the creation of the IMF the British argued that, for some time after the war, their economy was bound to be weaker than the American and the pound bound as a result to be under continual pressure in relation to the dollar. They could only accept the obligation to make it in due course freely convertible into dollars if they could be sure that the Americans would take some share in the task of adjustment. Agreement became possible because the Americans showed awareness of this need, and a clause was inserted giving the Fund power to declare a currency 'scarce' when the demand for it is such as to exhaust the Fund's own supplies of it. Other members would then be relieved of the obligation not to put up discriminatory barriers against the goods of the surplus country (thus freeing them to levy duties on that country's exports and so artificially raise the prices). In fact however the Scarce Currency Clause has never been invoked, upward revaluations having been used instead.

The International Bank for Reconstruction and Development, the third pillar of the Open World system, was intended to provide international capital for countries which were anxious to embark on investment projects but unable to find the necessary money themselves. But the funds put at the Bank's disposal were limited in size and the need to use them prudently was emphasised, with the result that it was condemned to a minor role in the immediate post-war years.

The authors of this system hoped that it would be world-wide in membership. When the Foreign Ministers of America, Britain and Russia met in Moscow in 1943, Hull

> in long discourses tried to win Stalin and Molotov over to the programme he had in mind for the world. Toward his effort Molotov showed polite but unhelpful admiration. He seemed impressed with Hull's idealistic zeal and genuinely perplexed as to how Hull's doctrines of freer trade could be harmonised with the Communist trade methods. This failure distressed the Secretary of State.

An article similar to VII in the British Lend-Lease Agreement was included in the Russian. All that the Soviet Government would have been required to do in joining the IMF would have been to fix a value for the rouble, make it convertible, and disclose the size of their gold stocks. They sent a delegation to Bretton Woods which took an active part in the work of the Conference. But the chief concern of its members seemed to be in what loans the Soviet Union could obtain from the Fund and the Bank to help in reconstructing their country. When they found that they could expect nothing from the first (because reconstruction was not one of its objects) and very little from the second (because its resources were too small), they lost interest and their signature to the articles was never ratified. Those responsible for drafting the Trade Charter included in it a section on State Trading and expressed the hope that representatives of the 'command' economies would offer to discuss what was there proposed. That never happened.

The Anglo-Americans realised that the financial and commercial methods of Communism were not those of private enterprise. They recognised also that centrally planned and controlled economies were unlikely to disappear. They supposed, however, that both types had in common a desire for stable economic conditions and for an increase in the quantities of goods produced and made available to consumers. What they left out of account was that Communists desired to strengthen their own economies to the disadvantage of those in which enterprise was still free, and believed that unfettered competition would have the opposite effect, exploiting the weak to the benefit of the strong. The advocates of freedom considered themselves broad-minded for being prepared to tolerate state trading; they could hardly have brought themselves to desire its spread, as the Communists did. Participation in a world seeking to maximise the free movement of men, money and materials over state frontiers does not come easily to an economy which is centrally planned. And central planning is closely bound up with the control of the Party over society which is a dominant characteristic of Communism. There was never much chance of an open economy being brought about on a world scale by voluntary agreements.

CHAPTER 2

1945-7

1 Truman and the Roosevelt legacy

Harry S Truman had been wished on to Roosevelt as candidate for Vice-President in the 1944 election because the Democratic leaders considered Henry Wallace, the previous holder of that office, insufferably radical – they had heard it said that he wanted to give every Hottentot a quart of milk a day! Truman's political apprenticeship in Kansas City under its boss Tom Pendergast hardly augured well for his performance in the White House. But the reputation which he had won for good sense during ten years in the Senate afforded more promise and proved more characteristic. He compared stepping into Roosevelt's shoes to having a ton of hay fall on him but set out undismayed to proceed in the direction which their previous inmate seemed to have been taking. The Open World which this appeared to be was not something he knew much about, having only quit the US to serve as an artillery captain in France in 1917. But his native Missouri adjoins Tennessee and he must have found a good deal that was congenial in Hull's outlook.

In so far as definite intentions about the post-war world can be assigned to Roosevelt, they were to unite as many nations as possible under the new organisation to be born at a Conference in San Francisco in May 1945. But to do this effectively the five Great Powers would have to remain united. Their right to a veto in the UN Security Council had been accepted, though the Russians had been persuaded to let its application be limited to proposals for action, not to discussion. Of the five the US, as the only one which had not been fought over, were bound at first to dominate, and the length of that dominance would be extended if the impending tests showed their atomic bomb to be as devastating a weapon as science predicted. In the economic field the Fund, Bank and Trade Organisation were to provide the prosperity which would reduce the temptation for states to solve their internal problems by war. The three countries whose attempts to do this had ended in defeat were to be rendered harmless for the foreseeable future but were not to be left permanently incapable of contributing to the world's wealth.

That this should never have been more than a dream was perhaps inevitable. Experience is constantly showing up as fallacious (since over-simplified) the hope that, because it is to the advantage of sovereign states to agree, they will. But two major reasons can be identified to explain why in this case reality ran so far behind expectation. In the first place, the problems of reconstruction were gravely underestimated. In the second, the leaders of the US failed to reach, let alone act on, a consistent view as to whether, in the Soviet Union, they were faced by a nation, motivated by the usual considerations of security and advantage, or by a religion which would not rest until it had converted the whole world. As a result the chances of opening the entire world were shewn, within two years, to be minimal, both economically and politically.

2   America and the reconstruction of Russia

American Lend-Lease exports to Britain between 1941 and 1945 totalled $13.8 billion and by the end of the war were providing in aircraft and food 25–30 per cent of available supplies. Exports to the Soviet Union totalled $9.5 billion; here also aircraft and food took the lead but probably represented a smaller percentage of supplies (transport equipment was also important). Russian tanks proved better than American (and even than German) and relatively few guns were sent. Thus Lend-Lease did as much to enable America's allies to live as to enable them to fight – and living was something which they would need to go on doing after they stopped fighting.

But a Senate Committee with Truman as chairman said in November 1943 that 'every effort should be made to reduce to a minimum the cost to our taxpayers', while the US Armed Forces looked with a baleful eye on a policy which reduced the quantities available to themselves. All those involved, from Roosevelt downwards, were keen that Lend-Lease should remain a wartime expedient and that post-war reconstruction should be financed by loans or credits. Congress was distrustful of the Administration's promises that Lend-Lease would end when hostilities did and wrote into a new Act in April 1945 a proviso that all goods supplied after the end of the war were to be paid for. Three days before Roosevelt died an amendment to tighten the conditions still further was only defeated by Truman's casting vote as Vice-President. The view was also gaining ground that nothing more should be given unconditionally to the Russians but that they should be made to choose between going without and paying more attention to American wishes.

If therefore the Administration had taken no steps to curtail Lend-Lease after the war in Europe ended on 8 May 1945, Congress would rapidly and with justification have insisted on action. But there were complications. To begin with, Japan had still to be beaten, a process in which both Britain and Russia had promised to join (although Russia's promise was still secret); until the Far Eastern war ended, further (if fewer) Lend-Lease supplies would be needed. Second, the Russians had been invited in the previous March to put in a list of the supplies which they wanted to receive between July 1945 and June 1946. Nobody pointed out to them officially that, once the fighting stopped, there were to be major changes in policy over aid and, although their representatives in the US must have realised this, the realisation may not have penetrated to Moscow. Further, the flow of aid was cut off with clumsiness owing to new hands at the top not realising all that was involved and zealous subordinates taking their chance to end something which they had never liked; ships already at sea were ordered back to port and cargoes of some still in port were off-loaded. The impression given by these excesses was harder to cancel than the measures themselves. Supplies were resumed for the time being but the end of the Pacific war in August brought them to another abrupt stop – this time final. One way of giving aid was thus halted before there had been any serious discussion about the form of the alternatives which were so obviously going to be necessary; arms might no longer be important but equipment for peacetime production was and for some time the US was likely to remain an indispensable source of food.

For Central, Eastern and Southern Europe outside Russia and Germany, the United Nations had set up in 1943 a Relief and Rehabilitation Administration (UNRRA), while the Allied military authorities were made responsible for immediate food relief in the West European areas which they liberated. To finance UNRRA each UN member was called on to pay one per cent (later doubled) of the national income; large as this sum seemed to be, the needs were even greater. The intention had been that those of the Soviet Union would not be met by UNRRA but by loans or grants. In August 1945, however, Moscow claimed $700 million from UNRRA – a quarter of the total available; in the end $250 million was allocated to the Ukraine and White Russia, the two areas which had suffered most from the German invasion. Even this might not have been forthcoming if Russian agreement had not been needed for extending UNRRA aid to Italy. Accusations were later made in the US that the aid given to the USSR and to Eastern Europe generally had been distributed on the basis not of need but of importance in and to the Party.

The limited amount of aid which the Russians could look for from Lend-Lease and UNRRA made all the more significant expectations of loans and grants which they had been encouraged to entertain. Hull had taken to Moscow in October 1943 a memorandum expressing the desire of the American people to co-operate fully in the rehabilitation of war damage in the USSR and recommending that negotiations be opened as soon as possible. Harriman, just appointed as US Ambassador, said much the same with Roosevelt's blessing, and so did other influential Americans. Contracts for Russia were considered important as a means of keeping US industry employed once the war was over; Russian raw materials were rather optimistically expected to serve as payment and fill serious gaps in US supplies. But when in January 1944 Mikoyan, the Commissar for Foreign Trade, proposed a loan of $1 billion, the Americans proved unprepared to start negotiating. An essential preliminary was the amendment of a couple of laws and Roosevelt was not willing to tackle this hurdle till the November elections were over; it was only in January 1945 that he asked Congress to make the necessary changes. In the same month Molotov proposed a loan of $6 billion, but by this time the anti-Russian feeling was gathering strength. Harriman was still in favour of granting credits but wanted to make them conditional on Russian good behaviour; Roosevelt decided to play for time and the question was left undiscussed at Yalta. The Russians were later told that America was not in a position to make any definite commitment; to judge by what they said in making their application to UNRRA, they took this reply as equivalent to a refusal.

In August 1945, however, after the legislative obstacles had been overcome, Molotov, at Harriman's invitation, put in a renewed request, this time for $1 billion at $2\frac{3}{8}$ per cent (in spite of the fact that Congress had fixed 4 per cent as the minimum rate for such loans). Truman agreed that negotiations should be opened but the question had first to be settled as to what political conditions (if any) to attach. The final end of the war had brought reorganisation and with it confusion to Washington; the new brooms had many things to think about, including the negotiation of a loan to Britain (p. 48 below). Only at the end of February 1946 did the State Department wake up to the fact that Molotov had never had an answer. On 1 March the Russians were invited to start discussing the loan. But they were also called on to negotiate at the same time about a wide range of other matters including compensation for US property seized in liberated areas, arrangements to protect US patents and copyrights, freedom of navigation on the Danube and other rivers and the right of the US to a greater say in assisting the peoples of Eastern Europe to solve by democratic means their pressing problems. To Moscow bargaining on such a scale appeared 'inexpedient'; the Russians failed to take up the offer and it was not repeated. The idea of the chief exponent of free enterprise helping to rebuild the chief exponent of Communism was finally discarded.

In 1943 Harriman had told Roosevelt that the Russian Government ranked the question of reconstruction as second only in importance to victory. That Government was also very conscious that fifty Russians had died in the war for every American death (though, given the resource endowment of the two countries and the greater American productive efficiency, a strategy which enabled the US to fight a capital-intensive and the Soviet Union a labour-intensive war may have been the most effective way for them both to win). During the war (and particularly when no landing was staged in Western Europe in 1942 and 1943), Moscow had suspected the Anglo-Americans of deliberately leaving Germany and Russia to exhaust one another so as to emerge themselves relatively strengthened. When the Soviet leaders found their moves to get reconstruction aid through Lend-Lease, UNRRA and a loan (not to mention the IMF and the International Bank) successively frustrated, the suspicion would have come naturally to them that the same sort of calculation was still at work and that all the wartime asseverations of debts to brothers-in-arms had been hypocritical. Stalin said as much in May 1945 when Truman sent Roosevelt's trouble-shooter Harry Hopkins to clear up misunderstandings. Even if they had not had spies inside the Western camp to tell them, they only needed to read American newspapers to discover how many people were urging that aid should be used as a lever for extracting concessions from them and making them take steps which in their view would impair their system and reduce their security. Stalin also told Hopkins that, if the refusal to continue Lend-Lease was intended as pressure on the Russians 'in order to soften them up', it was a fundamental mistake; when Russians were approached frankly on a friendly basis, much could be done, but reprisals in any form would bring exactly the opposite effect.

Relations between Russia and America at this period were complicated by false appreciations which each side made of the other's prospects. The Russians were convinced that, as many Americans believed and communist doctrine taught, the United States would find themselves in another depression as soon as the damage done by the war had been made good. They underestimated, as did many Americans, the scale on which reconstruction would take place and disregarded the effect of the new Keynesian doctrines about the duty of the State to stimulate demand by positive action. They thought that before long the Americans would be only too glad of Russian orders and that as a result time would work in their favour. The Americans for their part were impressed by the scale of war damage in Russia and many (though not all) of them thought that for her to make it good from her own resources would take an interminable time; during the interval public demand for some improvement in living standards would menace the regime. They therefore saw themselves as being in a position to dictate the terms on which they would consent to help and wanted to use this advantage to extend the free world system in which they believed. But the Russian leaders for their part believed in their own system and, having successfully repulsed Germany's attempt to destroy it by violence, were determined to resist American attempts to do so by economic pressure, even if such resistance involved sacrifices. Certainly the Russian economy was in a bad way and its prospects of recovery were not improved by the need to devote considerable resources to the home production of an atomic bomb, without which they could not expect to make their influence felt in world affairs. But, as events proved, the task was feasible; the population was used to obeying orders and having sacrifices imposed on it. The results of having done so in the 1920s and 1930s were there for all to see in the victory over Hitler.

The gap in thinking between the policy-determining elites in the two countries was so great as to throw doubts on the feasibility of a loan being enough to transform the situation. The process of negotiating one might have made things worse. The conditions which Congress were to apply to a British loan were harsh enough; for a Russian one they might have insisted on terms which Moscow would never have accepted.

What is regrettable is that the American leadership never made a clear choice between (a) refusing to grant a loan at all, (b) granting one unconditionally, and (c) determining conditions as an integral part of a consistent overall policy. Instead they procrastinated until so late in the day that the conditions which they were by then bound to demand were ones which the Russians were bound to refuse. This was not just the result of Roosevelt dying at a critical moment. It was due even more to the fact that American views about Russia – and many other things – were undergoing rapid change, making durable decisions hard to take.

3   Compromise in Germany

Before the German forces surrendered unconditionally (a process in which the Russians showed themselves intensely and unjustifiably suspicious of Western good faith), the victors had reached, at Yalta and elsewhere, certain decisions as to how the country was to be treated. The whole of it was to be occupied and three (later four) roughly equal Zones had been delimited to decide whose troops would garrison which parts; the Russians were to be in the east, the Americans in the south, the British in the north-west. The total occupied area was to be treated as a unity, although there was to be for a while no central German Government, power passing instead into the hands of an Allied Control Council consisting of the Commanders-in-Chief sitting in Berlin (which, although in the heart of the Russian zone, was to be a four-power enclave with each Power garrisoning a separate Sector). The Council had to be unanimous. Thus no Zone Commander could have decisions imposed on him which he did not like and, if on any particular subject the Council failed to agree on what to do, he was free to act as he (and his government) chose. The carrying out of the Council's decisions would however normally be left to the Germans, although there was not at first any precise idea as to how this would be effected. At Yalta the British had prevailed on the Americans and Russians to give the French a Zone in the south-west (made up from parts of the British and American Zones), a Sector in Berlin, and, with more difficulty, a seat on the Control Council.

The German Armed Forces were not merely to be demobilised and cut down in numbers; they were to be disbanded completely. All war equipment and installations were to be destroyed, including all armament factories. The Nazi Party, Nazi laws, organisations and institutions were to be wiped out, and all Nazi and militarist influences removed from public life. There was some uncertainty as to how far this involved a ban on the employment of anyone who had worked for the Third Reich but elaborate plans had been prepared for interning all who had held certain posts or reached a certain rank in certain organisations like the SS. All war criminals were to be brought to just and swift trial (see Section 4 below).

Three further matters had been discussed but not settled at Yalta. One was the question of breaking Germany up into smaller states. A committee was set up to decide how to do this, and, in the interval before it met, all three Powers decided that they no longer wanted to do it. Western fear of Russian intrigue in a divided Germany, Russian hopes of extending influence over a united Germany, fear that a divided Germany would be an impoverished one needing financial help from outside, fear that division might merely stimulate a nationalist German movement for reunification, all would seem to have played a part in the change of mind.

But if Germany was not to be divided, what were her frontiers to be? The general answer was 'those of 1937'. It had however been agreed that Poland should be compensated for her loss of territory to Russia in the east by receiving some German territory in the west. The British and Americans had been prepared at Yalta to agree that the new German–Polish frontier should run up the Oder river to its junction with the eastern Neisse and then along that river to the Czech border. The Moscow Poles however had demanded that it should run along the Oder and another Neisse, considerably further to the west; the Soviet Government supported the demand. But it meant taking away from Germany virtually the whole of Silesia instead of about a third of that province; its grant would mean increasing by several millions the number of Germans who would either come under Polish rule or have to find a new home further west. The British and Americans refused to agree and the matter was left for later discussion. But before it could be discussed again the Russians conquered the whole of the area up to the Western Neisse, and turned it over to the Poles to administer, declaring it excluded from the authority of the Control Council. Many of the German inhabitants, though fewer than the Russians alleged, had not waited for them to arrive.

The third question was reparations. Russia demanded that Germany should pay these to her; Roosevelt and Churchill, though wanting little for their own countries, agreed. It was further agreed, in the light of the

An Iron Curtain in place of an Open Door

Should the German people lay down their arms, the agreement between Roosevelt, Churchill and Stalin would allow the Soviets to occupy all Eastern and South-eastern Europe together with the major parts of the Reich. An iron curtain would at once descend on this territory.

Goebbels, 25 February 1945

An iron curtain is drawn down upon the Russian front. We do not know what is going on behind.

Churchill to Truman, 12 May 1945

From Stettin in the Baltic to Trieste in the Adriatic, an iron curtain has descended across the Continent.

Churchill in his speech at Fulton, 5 March 1946

In the [State] Department's view, our eventual objectives with respect to the economic treatment of Germany should be (a) the abolition of German self-sufficiency and (b) the elimination of the instruments for German economic aggression. These two objectives conform to the general economic foreign policy of the US.

They are closely related. Abolition of self-sufficiency requires the removal of all protection and subsidies to high-cost domestic production. Elimination of the instruments for German economic aggression requires the prohibition of all discriminatory trade controls, clearing agreements and international cartel agreements.

The eventual objectives imply the assimilation – on a basis of equality – of a reformed, peaceful and economically non-aggressive Germany into a liberal system of world trade ....

It is important that development of the German economy should not be so drastically restricted [during the control period] as to prevent the maintenance of a basic livelihood for the German people.

State Department Briefing Paper for Yalta

failure to extract reparations in money after 1919, that they should now take three forms: removal of equipment, annual deliveries of goods and the use of German labour. The removals were to come from all over the country, which made Russia keen to see Germany treated as a single unit. The question was 'How much?'. The American and British answer in effect (though none too clearly formulated) was 'as much as Germany can afford to pay without becoming a burden on other countries' (and in particular the Occupying Powers). The Russian answer was a precise sum – $20 billion, of which Russia was to get half.

This, if agreed, was presumably to be extracted regardless of its effects on the Germans. The Russians were unlikely to mind if, in order to pay, the Germans starved; in any case, most of Germany's food had been produced in their Zone. The Western Powers, who wanted in the long run a flourishing and contented (and therefore peace-loving) Germany to make its contribution to world prosperity, were not prepared to be so ruthless. The British at Yalta refused to let a sum be named; Roosevelt, to appease the Russians, was ready to let their figure be used 'as a basis for discussion' by the Commission set up to work out the details. As the Russians advanced into Germany they appropriated, both collectively and individually, a wide range of equipment from watches through railway lines to atomic scientists, and took them off to work for the Russian economy.

The division of Germany into Zones had of necessity to be agreed in advance at a time when it was impossible to foresee exactly how far forward the various armies would get before fighting stopped. In the event the Americans reached places 120 miles east of their Zone boundary, and met the Russians on the Elbe; indeed they might well have reached Berlin if they had not been halted, though they would not have done so in sufficient strength to storm the city. Churchill pressed Truman to leave his troops where they were and refuse to withdraw until the Control Council had started work and the Russians had agreed to supply food to the Western Zones. But although Truman told Molotov in no uncertain terms that he considered the Russians to be breaking their promises over Poland and reparations, he refused to put pressure on them by following suit. It was and is clear that, if he had done so, the Russians would have retaliated by not allowing Western troops to occupy the Sectors allocated to them in Berlin (which could only be reached through or over Russian-held territory). In that case the whole arrangement for setting up the Control Council and governing Germany from Berlin on a Four-Power basis could not have been put into operation. Nobody could at that stage have foreseen that this would probably not have made East–West relations any worse than they were going to be anyhow and posterity would probably have placed on the West a proportionately larger responsibility for bringing about the conflict with the East.

When the three leaders met at Potsdam on 17 July, they were able without much difficulty to fill in the details as to how a denazified Germany was to be ruled in the immediate future. Though no central Government was to be established, central administrative departments in the fields of finance, transport, communications, foreign trade and industry were to receive instructions from the Control Council and either execute them or pass them on to subordinate authorities; locally, self-government was to be restored as rapidly as was practicable. Decentralisation was to be the aim but dismemberment was not mentioned. Political parties and free trade unions were to be allowed and encouraged; so was freedom of speech, press and religion. The judicial and educational systems were to be reformed to eliminate Nazi and militarist ideas and establish justice under law with equal rights for all. So far as possible, the population were to be uniformly treated throughout the country.

A number of imprecise phrases in these political clauses were later to provide grounds for arguing whether they were being honestly carried out; the very word 'democratic' proved open to varying interpretations. But the burning question was how Germany should be treated economically. On this the Americans had been slow to make up their minds over a controversy started in the previous September by Morgenthau's notorious plan to prevent Germany from ever again going to war by destroying her industrial plant and turning her into a primarily agricultural country; the suggestion had even been put forward that any population thus made surplus to requirements should be dumped in North Africa! Strictly speaking, the future of Germany was not the business of the Secretary of the US Treasury, but Morgenthau was an old buddy of Roosevelt's and Roosevelt had all along been inclined to treat the Germans severely. Although the Plan in its extreme form was soon shot down, the episode had the effect of discrediting the milder plans previously prepared, mainly in the State Department. These had proposed, along with disarmament and reparations, the ultimate integration of the defeated country into 'the type of world economy envisaged by the Atlantic Charter. ... An indefinitely continued coercion of more than sixty million technically advanced people ... would be at best an expensive undertaking and would afford the world little sense of security.'

Wrangling went on in Washington all through the winter between the State, War and Treasury Departments and definite instructions were not sent to Eisenhower, as US Military Governor in Germany, until 11 May 1945, three days after the surrender; for a further five months they remained secret. Germany was to be occupied as a defeated enemy country rather than a liberated one and the Germans were to have it brought home to them that they were responsible for the chaos and destruction which prevailed. The principal aim of the occupation was to prevent Germany from ever again becoming a threat to the peace of the world. Controls might be imposed on the German economy to support these objectives, to protect the safety and meet the needs of the Occupying Forces and assure the production of goods and services required to prevent starvation or such disease and unrest as would endanger those Forces. No action was to be taken which would tend to support basic living conditions on a higher level than that existing in any of the neighbouring UN members. No action was to be taken looking towards the economic rehabilitation of Germany or designed to maintain or strengthen the German economy. The document satisfied Morgenthau but by the time it was issued his influence was waning. Truman had no liking for him and, having a tidier mind than Roosevelt, turned for advice to the men and institutions set up under the Constitution to provide it. As regards foreign policy, this was the State Department. Morgenthau asked to be taken to Potsdam, was refused and resigned.

The British, while determined to see Germany thoroughly disarmed and justice done to those guilty of inhumanity, were well aware that German prosperity was essential to that of Europe, and nervous lest they should have to spend many of their inadequate resources on keeping a defeated enemy from chaos and starvation. They also attached more importance than the Americans to seeing that thoroughgoing changes were made in German society so as to reduce the glorification of the state, the power of landowners and industrialists, and the prestige accorded to the military. The two overriding concerns of the Russians were security and reparations. They wanted to make as sure as they could that there would never be a third German invasion of Russia and they urgently needed all the help they could get in reconstructing their country; reparations were made more important as a means to this end by their disappointments over other forms of aid. They wished to see Germany held down as a whole and they wished to draw reparations from all parts of it, notably from the Ruhr (which was in the British Zone).

The economic terms agreed at Potsdam largely followed American ideas. Germany was to be treated as a single unit. Essential commodities were to be distributed equally between the Zones. 'Primary emphasis' was to be given to 'the development of agriculture and peaceful domestic industries'. But enough industrial capacity was to be left (a) to meet the essential needs of the Occupying Powers, (b) to maintain an average living standard not exceeding the average in other European countries except Britain and Russia (whatever that negative formula might mean), (c) to pay for essential imports, so that Germany could subsist without external help. Everything superfluous to these three requirements was to be dismantled and either destroyed or made available for removal in reparations. But until the figures had been worked out, it was impossible to tell how much plant would be left and therefore how big reparations could be. The Russians, however, wanted to see a figure set and overriding priority given to its fulfilment, rather than to the fulfilment of the other requirements. This the Americans (and the British) resolutely refused. To overcome the resulting deadlock Byrnes (a Supreme Court Justice and former Senator who had replaced Stettinius as Secretary of State just before the Conference) proposed that each Power should take its reparations in the first place from its own Zone, that Russia should be entitled to half the total taken and that, as Russia's Zone was believed to contain 40 per cent of Germany's total plant, she should also receive 10 per cent of the total removed in the Western Zones (as well as a further 15 per cent in return for food and other supplies).

To compensate the Russians for abandoning their demand for a fixed sum in reparations, the Americans agreed to accept the transfer of the lands east of the Oder-Western Neisse to the Poles (though with the face-saving proviso that a final decision as to this should not be taken until the Peace Conference, then expected to follow quite soon). The Potsdam meeting thus ended in a compromise, with each side having its way where it had power to do so, since the Russians could not take plant from Western Germany without Anglo-American consent any more than the Anglo-Americans could enforce their views about Poland's frontiers.

The refusal of the Russians to open their records prevents us even today from knowing how clearly they saw the dilemma facing them in Germany. To satisfy both their major aims, they needed to have the country treated as a whole. Not only did they want their share of reparations to include equipment from the Ruhr and the rest of the Western Zones. They wanted Germany held down as a whole; one of Communism's dogmas was that the capitalist world would seek to destroy it and they must have been aware of the danger that the resources of Western Germany would be rebuilt for this process. There are signs that they were ready to make concessions which would keep control functioning on a Four-Power basis. Thus they gave up the idea of dismembering Germany. They did not entrust exclusive power in their Zone to Communists (in spite of having brought with them a hand-picked German group who had spent the war in Russia) but instead set up 'Anti-Fascist' Committees in which anyone with a claim to have opposed Nazism was encouraged to join (though they took care to keep the more vital posts in communist hands). They allowed three other 'democratic' parties besides the Communists to be started. While they took under state control heavy industry and firms which had belonged to Nazis, they left small firms and retail trade in private hands. When in the late summer of 1945 they carried out a land reform designed to break the power of the big proprietors, they did not turn the estates into state farms but distributed them among peasants. On reparations and frontiers however they were not prepared to let American views prevail, although the effect of their refusal on American opinion probably resulted in their obtaining in the long run less security and no more reparations.

Much the same applies to their relations with Germans. Both then and since there has been argument as to how far they sought to turn Germany Communist. Stalin once said that Communism fitted Germany as badly as a saddle fitted a cow. While this is hardly conclusive evidence of his intentions, there were signs that Russian hatred of the people who had devastated their country did not turn into love immediately a German became a comrade. The Germans for their part had long despised Slavs and this attitude was not wholly dispelled by the fact that the Slavs had beaten them. Advancing the cause of Communism in Germany was therefore likely to be uphill work which would however have been eased if it could have been associated with prosperity and success. Instead the cruel and uncivilised behaviour of the Red Army to the German population (something possibly beyond the control of the Russian leaders) had increased German antagonism which the exaction of reparations in full was not going to diminish. Some evidence suggested that the Russians could not agree among themselves about where to strike the balance but those of them who had the job of removing the plant usually seemed to get the upper hand over those who were trying to govern the Zone. Yet if the Russians were not prepared to meet the wishes of the Anglo-Americans and preferred to run the risks of a quarrel, they would find themselves wanting to win the friendship of the Germans against the West. On balance the security and prosperity of Russia itself (and of the Soviet regime in Russia) would seem to have been given priority over the chances of advancing security and spreading Communism further afield.

The Anglo-American dilemma was the mirror image of the Soviet one. It involved choosing between retaining the co-operation of the Russians and pursuing the goal of an Open World. By refusing to toe the Russian line, the West certainly ran the risk of splitting the world into an open half and a closed one. But as the Russians seemed bent on keeping their half closed anyhow and as the acceptance of any demand on which they insisted seemed likely to turn Germany from an asset into a liability, half a sound loaf had many attractions over a whole one with bugs in it. But on both the Russian and the Western side the choice was not made after calm, clear assessment of the situation and of the alternatives which it offered but, as always in human affairs, by men trying to sort things out under pressure in a protracted debate amid a mass of fears, prejudices and misapprehensions. The fact that only on one side was the debate conducted openly does not mean that it did not occur on the other as well. Truman at Potsdam got the impression that Stalin's relations with the Politburo were much like his own with Congress.

4 The punishment of war criminals

As the war went on and evidence of Nazi inhumanities mounted, calls for justice on the perpetrators became more insistent. To implement the calls was not however a straightforward matter. The Allies emphasised that they were fighting for justice and the rule of law. Could they then consistently punish anyone without a fair trial? But if not, before what court could the trial take place? If the alleged crimes had been committed against non-Germans outside Germany in violation of the peacetime laws of the country concerned, then the perpetrator, once found, could be handed over for trial in that country (as many were in, for example, France, Norway and Holland). But often the alleged crimes had been committed in Germany without violating Nazi laws, or else the exact geographical location was unimportant. If the answer in such cases was to set up a special court, what law was it to administer (in the light of the maxim that nothing is a punishable crime unless a law making it so already exists)? If the Court's judges were drawn entirely from the victors, could they be regarded as impartial?

The question of what constituted a crime was also complex. To kill a civilian in cold blood, or a soldier who had surrendered, clearly violated the international laws of war. To order someone to do so was equally criminal. But what about carrying out orders? Obedience is a fundamental principle of most armies and police forces. In war, many acts are permitted which in peacetime are crimes. But how wide should the licence be stretched? What about the decision to make war? The Allies, in the heat of battle, made much of the fact that the Germans had deliberately started the war by attacking Poland (and subsequently other countries) although a German Government had in 1928 signed the Kellogg Pact renouncing aggressive war as an instrument of policy. But how are nations, if dissatisfied with the *status quo* and unable to get it reformed by agreement, to achieve change except by violence? Does aggression merely become a crime, as treason has been said to do, when it is unsuccessful?

In January 1942 a Nine-Power Conference in London agreed that Germany must answer for her acts of aggression, her imposition of reigns of terror and other acts of violence and oppression. A Commission to list crimes and criminals began work in 1943. But, in spite of pressure from Allied governments in exile and Jewish organisations, as well as much discussion behind the scenes, nothing further had been agreed by April 1945. But justice was an essential element in the American world picture and on 2 May, six days before the war in Europe ended, Truman, without consulting other governments, appointed Supreme Court Justice Robert Jackson to act as Chief Counsel for the US in preparing charges against such war criminals as the United Nations might bring for trial before an International Military Tribunal, thus virtually excluding such other courses as summary execution, which some, including the British Cabinet, had preferred. A Conference of American, British, French and Russian jurists met in London on 25 June to settle the nature and jurisdiction of the Tribunal but the agreement which they reached, after hovering for six weeks on the verge of breakdown, left many problems inadequately considered. The Tribunal was to consist of a judge and an alternate from each of their countries; the crimes were classified as those against peace, those against humanity and those violating the laws of war. The accused were also to be indicted for participating in a common plan or conspiracy to commit these crimes.

The Tribunal, over which the British judge presided, met in the ruins of Nuremberg on 20 November 1945 to try twenty-one Germans prominently associated with the Hitler regime (Bormann being tried in his absence as it was uncertain whether he was dead). On 1 October

1946 it condemned twelve of the accused to death, imposed prison sentences of varying lengths on six others and acquitted three. It declared in addition that the SS, Gestapo and 'Leadership Corps' of the Nazi Party had been criminal organisations, but found that this description did not apply to the Reich Cabinet, German High Command or Nazi Storm Troops. The American Occupation Authorities thereafter held twelve further trials of these and other organisations, and of prominent persons who had belonged to them. These continued until 1949 and resulted in a number of sentences. As has been mentioned, a number of Germans were handed over for trial by the countries where their crimes had been committed and many of these were sentenced, some to death.

Meanwhile inside Germany the British and Americans had interned some 136,000 persons who had held responsible positions under Hitler and removed some 300,000 more from office. During the ensuing years down to 1949, some five million people were charged before Allied or German courts, and well over a million sentenced. (There had probably been some four million hard-core Nazis in Germany, while the Party and its various affiliated organisations had some twelve million members.) The Russians and French, though in many ways more hostile to the Germans in general, were less systematic in dealing with them and left more discrimination to German courts. After the Federal Republic was set up, many of the sentences were cancelled or reduced. In 1951 a law was passed requiring the reinstatement at their former rank of all who were not actually serving prison sentences (on the ground that to keep them out of the posts longer would mean punishing them twice for the same offence); their replacements, who had often been victims of Nazism, had in many cases to make way for them. All who had passed the age of retirement were paid their normal pension. But after 1958 a fresh series of trials was started by the Germans themselves on the basis of new evidence, all based on charges of inhumanity. (In some cases people who had been reinstated were put on trial again, though for crimes other than those for which they had previously been condemned.)

There have been many criticisms of what was done; there would have been more if nothing had been done or if lynch law had been allowed to prevail. Some amount to arguing that no crimes should be punished because all are not. The claim that people should not be punished for obeying orders implies, in a leadership state, where all orders in theory come from the top, that only the Führer was guilty.

The presence of a Russian judge offends many, seeing how many inhumanities his Government has committed. But in the immediate post-war atmosphere, it would have been difficult to keep him out. What can be regretted is that no serious consideration seems ever to have been given to the possibility of including neutrals among the judges, but whether any suitable ones willing to serve could have been found in time is doubtful. During the war anti-Nazis in Germany often insisted that justice must be left to them, but the German failure to take any action after the First World War did not inspire confidence that they would do better if given a second chance. Some hold that area bombing of cities and the forced repatriation of Russians and Poles after the war deprived the British of the right to pass judgment. But the first was undertaken because it was genuinely believed at the time to be a means of hastening victory, while the second would not in itself have been questionable if it had not been for what other people did afterwards. The process has taken a regrettably long time but that is partly due to the difficulty of catching the criminals and collecting the evidence, partly to the effort to make all trials fair.

The trials called attention to much evidence about German misdeeds which might otherwise have escaped notice and they have led to a tightening up of international law of peace and war. Few if any people were condemned for acts which they had not committed and there would be general agreement that what they did was morally reprehensible, even if it did not always clearly break an existing law. To have concentrated exclusively on cruelties done to individuals (as some have advocated) would have meant letting many of the accused off lightly, since their influence had largely been indirect; as it was, the Tribunal was cautious in interpreting the right given it in its Charter to punish 'conspiracy', 'aggressive war' and crime by membership of an organisation.

5   Control of the atomic bomb

On 16 July 1945 the experimental atomic bomb was exploded in New Mexico. The principles underlying the bomb had been known to scientists for some time. The unanswered questions were whether technical means could be found of bringing about an explosion and how much devastation such an explosion would cause. The answer to the second was not fully clear until the first operational bomb was dropped on Hiroshima on 6 August. Not only was one aircraft with a single bomb able to do as much damage as two hundred of the hitherto conventional kind but there were lasting radioactive and genetic consequences.

The Russians had known through spies about the bomb for some time. The news of the successful test, which Truman gave to Stalin without describing the weapon in any detail, told them that the engineering problem could be solved; it did not tell them how, but stimulated their search for the solution. US scientists had little doubt that the search would succeed before long, though the soldiers and politicians chose to overestimate the timelag. There is nothing to show that awareness of the feasibility made the Americans more intransigent at Potsdam or the Russians more compliant; the compromise which ended the conference (p. 37) involved, if anything, more yielding of ground by the former than by the latter. The bomb certainly made a full-scale Russian attack on America out of the question for some time but nobody even in America had supposed that Russia in her exhausted state would venture on such a thing. This however made Communist subversion in third countries all the more attractive as a means of weakening the US.

At first the Americans were inclined to suppose that the bomb had made them masters of the world, able to impose their will wherever they wanted. But the more they thought about the matter, the more doubtful this seemed. For so terrible were the bomb's effects that nobody would use it lightly, least of all a people convinced that freedom and peace went together. But if it was to be regarded as a weapon of last resort, justified only in defence, it could not be used as a means of forcing compliance on an adversary who made no direct attack.

There was however one way in which there seemed to be a possibility of the bomb being used to increase international security and peace. During the autumn of 1945 there was much discussion in America and Britain about entrusting monopoly control of atomic development to the United Nations, so as to strengthen the authority of that body. Individual nations would be required not merely to renounce the possession of bombs and preparations for making them but also to disclose what they were doing about stocking and using fissionable material for peaceful purposes (which were still at that time unexplored) and to allow UN inspection of their activities. On 3 October Truman told Congress that he intended to work for such an agreement and, after the British and Canadian Prime Ministers had given warm support,

Byrnes induced the Russians to agree that details should be discussed.

In the first half of 1946 an American plan was drawn up by which a UN Atomic Development Authority would take control of all fissionable material and make it available for peaceful purposes only; once the Authority was operating, the US would destroy its stock of bombs. Congress, which would have to approve any such agreement, overestimating the advantage which the bomb gave to the US and the likely durability of that advantage, was highly suspicious of the whole idea of sharing the weapon and the knowledge behind it with other nations. In an effort to allay such suspicions, Truman gave the job of presenting the Plan to the UN in June to the elderly New York banker Bernard Baruch, who insisted on adding a clause to deprive the Great Powers of their right to veto the Authority's proposals. The Russians, who were not prepared to see themselves deprived of such an opportunity for obstruction and bargaining, rejected the Plan, proposing instead an immediate ban on the production and use of weapons followed by the destruction of all those in existence, without simultaneously providing a reliable means of making sure that this was done. Naturally Truman was not willing to renounce the American head-start on such terms and, even if he had been, Congress would not have allowed it. But such a renunciation was the smallest concession needed to attract the Russians, who believed (correctly) that they could have a bomb ready themselves within a few years. How far information from their various spies accelerated their progress is hard to say but many Americans came to believe that it had been indispensable.

As often happens the Plan's chances of success hinged upon the order in which two steps were to be taken – in this case, surrender by the US of their existing weapons and submission by the USSR to effective control. Whether the Russians would in any circumstances have allowed the latter is doubtful; they have always been reluctant to let the outside world pry into their internal doings, both to conceal their weakness and to foster an exaggerated idea of their strength. They would never have agreed to do so except in return for absolute certainty that the US would surrender its bombs, without trying to extort concessions first. But the US would never make such a surrender until they were absolutely certain that the Russians had become incapable of making bombs themselves. The Plan posited the existence of that very mutual trust, the absence of which it was designed to remedy.

6   Britain after 1945

When the results of the first British General Election since 1935 were declared on 26 July 1945, even the Labour Party were surprised to find that they had won 396 seats out of 648 (albeit only gaining 48 per cent of the votes) and thus obtained a clear majority for the first time. But such figures should have been expected. Though the British people were profoundly grateful to Churchill, they were also a good deal less enthusiastic about his Conservative colleagues and knew that his own record as a peacetime Minister was less impressive than his war-time one – as he demonstrated afresh by mishandling his election campaign. Many influences had been disposing the public as the war went on to wish for sweeping changes after it was over; as long ago as June 1943 47 per cent of a sample poll had said that they intended to vote Labour or Liberal, while by April 1945 the percentage of those intending to vote Conservative had dropped to 24.

The Labour Party believed firmly in both liberty and equality. They had thought little about which should have priority if the two became hard to reconcile. They wanted to socialise 'the commanding heights of the economy' which in practice meant taking into public ownership transport, energy and steel. They had not thought much about how best to do this, with the result that they contented themselves with replacing boards of directors with boards of government-appointees and did nothing to give the workers a greater say in management or a greater share in profits. For the rest, private enterprise was to be left free but be regulated in the public interest. In the case of the coalmines and railways state intervention was inevitable since they were virtually bankrupt. The rising costs of medical treatment also pointed to the need for a state-run scheme, though the National Health Service owed to Aneurin Bevan as Minister of Health its actual form as a nationwide system financed out of taxation rather than by insurance. Insurance was used to provide funds for pensions, unemployment pay and other social services. An Act passed in 1944 had already provided for free secondary education. These extensions to individual welfare were however made in the face of an economic situation which was highly unpropitious.

Even before the war Britain had not been properly paying her way in the world and wartime sacrifices had weakened her still further. To produce the arms needed for fighting, she had had to run down her output of peacetime goods and in 1944 her exports only amounted to a third of those of 1938. One of the conditions of Lend-Lease had been that nothing obtained under it could be exported or used to make goods for export. Before Lend-Lease began to operate, a quarter of Britain's overseas investments had been sold to pay for American supplies (p. 17) and many of those which were left were not easy to realise. Although she still had assets worth £3,000 million abroad, she had run up an equal amount of debt on which interest had to be paid; these debts were being increased by heavy Government expenditure overseas. Gold and dollar reserves had been run down from $4,190 million to $1,409 million; instead of being large enough to pay for a year's imports, they would barely last for four months. Many of the country's suppliers and markets, both in Europe and Asia, had been devastated and disrupted; they could not for the time being provide their usual goods. The bulk of the supplies which were essential had to come from North and South America. But, with Lend-Lease ended, how were they to be paid for? Owing to the reasons just given, there was not enough money available and before Britain could offer goods in exchange, she had not only to make them – which first involved converting her factories back to their peacetime uses – but also obtain the materials, which involved the same problem of how to pay. In the interval, she had to keep her population fed. The expectation was that it would take her three years before she could pay her way again and during the interval she would need to borrow $6,000 million if she was not to starve.

Though rulers and ruled had already been working under stress for nearly six years, they met this challenge with remarkable success, as the table illustrates. By the time the war ended, the economic system was being run all out, with virtually no unemployment. This unprecedented level of full employment was maintained for the next five years (except for a few weeks in the spring of 1947 when the transport system was

Britain's economic record 1946–50

	1946	1947	1948	1949	1950
Employment in industry	100	108	111	112	115
Industrial production	100	108	121	129	140
Personal expenditure (at 1948 prices)	100	103	103	103	108
Volume of exports	100	139	139	139	177
Volume of imports	100	114	119	129	130

From G. D. N. Worswick and P. H. Ady, *The British Economy 1945–1950*, p. 3.

paralysed by bad weather, power stations as a result ran out of coal and electricity had to be cut off). Industrial output was raised at a steady rate of 8 per cent, initially by demobilising workers from the Services and then by improving methods of production. The target of increasing exports to one-and-three-quarters their pre-war level by 1950 was met, helped by the worldwide demand for goods and the temporary absence of Germany and Japan, two major pre-war competitors. Imports remained low, partly because world scarcity meant that more were not to be had. Indeed British payments would have been comfortably in balance as early as 1946, had it not been for the heavy expenditure which the Government had to make abroad as a result of commitments undertaken during the war to occupy Germany and help in re-establishing order in various other countries. As a step towards cutting down such expenditure, the Government announced in February 1947, after the fuel crisis, that it could no longer afford to keep troops in Greece or give financial help to Turkey (p. 70). But the much more important decision to withdraw from India in August 1947 was not taken in order to save money but because the Labour Party believed that the Indians were entitled to govern themselves.

At home, investment in new machinery was roughly double the pre-war scale. But such a rise was not merely needed to make up for the peacetime investments which had had to go unmade during the war. Since the closing decades of the nineteenth century Britain had not been investing as much in new plant as her main rivals, such as the US and Germany. An even higher post-war rate of installation and replacement would therefore have been desirable to make up fully for lost ground. But the problem was to find the necessary resources. With the economy at full stretch there was no unused capacity to draw on. Exports had to keep their priority. As the table shows, personal expenditure at home, which had been cut to the bone during the war, only increased by 8 per cent, and this had to be spread among a growing population. (Taxation however reduced the share of the rich and the new welfare benefits increased that of the poor.) Only 840,000 houses were built during this period, in spite of four million having been destroyed or damaged during the war; in any case materials saved by doing less building would have been little use for making new machines.

To achieve these results the Government kept in force nearly all the wartime controls. Food, clothing and domestic coal continued to be rationed; bread rationing, which had never been resorted to during the war, was brought in to help in feeding Germany. Licences were still required for many imports and for building, while steel was allocated. The only important power allowed to lapse was that of directing labour to particular jobs. There were some in the Labour Party who favoured making such a system permanent. It was to be used as a means of planning the allocation of national resources, as had been done in Russia. From 1947 onwards the Government brought out each year an Economic Survey which set out targets for future production, exports, investment and the like. After the fuel crisis a Central Planning Staff was set up. But the controls were far from popular; although the Government made great efforts to explain what their object was, the public found it hard to understand why they were prevented in peacetime from living as they liked. As time passed and supplies grew ampler, the Conservative opposition and the business community called for derestriction. The Government made concessions to the demand, perhaps without full awareness of the implications; from 5 November 1948 onwards there was a series of 'bonfires' of controls. The relaxation, however, increased the difficulty which the Government were already finding in making the economy move in the direction which they desired. The targets in the Surveys gradually degenerated into 'best available guesses' as to what, on the basis of past performance, might be expected to happen in future. The main achievement of planning was to give a little more consistency to the various parts of the Government's policy. Even the nationalised industries were not properly co-ordinated.

The story would however have been even more austere if Britain had had to depend entirely on her own resources. The hopes which some of her leaders had had of getting help from the US as a gift or interest-free loan were disappointed but in 1946 Congress agreed to a loan of $3,750 million at 2 per cent, to which Canada added a further $1,250 million. Even so, there were Americans who said that the sum was unnecessarily big, just as there were some Britons who said that the terms were impossibly harsh. For as an integral part of the loan the British Government were required to sign the Bretton Woods Agreement and thereby repeat the commitment to freedom of trade and payments which they had accepted in Article VII of the Lend-Lease Agreement. Conservatives objected to this commitment as impeding Britain's ability to impose effective tariffs, Left-wing Socialists as impeding effective planning of the economy. Moreover the Government was required to make sterling freely convertible into other currencies (including the dollar) a year after the loan began to operate (which in practice meant 15 July 1947 – five years earlier than was required by the IMF). For sterling to become freely convertible was an essential element in any free international economic system, since it was still a major world currency. Moreover the Americans had some justification for pressing the British, who were inclined to be over-cautious. But as things turned out the commitment to convertibility at a definite date, made eighteen months ahead, was too rigid and took too little account of what the situation might be when the time came for it to be carried out.

Hand-in-hand with the convertibility of currencies went the removing of barriers to trade. Immediately after the war these consisted not merely of tariffs but even more of 'quantitative restrictions' or 'quotas', involving the limitation by a government of imports to those goods for which it had issued a licence. For all countries were short of gold and dollars, were not prepared to pay out gold and dollars for any imports not essential to them and were reluctant to accumulate in payment for their own goods currencies which were unconvertible. They therefore concluded bilateral agreements with the countries from which their principal supplies came, by which they undertook to licence for import into their territory from the other country in the agreement 'quotas' of goods worth roughly the same amount as the other country was prepared to import from them, the aim being to pay for goods with goods so that no money need pass. Before the war, by contrast, Denmark might have paid for imports of steel from Belgium by exporting butter to Britain, leaving the British to pay the Belgians by selling them cars; some trade was even more roundabout. Bilateralism and quotas reduced the possibility of such deals and thus cut down international trade. Instead Belgium refused to sell steel, which was much in demand, unless purchasers also agreed to issue import licences for azaleas, which Belgium produced but could not otherwise find a market for.

In the autumn of 1946 a United Nations Conference on Trade and Employment met in London to prepare a Charter for the International Trade Organisation (above, p. 20). The US Government submitted a draft which had been made in consultation with the British. It was in two parts, of which the first proposed a general pledge to adopt policies leading to full employment. The other provided for the progressive reduction of tariffs and the elimination of both preferences and quotas. The British were nervous about renouncing anything which might help them to rebuild their export trade and there was much opposition, particularly among Conservatives, to the demand that Imperial preferences (i.e. agreements by which lower duties were charged on goods from Commonwealth countries than on those from elsewhere) should be given up. In the end it was agreed that existing preferences might be kept but that no new ones should be created. As time went on, with tariffs being lowered and prices rising, preferences, which were usually expressed in terms of cash rather than as percentages, dwindled in value. But the controversy over them raised feelings on both sides out of all proportion to their importance.

The Americans for their part had decided that Congress would never agree to any international scheme which involved all US tariff rates being reduced by a uniform percentage and that the only way of progress was to get authority to negotiate mutual reductions with their principal suppliers and then extend those reductions to all other countries which joined the Trade Organisation. Thus America might agree to reduce its tariff on motorcars in return for a corresponding reduction of the British tariff on office machinery; the new rates would then apply to all member countries and not just to the two striking the bargain. The advantage of this method was that these individual agreements did not need to be submitted to Congress. The first bargaining session, at Geneva in 1947, resulted in 45,000 reductions covering trade worth $10 billion. To regulate the negotiations the participating countries signed a 'General Agreement on Tariffs and Trade' (GATT) which was originally regarded as a stopgap measure, to be replaced by the Charter of the ITO when agreement on the draft prepared in London had been finally reached in a wider Conference held at Havana in the winter of 1948-9.

7 France and Italy

France had been in decline for some time before 1940. In the century after 1846, the population only rose by 15 per cent whereas those of Britain and Germany doubled. The war of 1914–18 involved much destruction and loss of life; production in 1929 was little higher than in 1913 and fell away again thereafter. The revolutions between 1789 and 1870 had given political power to the small men in business, in the shops and on the land; they were antagonistic to economic change for fear it would favour large-scale enterprise to their disadvantage. Social change was resisted by the upper classes who were never wholly reconciled to their loss of political predominance; some of them would have preferred to see Hitler (i.e. the Fascists) in power than Blum (the Socialist leader of the 1936 Popular Front). Working-class discontent brought votes to the Communists who in 1939 were ordered by Moscow to sabotage the war effort. Defeat was thus due as much to internal as to external factors. Thereafter a cruel enemy occupation brought impoverishment and made disaffection patriotic.

The damage done by fighting was however relatively superficial and the loss of life limited. Though the system for distributing food was temporarily dislocated, France still possessed the great advantage of being able to feed herself in most things. Moreover there were grounds for hope that the unity which had been established in the Resistance could be carried over into peacetime politics. The actions of the Vichy Government between 1940 and 1944 had discredited those authoritarians who put Fascism before France, while those who did the reverse had learnt to work with the left. Moscow was now telling the Communists to support an anti-Fascist coalition. Nazism had taught the Catholic Church that liberal tolerance of thought was preferable to totalitarian persecution of Christianity; the result might be a softening of the antagonism between radicals and clericals which had done so much to weaken the Third Republic. Finally the nation had in de Gaulle a leader whom most people respected.

Politically these hopes were disappointed. An attempt by Blum to convert the Socialists into a party of moderate reform was defeated by doctrinaire Marxists. This made co-operation impossible with the Mouvement Républicain Populaire (MRP), a party of Progressive Christian Democrats whose Resistance record led to them winning second place in the 1945 election. Nor were the Socialists prepared to merge with the Communists. De Gaulle, who from the Liberation in August 1944 until the election of a Constituent Assembly in October 1945 was virtually a dictator, considered that his duty was to unite the nation and made no effort to organise a party of his own. He gave first priority to restoring France's morale by re-establishing her as an independent power. He resented Roosevelt's tardiness in recognising him and the American tendency to treat France as a second-class state. The fact that she was for the moment dependent in many ways on the US only reinforced his determination to assert himself. As one sign of this, he refused to relinquish Indo-China and instead sent an army to restore French authority over it.

As a symbol of the unanimity which the nation was supposed to have recovered, de Gaulle's first Cabinet included members of the four main parties, Radicals, MRP, Socialists and Communists. The Communists, however, were kept out of all the key posts, even after the election showed them to be the strongest party. The Government proceeded to put into effect many of the plans which had been worked out during the Resistance, especially measures of nationalisation and social security. Women were given votes for the first time. But when in January 1946 the Assembly rejected the Budget, de Gaulle resigned. He regarded the move as a sign that the party politicians were bent on putting the Government at the mercy of Parliament. This he considered to have been the biggest flaw in the Third Republic and was determined to have no part in another such system. He may also have foreseen a period of economic shortages and Communist threats which would frustrate his ambition to increase French influence by standing as a free agent between East and West.

The Constituent Assembly did produce much the sort of constitution which de Gaulle had feared, only for it to be rejected in a referendum, largely on the ground that it might allow the Communists to manipulate the legislature. When a second attempt was put in hand, de Gaulle propounded his alternative of a strong executive but failed to get the draft changed in the way he wanted. In a second referendum in the autumn of 1946, however, almost a third of the electors voted 'No' to the Assembly proposal while another third failed to vote at all, thereby suggesting that though the nation feared a strong government, it had no enthusiasm for a weak one.

In practice the Fourth Republic did turn out very like the Third, with numerous parties, short-lived ministries and governments at the mercy of the Assembly. The growing East–West tension made it increasingly difficult for the Communists to go on supporting the Government and when in April 1947 their Ministers backed a strike in the publicly owned Renault works, the Socialist Prime Minister Ramadier acted on the promptings which he was getting from Washington and made them resign. For a moment in the early summer of 1947 it looked as though the economic crisis might play into the Communists' hands and, after the Marshall Plan was launched (p. 82 below), the Party acted on the promptings it was getting from Moscow and went over to a policy of violent opposition; the strikes which they called were ruthlessly suppressed by the Socialist Minister of the Interior Moch. In 1947 also de Gaulle returned to politics at the head of a new organisation called the Rassemblement du Peuple Français which had more authoritarian traits then he perhaps intended. With influential groups on each wing of the Assembly thus hostile to the Republic, the burden of maintaining it fell on the parties of the Centre and, as the votes of all of them were needed to get a majority, positive proposals for change were hard to carry out. In 1951 the Socialists became impatient and withdrew from the Cabinet but by their absence only increased the influence in it of the forces favouring inaction. After gains in the 1956 election they came back to power but found that they could only continue to hold it by jettisoning most of their own policies. Thus the Left never succeeded in giving practical effect to the strength which they had displayed immediately after the war and the period was characterised by a steady rightwards drift. One symptom was that the MRP dwindled to insignificance.

Yet the Fourth Republic saw the French economy recover a new lease of life. The population suddenly grew by 10 per cent in a decade. The gross national product increased until, in the last three years before the regime collapsed, it went up at an annual rate of 8 per cent, the highest in Western Europe. In part this was due to the forces which were at work all through that area. But part of the credit must go to a small group of officials in the Planning Commission, led at first by Jean Monnet, who systematically worked out the production capacity which France would need in order to reach a target level of economic activity. They communicated the results to the executives of a few big firms who then saw to it that, with state help, the necessary investments were made. The process was made easier by the extent to which industry (including banks and insurance companies) had been nationalised, by the common background of the officials and executives concerned (especially through their training in the National School of Administration and other Grandes Écoles) and by the long habituation of French business to an extent of government 'guidance' which would never have been tolerated in the United States or Britain. What was remarkable was that this process of planned expansion almost completely escaped political control. The Planning Commission was brought into existence by a ministerial decision soon after the war but its actions thereafter required no legislation. Ministers changed too often to have much influence on, or even knowledge of, what was being done. The parties behind the Governments, and the small men for whom they largely spoke, were unobtrusively circumvented. So were the trade unions.

Economic development in Western Europe was destined to be most intense within the area bounded by a line drawn from Rotterdam through Le Havre, Marseille, Trieste and Hamburg back to Rotterdam. A considerable part of France (including much which voted for the Left) was outside this. But in Italy the contrast between the industrialised north and the agrarian south was even more marked. Italy is almost half the size of France yet since the 1930s has had a larger population. She lacks most industrial raw materials, has little or no coal and had lost about a third of her wealth during the war. Not surprisingly therefore her gross domestic product per head was both in 1937 and in 1950 less than half as big as the French.

Paradoxically it was the south, never conspicuous for democratic ardour, which was freed first. Another eighteen months of fighting was needed to complete the process of evicting the Fascists and their German masters. The monarchy, which had lost credit by collaborating with Mussolini, saved itself from immediate overthrow by taking the initiative to remove him. The bayonets of the Anglo-Americans, whose Military Government kept its control of the north until 1 May 1946, militated against the chances of resistance activity in that area, where it was predominantly Left-wing, leading on to a social revolution. As in France the Communists were at the outset ordered by Moscow to support an anti-Fascist Coalition and the Cabinet continued to contain Communist ministers until they were turned out (along with the Socialist ones) in May 1947. Had the Party tried to seize exclusive power, it would undoubtedly have been suppressed.

The Catholic Church put its very considerable influence behind the new Christian Democratic Party whose able leader, Alcide De Gasperi, had been protected from the Fascists by being given a job in the Vatican Library. The premiership has remained a perquisite of his party ever since he took it over in December 1945. A referendum in June 1946 resulted in the substitution of a Republic for the monarchy (by 55 per cent, predominantly in the north, against 45 per cent, predominantly in the south). Elections to a Constituent Assembly in the same month gave the Christian Democrats 207 seats against 115 for the Socialists and 104 for the Communists. But the smaller parties of the Centre like Liberals and Republicans were strong enough to provide a majority for the DC without there being any need to rely on the Left. Unless a crisis occurred, there was clearly not going to be a fundamental recasting of Italian society. In return America, through UNRRA and directly, provided $1.6 billion in aid up to June 1948 and by the end of 1947 production had been brought back to the 1938 level. But Italy's fidelity to the West was to have lasting consequences for her politics. The strength of the Christian Democrats, when taken with the refusal of the remaining parties (other than the Socialists) to enter into a coalition with the Communists, meant that the opposition, though representing 40 per cent of the voters, could never take over the government. By contrast the Christian Democrats could rely on being always in the Government.

The birthrate in the poor South was almost double that in the rich North, thus exacerbating the area's overpopulation and creating a perennial need for new jobs. Until the 1920s the traditional safety-valve had been emigration to the Americas but they then set up barriers to check entry and in 1945 alternative destinations were hard to discern. Alleviation was also provided by posts in the civil service, which saddled the country with an excessive, conservative and obstinate bureaucracy, adept at frustrating the intentions of reforming Ministers and at feathering its own nest. In the years after 1945 most relief was to be provided by the labour needs of affluent and expanding countries like West Germany and Switzerland and by North Italy itself. A sustained drive was also made to channel industry and its jobs southwards, though this proved easier to plan than to achieve.

The Italian economy was dominated by half-a-dozen large private firms (of which Fiat, producing 90 per cent of the cars, was the best known) but even more by the Istituto per la Ricostruzione Industriale (IRI), set up by Mussolini in 1933 to take over a number of firms which were going bankrupt. By 1945 the State, through IRI, owned various banks, the steel, ship-building and cement industries, the main shipping (and later air) lines, the telephone and radio networks and a number of firms in heavy and light engineering – even a chain of confectioners. A similar body ENI was set up in 1953 to exploit the fields of natural gas whose discovery gave such welcome relief to the country's energy problems. Most of the companies were run as profit-making concerns, without subsidies, raising their funds on the open market. IRI and ENI together became responsible for over a fifth of all capital investment in manufacturing, transport and communications. The considerable success which they were to achieve was partly due to the independence on which their managers, like Renaissance *condottieri*, insisted rather than to any centralised planning to which the small number of decision-taking centres might have been expected to lend itself. On the other hand their ultimate control by the state gave to Ministers a wealth of patronage which added considerably to the attractions of office.

Italian industry thrived on the low cost of its labour, combined with the high skills of its engineers and designers. It made money by converting imported raw materials into the durable and soft goods which the consumers of the West were to take to their hearts as their taste rose in line with their incomes. Italian silks, stiletto heels, cheeses, coffee-making machines, films, typewriters, refrigerators, mopeds and motorcars became the vogue.

8   The US and the USSR in Eastern Europe

The experience of Potsdam blunted the appetite of the leaders for further encounters; there was not to be another 'summit' meeting for ten years. Instead the Foreign Ministers (including those of France and China) were given the job of tying up the ends which had been left loose. The Ministers first met in London six weeks after Potsdam broke up – and four after Japan surrendered. At the top of their agenda came the preparation of peace treaties with Italy, Finland, Hungary, Rumania and Bulgaria; Germany was left till the last not so much because she was the most important as because some time was bound to elapse before she had a government to give undertakings on her behalf. At Potsdam the three leaders had agreed to 'examine in the near future, in the light of the conditions then prevailing', the establishment of diplomatic relations with each of the four satellites (other than Italy); this phrasing was designed to cover up the flat refusal of America and Britain to establish relations with Rumania and Bulgaria until the puppet regimes which the Russians had put into power there were made more representative and free elections held. The Russians were behaving in the Balkans on the basis of the arrangement as to spheres of interest which Churchill had concocted with Stalin in the previous October (above, p. 12) and, even allowing for the different interpretations which they put on phrases like 'democratic means' and 'governments responsive to the will of the people', their actions were hard to reconcile with the Declaration on Liberated Europe which they had signed at Yalta (above, p. 13). It is of course a dogma of the Communist creed that sooner or later their form of society will prevail everywhere; what holds it back is the exploitation and deception of the masses by capitalist masters. The Russians would probably have excused their pursuit of their own interests in Eastern Europe by arguing that their forcible intervention, which prevented the pre-war regimes from being restored, was allowing the 'real will of the people'

Two thoughts but with a single word

Ambiguity is the price of unanimity.

James Madison

There is too much difference in the ideologies of the US and Russia to work out a long-term programme of co-operation.

James Byrnes at Potsdam

The American insistence on the fulfilment of the Yalta Declaration on Liberated Europe was denounced in the Russian press as a thinly-veiled move 'to undermine the still-unfirmly-cemented democratic regimes in Eastern Europe', the internationalization of the Danube as an attempt to turn back the wheel of history to the Balkanization policy pursued by the imperialist Powers in the nineteenth century, 'equal opportunity' and the 'open door' as 'slogans of monopoly trusts', a 'quasi-liberal guise' to take advantage of the temporary enfeeblement of the vanquished countries in order to deprive them of economic independence.

G. C. Herring

Apparently in Greece the US press correspondents were happy but the people were not, whereas in Rumania the people were happy but the correspondents were not. The Soviet Union considers the people more important than the correspondents.

The Rumanian Government was liked by the Rumanian population but not by the American Government. What should be done? Should they overthrow it because it is not liked by the American Government and set up a Government that would be unfriendly to the Soviet Union?

Molotov in Council of Foreign Ministers, 21 September 1945

We must recognize that the words 'independent but friendly neighbour', and in fact 'democracy' itself, have entirely different meanings to the Soviets than to us. Although they know the meanings of these terms to us, they undoubtedly feel that we should be aware of the meaning to them. We have been hopeful that the Soviets would accept our concepts whereas they on their side may have expected us to accept their concepts, particularly in areas where their interests predominated. In any event, whatever may have been in their minds at Yalta, it now seems that they feel they can force us to acquiesce in their policies.

Averell Harriman (US Ambassador in Moscow)
to State Department, 6 April 1945

to express itself, in what were described as 'people's democracies'.

In Hungary (where Churchill's Kremlin bargain had given each side an equal say) a coalition government with a non-Communist majority was set up and confirmed by elections; it was recognised by the US at the end of September 1945. Finland presented even less of a problem. In Yugoslavia (the other case of fifty–fifty) Tito had ruled the country from the moment of its liberation by the Russians in the autumn of 1944 and disregarded Stalin's advice that he should form a coalition with the government of King Peter; and though the monarchy was not formally abolished for another year, King Peter had no effective authority. The elections held in November 1945 may not have been conspicuously free, but Tito's National Front got 80 per cent of the votes. Moscow was not merely confined to the role of friend and adviser but used its influence to restrain rather than to foment, though the Anglo-Americans were slow to realise that the tail was wagging the dog. In Bulgaria less than 5 per cent of the population were said to be Communists, while in Rumania the strength of the 'National Democratic Front' certainly did not entitle them to fourteen places in a Cabinet of eighteen.

At the London Conference the Americans presented draft peace treaties which began by saying that they would only be negotiated with regimes broadly representative of all democratic elements and pledged to early and free elections; Molotov was only prepared to let elections be held if the US would first recognise the regimes. Byrnes, whose long experience as a Senator inclined him to compromises, might have clinched the deal if other members of his delegation, led by the Republican lawyer John Foster Dulles, had not threatened to attack such a course as 'appeasement'; as a result the Conference broke up without agreement. Three months later Byrnes went to Moscow without Dulles, and did reach a settlement on much those lines; the Rumanian and Bulgarian cabinets were to receive the cosmetic addition of a few more non-Communists, after which the US Government would recognise and conclude Peace Treaties with them. Turning this arrangement into actual treaties took until January 1947 and the interval saw a major shift in Byrnes's attitude, under the pressure of public opinion at home.

Roosevelt, helped by the emergency of war, had understood how to secure and exercise a relatively free hand in foreign affairs, though even he knew better than to move too far ahead of his public. Byrnes, who could never forget that he had nearly been made Vice-President instead of Truman, imagined for a time that he could play his own hand. Like FDR, he considered that a policy could only be effective if there was adequate power available to back it up and that when such power is absent, as it was for the US in Eastern Europe, bargains offer the only chance of influencing events. But when standpoints differ, bargains involve the compromising of principles. Both in the American administration (notably in the State Department) and in the nation (as reflected in Congress) there were substantial groups who did not appreciate or refused to accept this.

Such groups advocated a firm stand on their interpretation of the principles which had been set out in the Atlantic Charter and reaffirmed in the Yalta Declaration. As Truman said in his first major speech on 27 October 1945, US foreign policy should be based on fundamental principles of righteousness and justice, which embraced self-determination and the Open Door. People who thought in this way accepted that only where America (or her allies) had forces on the ground were they in a position to secure the observance of these principles. But they would not openly admit their impotence any more than they would surrender their principles. They were equally reluctant to use such bargaining cards as did exist to obtain Soviet compliance in other directions, since that would involve returning to the old methods of compromise, balance of power and spheres of influence. They further favoured caution in the steps which US diplomats took in the areas concerned, so as to avoid giving the Russians grounds for charging them with infringement of the sacred right of every people to manage its own affairs, or prejudicing the right of appeal to the United Nations. The underlying attitude was that, if the Russian Government was not prepared to respect the American standpoint, it was not merely going back on its acceptance of the Atlantic Charter but thereby disregarding fundamental human rights. Any government which so behaved must expect to incur the systematic hostility of the United States, a hostility which would be maintained as tenaciously as the Russian adherence to their own positions. Moscow had to learn to be done by as it did.

Manner had its effect as well as matter. Negotiating with the Russians was a protracted and thankless business. 'If you treated Molotov badly', said the British Foreign Secretary Bevin, 'he made the most of his grievances and, if you treated him well, he only put his price up and abused you next day.' Soviet officials were sent to meetings with lines laid down for them by their superiors which they had little

Molotov

Real name Scriabin, a nephew of the composer ('Molotov' means 'hammer').

The best filing clerk in Russia.

Lenin

Looking rather like a head-gardener in his Sunday clothes.

Macmillan, at the signing of the Austrian Treaty

[Molotov] was the city dancer among us. He had grown up in an intellectual family, and as a university student, he had been at many student parties and knew how to dance the way students did. He loved music and could even play the violin.

Khrushchev Remembers

There are those who say that passion was not absent in the man whom Churchill described as carved from a slab of cold Siberian granite. Suspicious by nature and by Stalinist training, he took no chances. ... At Chequers ... and at Blair House, the President's mansion for distinguished visitors, he slept with a loaded revolver by his head. ... He ploughed along like a tractor. I never saw him pull off a delicate manoeuvre; it was his stubbornness that made him effective.

Charles E. Bohlen

... it suddenly came into Stalin's head that Molotov was an agent of American imperialism. And what was the evidence for this charge? It seemed that when Molotov was in the United States he travelled from Washington to New York by train. Stalin reasoned that, if Molotov travelled by train, then he must have had his own private railway car. And if he had his own private railway car, then where did he get the money? Hence, Molotov must have sold himself to the Americans.

Khrushchev Remembers

discretion to modify. Any new departure by the other side led to delay while they sought new instructions. Informal contact with non-Communists was discouraged for fear it might stimulate dangerous thoughts. The apparatchiks sought to gain their ends by causing embarrassment rather than by ingratiating themselves; in the hope of tiring an opponent into giving way, they put a strain on his patience. They were adepts at what came to be known as 'salami tactics' –

obtaining an appreciable share of the sausage by demanding a succession of thin slices, each of which seemed to involve too small a concession to justify halting negotiations by an uncompromising refusal.

9 Breakdown in Germany

Eastern Europe, where the Americans felt principles to be at stake rather than material interests, was undoubtedly the area in which they first became exasperated and alarmed by the Russians. In Germany where the consequences of disagreement would be more far-reaching, the will to co-operate was on both sides greater and the break slower in arriving. Indeed the French rather than the Russians proved the first stumbling-block. During the war Roosevelt had offended de Gaulle by refusing to take it for granted that that proud and determined man would emerge as the unchallenged French leader. When the Liberation vindicated the General's self-confidence, he invoked 'the superior interest of mankind' as requiring France to share in all decisions about Germany's future. But Stalin despised France for not having done much fighting during the war and was as opposed as Roosevelt to inviting her to Yalta. De Gaulle retaliated by refusing to meet the President afterwards and his penchant for presenting the Great Powers with accomplished facts in the occupation of Germany (as by trying to hold on to Stuttgart even though it was not in the French Zone) had to be curbed by cutting off his supplies. Such behaviour prevented him from being invited to Potsdam.

Although Churchill had complained at times during the war about 'having to bear the Cross of Lorraine' (de Gaulle's symbol), he believed that if the US was going to quit Europe within two years (p. 10) Britain would need French help to hold Germany in check. That was why he persuaded the other two leaders to give her a Zone and a seat on the Control Council. Nobody seems to have thought of making her assumption of that seat conditional on her acceptance of the policies laid down for that body at Potsdam, in spite of de Gaulle's clear statement that she would not be bound by any decisions in which she had not shared. Yet, as the Council's decisions had to be unanimous, this was tantamount to giving her a veto after the event. Smarting under her previous exclusion, embittered by defeat and by the memories of occupation, she objected to the treatment of Germany as an economic unity, as well as to the creation of administrative departments, political parties and trade unions on a nation-wide basis; her underlying object, besides that of making herself felt again in international politics, was to bring the whole area west of the Rhine under her sway, annex the Saar basin and get the Ruhr put under international control. From late September 1945 onwards her representative on the Control Council blocked all steps to set up central German agencies; de Gaulle's resignation in January (above, p. 52) brought no change in this attitude. France was still at this time dependent on the Americans for many supplies and no adequate explanation has ever been forthcoming as to why they did not use their whiphand to force her into compliance. The American leaders had many other things to think about. The State Department, which was primarily responsible for US relations with France and did not see eye to eye with the War Department, primarily responsible for American policy in the Control Council, was anxious to restore France's international status and reluctant to do anything which might gain votes for her Communists. The failure to get a central German administration working meant that the Zone Commanders had to act on their own and in doing so took different directions. Of course the Council, even if it had had Germans to order about, might well have disagreed on what orders to give them. But the underlying differences between the Occupying Powers would then at least have become clearer and the later division of Germany a little harder to achieve.

Meanwhile the Council's Economic Committee managed by March 1946 to produce an agreed plan for the future level of German industry. The figures did not bear close examination and many of the underlying assumptions were shaky. The British fought for a realistic view of what the minimum was on which Germany could subsist but American thinking was still dominated by reluctance to quarrel with the Russians and by Roosevelt's harsh attitude towards the Germans. As a result big concessions were made to the Russians and French whose main aim was to set as much as possible free for reparations. In theory at any rate the way was now open to decide how big reparations were to be. Almost immediately, however, the process of paying them was halted by the American Deputy Military Governor, General Clay, who on 3 May suspended further reparations deliveries from the US Zone. The importance of his action was largely symbolic, since the actual quantities involved were small. His aim was to get Germany treated as an economic unit, as agreed at Potsdam. For the US Zone was not self-sufficient and, as long as there was no exchange of food, materials and manufactures with other Zones, its population could only live and work if supplies were brought in from outside Germany – which meant in practice that the American taxpayer had to meet the bill for them. Not only were the French holding up central administration. They were also removing from their Zone for the benefit of their own economy many things which would have reduced the need for imports into Germany or, if sold as exports, helped to pay for such imports. They were further demanding a major share of the coal produced by Germany, regardless of the fact that, if Germany were deprived of so much, her economy would take all the longer to get going again.

But the French were not the only offenders; the Russians had never stopped plundering Germany from the moment they entered the country. They were keeping most of the German prisoners whom they had captured so as to make them work in repairing the damage they had caused. The Russians were also finding that the system of removing equipment from Germany for use at home left a lot to be desired; it was apt to get held up or lost *en route* and even if it did arrive, could often not be re-erected because the relevant documents had not been sent with it. They were therefore turning more and more to leaving the factories in Germany and taking the output instead; in June 1946 they listed two hundred plants in their Zone for such treatment. Reparations from current production had been contemplated at Yalta but left unmentioned at Potsdam. The Americans maintained that such reparations had been ruled out by the requirement that enough resources must be left in Germany to enable her people to subsist without help from outside; if the goods going to Russia (and France) had been sold as exports and the proceeds used to pay for imports, there would have been a smaller bill for the American (and British) taxpayer to pick up.

What those taxpayers were in fact doing (without realising it) was to subsidise indirectly the Russian people who had done so much to bring victory. If an alternative scheme for financing their recovery had been devised (as it was for the French who got a loan from the World Bank) the Russians might have shown more restraint. Instead, they answered the charge that they were breaking the Potsdam agreement by accusing Clay of doing the same. Moreover they were acting on their view that reparations should have priority over German living standards. The Americans, by contrast, were in practice interpreting the Potsdam requirement (above, p. 37) 'to maintain in Germany average living standards not exceeding the average of the standards of living of European countries' as specifying a floor rather than a ceiling – and moreover a floor which would rise as standards elsewhere in Europe went up.

Clay's intervention over deliveries had no effect upon Russian behaviour. Two months later Bevin threatened to suspend all exports from the British Zone and Byrnes, to prevent this, offered to fuse the US Zone economically with those of such other Powers as might be willing. The Russians did not react and the French made an ineffective counter-proposal. But the British, whose highly industrialised Zone was even less self-sufficient than the American, accepted with alacrity. The UK balance of payments was in no position to take the strain of feeding 22 million Germans; the net cost of imports for them went far to account for the £300 million which the Government spent abroad in 1946 (above, p. 47). A little later the US Government undertook to provide all the dollars needed to buy imports for both Zones; thereafter they used their position to halt the nationalisation of the German coal and steel industries on which the British Labour Government had decided.

On 6 September 1946 Byrnes, speaking in Stuttgart, said flatly that, if Germany was not to be treated as a unity, the Level of Industry Plan would have to be reconsidered. This would become even more essential if reparations went on being taken from current production. The United States was not prepared to co-operate in any arrangement which led to more reparations being exacted than had been provided for at Potsdam.

> Germany must be given a chance to export goods in order to import enough to make her economy self-sustaining. Germany is part of Europe and recovery in Europe ... will be slow indeed if Germany ... is turned into a poor-house.

In other words the experience of having to prop Germany up had put paid to the Roosevelt–Morgenthau policy of Four-Power action to hold Germany down. This was the view which the British had been pressing for some time. The speech also made clear that, far from going home after two years, the US would stay in Germany as long as the Occupation lasted. The Open World needed a prosperous Germany and America was prepared to make sure that Germany could prosper. She would also protect from retaliation all Germans who sided with her. To those who had watched at close quarters American attitudes gradually changing, the speech did not come as much of a surprise but, as far as the general public was concerned, it was a turning-point.

On 1 January 1947 the new entity 'Bizonia' began to function. Although it was supposed to have no political significance (so as not to prejudice the chances of reuniting all four Zones later), it was run (under Anglo-American supervision) by German boards representing the eight provinces (*Länder*) which had by that time been created in the two Zones and was unmistakeably a temporary halting-point on the road towards a West German Government. If the Russians wanted to prevent further progress down that road, they would have to offer an effective threat or an attractive alternative.

They however were moving, or encouraging the German Communists to move, along a different road but in a parallel direction. As was only to be expected after Russian behaviour, few Germans felt much sympathy for the Communist Party and the preference of the German working class for the Socialists was everywhere evident. But many people still felt that the feud between Communists and Socialists from 1919 to 1933 had played into the hands of Hitler. As a result they had found themselves side by side in the concentration camps. Should they not remain side by side to tackle the problems of defeat? Late in 1945 the Communists in the Russian Zone tried to exploit this feeling by starting a movement for the amalgamation of the two Parties and in January 1946 the Communist theorist Ackermann published an article arguing that different countries could take different ways to Communism. As the capitalist masters were no longer in control of the German state, revolution was no longer necessary there and the goal could be reached by political action alone. In the following month the Socialist executive in Berlin was induced to vote for absorption into a new Socialist Unity Party (SED); two days later a mass meeting of Berlin Socialists voted against such a merger and at the end of March a plebiscite confined to the three Western Sectors of the city (since the Russians had refused to permit it in theirs) produced an adverse majority of 82 per cent. Accordingly the Western Powers refused to recognise the new Party or to allow delegates from their Zones to attend its meetings in Russian-occupied areas. The Russians by contrast showed it open favouritism and in *Land* elections held in their Zone in September it won almost as many votes as all the other parties combined; on the strength of this, cabinets were set up which in three cases gave the SED a majority and in the other two parity. But in a simultaneous election in Berlin (for which the Four-Power body controlling the city had surprisingly enough managed to agree on rules) it only won half as many votes as the Socialists. In the Western *Länder*, elections about this time resulted in cabinets where Christian Democrats and Socialists shared power while Communists were unrepresented. Thus the political complexion of West Germany was beginning to differ markedly from that of East Germany.

10 Hull's policies come to a halt

Russian behaviour in Germany was read by the Americans and British not in isolation but as an extension of the behaviour in Poland, Rumania, Bulgaria and the Baltic States. Other events strengthened the impression thus created. In the autumn of 1945 the Russians had asked to be given a share of the Italian fleet, to be made UN Trustees for Italy's former colony of Libya and to be allowed greater freedom of passage for their warships through the Bosporus. These demands may have represented merely the staking-out of claims to be used later as bargaining-counters but were taken by the British as evidence of designs to control the Mediterranean. The Russians also dragged their feet over evacuating Iran (which they and the British had occupied in 1941), and thereby alarmed the Americans who were beginning to realise how important the Middle East would be to them once Western-hemisphere supplies of oil ran short.

There had long been people in the Western world who were inveterately suspicious of the Soviet Union because of its open hostility to private property, to religion and to personal liberty. An important group of officials in the State Department, with personal experience of Russia, had for some time past emphasised the evidence which went to show that country's rulers as ruthless, hypocritical, dominated by a lust for power and suspicious of anyone, either at home or abroad, who might threaten their hold upon it. Such people had argued that Stalin and his henchmen were not to be trusted, were bent on the undermining of 'capitalism' and would only co-operate with the free world when they thought that by doing so they would strengthen themselves at its expense. This picture won increasing attention as more and more people from Yalta onwards began to ask 'How far do the Russians seek to go? Will they rest content with control over their neighbours or do they aim at dominating the entire world? Are they playing power politics or trying to convert mankind to their creed?'

In February 1946 a number of events combined to have a marked effect on opinion. The Russians chose a new Supreme Soviet and went through the motions of an electoral campaign; Stalin made one of his rare public speeches. His main aim was to justify a further three Five-Year Plans, involving many sacrifices for consumers, by showing what the first three had achieved. His target was 'Fascism' and the terms in which he described his former allies were restrained. But his remarks were widely interpreted in the US as showing that no peace was to be looked for until Communism had supplanted 'Capitalism'. A week later the Canadian Government announced the arrest of twenty-two of their citizens who had been trying to steal atomic secrets for the Soviets; that the operation had been successful presumably caused more surprise than that it had been attempted. On 23 February there arrived in Washington from the *chargé d'affaires* at the Moscow Embassy, George Kennan, what has become known as the 'Long Telegram', summarising his views about the Russians and the best way of dealing with them. It is interesting that Kennan was provoked to action, in part at any rate, by an enquiry from the US Treasury as to why the Soviet Union should be unwilling to join the IMF and International Bank (p. 24).

The Soviet leaders, according to Kennan, portrayed their country to its inhabitants as living in 'antagonistic capitalist encirclement'. They represented a battle between the world centre of Socialism and that of 'Capitalism' as being inevitable; it would decide the fate of the two societies throughout the world. The Soviet aim must be to see that the capitalist nations fought with one another rather than with the USSR, and to neglect no opportunity of advancing the relative strength of that country in international society. The leaders did not base these theses on any objective analysis of the facts but were motivated to accept them by inner-Russian needs. Marxism was embraced as justifying the rulers' sense of insecurity both towards other governments and towards their own subjects:

in this dogma, with its basic altruism of purpose, they found justification for their instinctive fear of the outside world, for the dictatorship without which they did not know how to rule, for cruelties which they did not dare not to inflict, for sacrifices they felt bound to demand.

The causes of this attitude meant that there was no chance of its being relaxed.

> We have a political force committed fanatically to the belief that with
> the US there can be no permanent *modus vivendi*; that it is desirable
> and natural that the internal harmony of our society be disrupted,
> our traditional way of life be destroyed, the international authority of
> our state be broken, if Soviet power is to be secure.

Kennan admitted that Soviet power did not work by fixed plans and was
not inclined to take risks. 'Impervious to reason, it is highly sensitive to
the logic of force.' It was also still far weaker than the West. The way to
deal with it was to determine in advance the points beyond which it
should not be allowed to go and make clear that any attempt on its part
to pass them would be met by force. Essential to such treatment was a
clear realisation by both the American government and people of what
they were up against, while the sympathies of other nations must be
enlisted by projecting a positive and constructive picture of an
alternative world.

There is general agreement that this document, by putting into words
what many people had been coming to feel, had a lasting influence on
American policy. The political strategy which it embodied became
known as 'containment', a term which implied accepting that the areas
already under Soviet control were lost to the free world. But though
given wide circulation inside official circles, the Long Telegram
remained for the time being unpublished. Within ten days, however, it
was supplemented by a speech which Winston Churchill delivered in
Truman's presence at Fulton, Missouri. The phrase 'Iron Curtain'
here made its first public appearance in English as a shorthand
description of what had happened to Eastern Europe. The main
purpose of the speech was to call for a 'fraternal association' between
the two English-speaking Powers, a concept which was so obviously
designed to improve the position of the more easterly of these powers as
to be received with considerable hesitation in the more westerly one.
The Americans, however, were much readier to agree that Communism
constituted 'a growing challenge and peril to Christian civilisation'. The
Russians, according to Churchill, wanted the indefinite expansion of
their power and doctrines. No one could know what were the limits of
these 'expansive and proselytising tendencies'. But 'from what I have
seen of our Russian friends ... I am convinced that there is nothing they
admire so much as strength and there is nothing for which they have
less respect than military weakness'.

Two months later Bevin's Private Secretary noticed that at the meetings of Foreign Ministers the Americans had become far tougher. The Senate after considerable debate approved the loan to Britain (above, p. 48) not because of Britain's war record or of any theories about world economics but because of the need to keep her out of Russia's clutches. The same stiffening of attitude lay behind Byrnes's initiatives over Germany (p. 64) and Baruch's ultra-cautious plan for controlling atomic weapons (p. 44). It was illustrated when in September 1946 Henry Wallace (p. 25) was sacked from the job of Secretary of Commerce not merely for saying that 'the tougher we get, the tougher will the Russians get' but also claiming that Truman agreed with him.

The parameters of American policy

Byrnes is bent on a break-down, presumably to teach the Russians international conduct. Byrnes is an admirable representative of the US, weak when the American public is weak, and tough when they are tough. At present they are tough.

Pierson Dixon (Private Secretary to Bevin), 14 May 1946

If we are not allied to that great democracy [Britain], I fear somebody else will be and God pity us when we have no ally across the Atlantic Ocean. God pity them too.

Sam Rayburn (Speaker of US House of Representatives) on question of loan to Britain, July 1946

The most important task in conducting US foreign policy is focusing the will of 140m people on problems beyond our shores [when those] people are focusing on 140m other things. The slogans 'Bring the boys home' and 'Don't be Santa Claus' are not among our more gifted or thoughtful contributions to the creation of a free and tranquil world. We believe that any problem can be solved with a little ingenuity and without inconvenience to the folks at large.

For all our lives the danger, the uncertainty, the need for alertness, for effort, for discipline will be upon us. ... We are in for it and the only real question is whether we shall know it soon enough.

Dean Acheson

Much is still obscure about Russian internal affairs at this time but Wallace may well have been right. By 1946 there was a loss of influence by the non-Party members who had been allowed a hand in winning the war and who were interested in developing contacts with the West. The gainers were dogmatic Communists led by Zhdanov, as suspicious of the West as they were ignorant about it and determined to minimise its impact on Soviet life. In their drive against the free world their hands must have been strengthened by the way in which the drive against Communism seemed to be gaining ground within that world. The interrelationship between US external and internal policy was further illustrated after the Democrats lost control of Congress to the Republicans in the mid-term elections of November 1946. The new majority, though inclined to 'bipartisanship' in foreign policy, had to be persuaded that acceptance of the Administration's objectives meant refraining from cutting taxes to the point at which the funds available for defence and foreign aid became inadequate. The obvious way for the Administration to bring this home was by highlighting the threat from Russia.

At this stage, however, practically nobody saw that threat in military terms. According to Kennan, Soviet policy wanted at all costs to avoid 'a war of intervention' against the USSR. According to Churchill, it was the fruits of war which the Soviet Union wanted rather than war itself. There was indeed something ridiculous in the idea of a Russia which lacked a fleet, which had never come near matching America as an industrial power, and which was now weakened by war, even beginning to contemplate an assault on the unscathed continent, the home of the world's most devastating weapon. True, the US did not yet have many bombs, but the Russians had none. The US had reduced their forces from 12.3 to 1.5 million – but the Russians had reduced theirs from 11.4 to 2.9 million. They had also removed as reparations one line of every double-track railway in their Zone of Germany, a considerable handicap if they wanted to move west.

Where a threat was with more justification seen was in the activities of Communists and fellow-travellers throughout the free world. Whereas populations who had been conquered by force might have to be held down by force, thus adding to the Soviet Union's burdens, comrades who managed to gain power in their native countries might thereafter manage to go on keeping those countries out of the capitalist camp. Americans who talked so much about the right of nations to decide for themselves how they wished to be governed might well feel inhibited from intervening to prevent that decision going in favour of the Communists. What first brought the issue to a head was Britain's decision in February 1947 that she could no longer afford the support which she had been giving to Greece and Turkey (p. 47). In Greece the struggle against the Communists was far from won, while Turkey, besides having one of the largest armies in Europe, controlled the passage from the Black Sea to the Mediterranean (p. 66). If a British withdrawal were to leave a power vacuum in the area many people considered that the way in which it would be filled was too obvious for it to be permissible, (although the Yugoslav Milovan Djilas has recorded that Stalin at this time said to him in Moscow: 'What, do you think that Great Britain and the United States ... will permit you to break their line of communication in the Mediterranean? Nonsense. And we have no navy. The uprising in Greece must be stopped, and as quickly as possible.') But was the danger evident enough to Congress and public for them not only to agree that the US should replace Britain but authorise the expenditure which that course would involve? Truman little needed the encouragement which he received from his officials to deliver on 12 March an 'all-out speech' dramatising the danger. The 'Truman Doctrine' presented America, and indeed the world, with a choice between alternative ways of life:

One way of life is based upon the will of the majority, and is distinguished by free institutions, representative government, free elections, guarantees of individual liberty, freedom of speech and religion and freedom from political oppression. The second way of life is based upon the will of a minority forcibly imposed on the majority. It relies upon terror and oppression, a controlled press and radio, framed elections and the suppression of personal freedom. We [the US] will not realise our objectives unless we are willing to help free people to maintain their institutions and their integrity against aggressive movements that seek to impose upon them totalitarian regimes. .... It is the policy of the US to support free people who are resisting attempted subjugation by armed minorities or by outside pressures.

The US might have given up as hopeless its efforts to alter what was happening behind the Curtain but would exert its full strength to stop that Curtain being brought any further westwards.

Greece and Turkey were only the beginning. By the spring of 1947 those with vision could see that the whole of Western Europe faced an economic crisis. The situation, which had improved in 1946, was getting worse again. Far fewer supplies than in the past were coming from Eastern Europe. At the end of the war considerable stocks of food and materials built up during it still existed, particularly in Germany.

Several Governments of occupied countries had, while in exile, accumulated funds and these they had been able to draw on for early purchases. Supplies brought from America to aid the war effort were turned over to civilian use at cut prices once fighting ended. But all these stocks were beginning to run out and nothing was coming in to replace them. We take for granted in everyday life that there is a chain of supplies reaching back in various stages of readiness from the point of retail sale to the producers of raw materials – behind the loaf on the shop counter, the flour in the baker's bin; behind the flour, the wheat in the miller's store; behind the miller, the farmer reaping; behind the farmer, the seedsman and maker of fertiliser. The process of movement through the pipeline takes months, if not years. What was happening in 1947 was that these pipelines were becoming empty and most of them could only be filled again by bringing supplies from outside Europe. Even where the supplies existed in Europe, they often could not be used without the aid of other supplies (most notably wheat and oil) which had to come from outside. Thus the production of ballbearings in France and Italy could not increase because they had no acceptable currency with which to pay for the special steel required from Sweden. The owners of commodities in short supply would only part with them in exchange for dollars and the European countries not only lacked the necessary dollars but had no hope of earning them until they had goods to export, yet could not make the goods until they had the materials. A 50 per cent rise in American prices, due to too many people trying to reconstruct at the same time, reduced the amounts which could be bought with such money as was available. The harsh winter of 1946–7 aggravated the situation, chiefly because the transport system broke down and such supplies as there were could not be distributed.

Germany was the worst case, as the country most seriously devastated, with a dislocated transport system and a population swollen by refugees from further east. A country where waterways are important was badly hit when they froze over. Already the US was having to pay for all the dollar imports 'necessary to prevent starvation or widespread disease or such civil unrest as would endanger the occupying forces' (to quote the conditions in the commander-in-chief's instructions which had to arise before supplies could be brought in for the German population); even so the ration level of 1,500 calories a day for normal consumers could not be sustained (the figure for the US army was 4,200 calories). Coal production was running at 30 per cent of pre-war. Italy, which had never been self-sufficient in fuel, was not much better off;

her Government could not see how to finance any purchases of coal or oil after September. France's harvest prospects looked unfavourable. She needed 70 million tons of coal a year and was herself only producing 30 million; as the run-down British coal industry, in spite of nationalisation, had none to spare for her, she wanted all she could get from Germany. Her Government threatened to halt at the end of August all imports other than coal and cereals. The ensuing shortages and unemployment would give a golden opportunity for the strong Italian and French Communist Parties to bid for power.

The fuel crisis in February 1947 illustrated the narrow margin on which Britain's economy was working. Export earnings worth £200 million were said to have been lost. The rate at which she drew on her North American loans accelerated ominously and by the end of June half the $5 billion had been spent. Worse was to follow, for most countries wanted to buy from America and, whereas few had dollars, many had pounds. As soon therefore as sterling was made convertible, in accordance with the condition attached by Congress to the loan (p. 48), they presented their pounds for conversion into dollars and in thirty-six days another $1 billion had been used up. The remainder would have quickly gone the same way if convertibility had not been suspended and a new set of bilateral agreements rushed through. When the US loan was being negotiated, the Americans were led to believe that, before the pound became convertible, the British Government would reach agreements with its creditors limiting the rate at which they could change their pounds into dollars. In some cases this was done but in others for various respectable reasons it was not. By the time it became clear that arrangements could not be reached with everyone, it was too late to get Congressional consent to convertibility being postponed. Either the objections to reaching agreements should not have been allowed to prevail or a postponement of the obligation should have been asked for earlier.

America's wartime plans for the peacetime world had been shown up as inadequate. The hopes of an international order which was both universal and free had vanished. From Vladivostok to Lübeck the individual was being denied a say in the character of his society and in the choice of his rulers. The United Nations, intended as the forum in which international differences would be smoothed out under the harmonious supervision of the Great Powers, was degenerating into an arena where insults were exchanged and disaffection fostered. The international organisations which had been designed to bring about the free movement of men, money and goods were either failing to operate or faced problems far beyond their capacity to resolve. The Communists had refused to join them but had extended the scope of their own command economies in which production was decided by what bureaucrats thought would be needed instead of by what the consumer was prepared to pay. Bilateral trading and quotas were widespread and showed no signs of disappearing. Few currencies were convertible.

Fate – or chance – had however put into positions where they could take effective action a few individuals who could both see what needed to be done and had the determination to ensure that it was done. Chief among them was the ex-haberdasher from Missouri who had become President of the United States. Next came George Marshall, the general who, after guiding the armed forces of the Union to victory as Chief of Staff, had been persuaded by his ardent admirer Truman to postpone retirement for a few years in order to take over from Byrnes the equally gruelling and responsible post of Secretary of State. Marshall in turn relied on his Under-Secretary Dean Acheson, the quintessence of a 'Wasp' (White Anglo-Saxon Protestant), whose spiritual home might appear at first sight to be Edwardian England but who could all the same see that 'Britain has lost an Empire and not found a role'. Along with them went various others including an illegitimate boy from the fringes of Exmoor who had worked his way via Bristol Docks and the trade union movement to become Britain's Foreign Secretary and a former philosophy don from Oxford. Between them they managed in a remarkably short time to transform the situation. But, to start with at any rate, their efforts earned them scant gratitude from the American people.

11   The unnecessary panic

The Russian refusal to dance to the US tune sparked off among the Americans a political witch-hunt almost worthy of their Puritan ancestors, though nobody was actually burnt at the stake and only two presumed spies – Ethel and Julius Rosenberg – executed. At first the running was made by the House of Representatives Committee on Un-American Activities, a body originally set up in 1938 which, after languishing during the war, was revived in 1945; one of its more effective, since less rabid, members was a young man called Richard Nixon who in 1946 was elected as a Republican Representative for California.

The same election saw Joseph McCarthy sent to Washington as Republican Senator for Wisconsin but he did not become prominent until in February 1950 he claimed in a speech to be holding in his hands a list of 205 Communists employed in the State Department. The charge was investigated and found to be 'the most nefarious campaign of half-truths and untruths in the history of this Republic'. That however did not prevent the incoming Republican administration in January 1953 from appointing him Chairman of a Senate Committee on Government Operations. For the next twenty-two months he made the most of his opportunities but then overreached himself, notably in launching an attack on the loyalty of the Armed Forces, and in November 1954 was censured by the Senate. Thereafter the campaign began to wane, or rather to become counterproductive. An unexpected factor was the attitude of Earl Warren, appointed by Eisenhower as Chief Justice of the Supreme Court in 1953 who, although a Republican, proved a much stouter defender of civil liberties than his Democratic predecessor had been; under his influence the Court began to give judgments considerably stiffening the evidence required for convictions. But the scare of a 'missile gap' between 1957 and 1960 (p. 179) meant that the wave of intolerant persecution did not finally die out until the early 1960s.

There were many unlovely features about the agitation, which brought out much that was worst in American society. Shaky evidence, often hearsay, was accepted without proper examination. Little allowance was made for the fact that in the 1930s many of the younger generation, such as Alger Hiss, despairing of free enterprise, had been attracted to Communism as an alternative; others shared the widespread admiration for the war record of the Soviet Union. Most of them thought better of their enthusiasm later, but the attitude of the prosecutors was 'once a Communist, always unreliable'. Wide-scale use was made of informers and agents, thereby attracting dubious characters, prepared to say anything for money; one of these was convicted for lying under oath that he had lied under oath! Some victims were charged not with conspiring to overthrow the government but with holding the opinion that the government ought to be overthrown, since the virtual absence of a radical party, committed to seeking major changes in the existing system, made many people regard rejection of 'the American way of life' as tantamount to treason. One man was accused of disloyalty because he said that the House Committee on Un-American Activities was a greater threat to civil liberties than the Communist Party.

In 1947 the Attorney-General drew up a list of seventy-eight organisations which were regarded as 'subversive'; to have had any connection with any of these was made a reason for suspecting the loyalty of any government servant, while in 1951 Review Boards were instructed to dismiss all whose loyalty was so much as doubtful. People fell under suspicion simply for failing to break off relations altogether with communist parents or other close relatives. Suspects were removed not only from public service but from any firm with a government contract (even if the accused had no connection with that side of the work). Those who lost their jobs had difficulty in finding anyone willing to employ them, yet were often refused passports to leave the country (though at an early stage the Attorney-General had said 'those who did not believe in the ideology of the United States should not be allowed to stay in the United States'). Persons who took advantage of the Fifth Amendment to the Constitution, according to which nobody was compelled to be a witness against himself, and refused to answer questions, were automatically presumed to be guilty. Yet even at the end of the war the Communist Party had numbered under 80,000 and by 1957 had fallen to 10,000. No case of serious sabotage was ever proven, no spy unearthed comparable to Tyler Kent in the US London Embassy for the Nazis, Fuchs and Philby in Britain and Felfe in West Germany for the Russians.

The phenomenon however, remarkable as it was, is fairly easily explained. The division of powers in the American Constitution automatically sets legislature against executive and deprives senior members of Congress of the sense of responsibility induced by becoming a Minister. By the elections of 1948 the Republicans had been out of office for sixteen years (by 1952 for twenty) and were desperate to recover it, while the Democratic Party, thanks to its history, has a split personality, with conservatives and grass-root populists from the south at cross-purposes with radicals from the big cities. The absence of a homogeneous left-wing party tempted radical critics of society to become Communists in protest – or at least Progressives, widely regarded as almost equally unreliable. Truman felt compelled to institute loyalty reviews and make them look rigorous for fear that otherwise he would give ammunition to his political opponents;

Eisenhower believed it to be the President's duty to get along with Congress.

The kind of people who were suspected were those who had been associated with Roosevelt and the New Deal, so bitterly hated by Big Business and its camp-followers; they included 'egg-heads' inclined to liberalism and familiar with Britain, advocates of involvement in world affairs and of the United Nations. Many Americans of German origin (numerous in McCarthy's Wisconsin) resented having been involved in war against their native country, former isolationists resented having been involved in war at all. Catholics hated Communism, Irish emigrants Britain, people of Slav extraction Russian behaviour in Eastern Europe. The movement was thus the outcome of past prejudices and present fears, in which electoral calculations played more part than rational reflection. It was exploited as a sensation by the press as well as by the novel medium of television (though in time the sight of McCarthy on the screen helped to discredit him).

Yet when all is said and done, the American system emerged with some credit. The number of people called before Congressional Committees vastly exceeded the number of cases brought into court, which in turn exceeded the number of convictions (though acquittals often took time to secure). The danger of losing one's livelihood was greater than that of losing one's liberty, let alone one's life. The barriers set up by the Constitution and by American tradition to intolerance, injustice and tyranny were temporarily dented but not permanently impaired. Too many people kept quiet until the storm had passed and failed to speak out against the rabble-rousers or for their friends. But there were exceptions, as the quotations on the next page show.

Moreover many of the charges brought, although exaggerated, had a basis. To say that sympathy for Communism on the part of General Marshall had been responsible for Chiang Kai-shek's defeat by Mao Tse-tung in China was of course as absurd as to suggest that Roosevelt's concessions to Russia at Yalta had been inspired by a junior member of the US delegation called Alger Hiss. But objective examination of the Hiss case has not yet acquitted him of the charge of having passed documents to the Communists and having afterwards denied doing so; the Rosenbergs openly admitted their Party membership. Nearly all the persons accused had been radicals, if not Communists; Communism does engage in widespread espionage. Membership of the Party is not a reliable guide, since it often directs its agents to pose as liberals or even conservatives. There are many

The Communists within our borders have been more responsible for the success of Communism abroad than Soviet Russia.

McCarthy

A Liberal is only a hop, skip and jump from a Communist. A Communist starts as a Liberal.

Lt-Col. Randolph, of US Army Intelligence,
to Truman's Loyalty Committee, January 1947

The simple fact is that when I took up my little sling and aimed at Communism, I hit something else. What I hit was the force of that great socialist revolution which, in the name of Liberalism, spasmodically, incompletely, somewhat formlessly but always in the same direction, has been inching its icecap over the nation for two decades.

Whittaker Chambers (accuser of Hiss), 1953

We must not burn down the house to kill the rats.

Adlai Stevenson (Democratic candidate, 1952)

If Stevenson were to be taken in by Stalin as he was by Alger Hiss, the Yalta sell-out would look like a great American diplomatic triumph by comparison.

Nixon

I will not turn my back on Alger Hiss.

Acheson (four days after Hiss's conviction in January 1950)

I watch his [Acheson's] smart-aleck manner and his British clothes and that everlasting new-dealism in everything he does and says, and I want to shout, 'Get out, get out! You stand for everything that has been wrong with the US for years!'

Senator Hugh Butler (Republican) of Nebraska, 1950

The right to dissent or, if you prefer it, the right to be wrong, is surely fundamental to the existence of a democratic society. That was the right which disappeared first in every nation which stumbled down the road to totalitarianism.

Ed Murrow (radio commentator), 1947

---

countries in which it has succeeded in infiltrating the public services, justifying precautions to prevent this (nobody has a constitutional right to a job with the government). Liberals perennially face the difficult problem of having to decide how far people who aim to overturn civil rights should be allowed to take advantage of them; examples are not lacking of over-generosity in this matter leading to catastrophe. The answer may be that the case for rigour varies in accordance with the gravity of the danger. If that is so, the real charge against the American 'Commie-hunters' is that the danger was nothing like grave enough to justify the methods employed.

12   A tragedy without villains

Who was to blame for that estrangement between the Soviet Union and the United States for which the American columnist Walter Lippmann in 1947 coined the title of 'Cold War'? Few subjects have been more debated during the last thirty years. The Russians of course have never shown any doubt as to their innocence, while for a time publicists and historians in the free world were almost as unanimous in endorsing the verdict of 'guilty' which the politicians passed on the Kremlin. More recently however the 'revisionist' school has put a major share of blame on the United States.

The first comment necessary is that throughout history the organised power-systems which we describe as states have found it remarkably difficult to live together in harmony; the term 'Cold War' merely attaches a new label to a long-familiar condition. The more powerful any two such states are and the closer their geographical propinquity, the greater the likelihood that they will find themselves at cross-purposes. Russia and America are more populous and possess ampler resources than any previous countries, entitling them to be described as 'Super-Powers'; modern communications have made insignificant the distance separating them. There was between 1945 and 1960 no third country menacing enough to drive them into co-operation. Harmony between them would therefore be much more surprising than antagonism.

Both countries are extensive in area and have wide varieties of climate and fertility. Each contains peoples of many different backgrounds who are in process of being integrated into greater uniformity. But in their backgrounds, histories and ways of thought they are more unlike than similar. As so often in the past, political rivalry is intensified by a cultural ideological difference which adds to the barrier of language a barrier of thought. This goes deeper than the familiar distinction between the systems. In the Russian *mir*, for example, the individual always counted for less and the community for more than in the American township; the Russians have always been ruled by autocrats, the Americans never.

There is no need for the historian to look for villains in explaining how the Cold War began. It is merely another example, though a major one, of the most fundamental of human problems — mutual understanding and trust between societies. The pathetic aspect of the tension is the firm belief on each side that the menace comes from the other. But divergent interpretations of events result both from and in incompatible values; men cannot stop themselves from wishing to see the world changed so as to accord better with their own values, even if they realise that the cost of enforcing such a change would outweigh any possible benefits. Moreover values are power, in so far as they move men to act or refrain from action. The knowledge that one's values are challenged makes them seem threatened and the resulting feeling of insecurity gives birth to emotion. Suspicion, bred of fear, is fanned by people whose own interests, altruistic as well as selfish, are advanced by its prevalence. For the United States, at the zenith of their power, to have feared the Soviet Union was ridiculous. For them to have feared the spread of Communism, especially in third countries, was more understandable. And the fear inhibited a rational assessment of Communist prospects, and of the length to which the Soviet Union would or would not risk its own national security in the interests of advancing its creed. Moreover strength is always prone to find respectable pretexts for taking advantage of weakness and the liberal tenet that right is in the long run bound to prevail is not only more of a faith than a fact but leaves out of account how unpleasant the short run can be.

CHAPTER 3

1947-9

1 Marshall Aid

James Byrnes, like many men who have reached top executive posts through politics, was not a good organiser and did not know or care how to use his staff; an exasperated subordinate said that 'the Department fiddles while Byrnes roams'. In the Armed Services, however, officers are trained to act as a member of a team. Marshall not only delegated work and sought advice; he introduced into the State Department from war-time operations the practice of trying to anticipate future events and plan in advance how to deal with them. Kennan described him as 'an orderly man'. He came back to Washington from a meeting of Foreign Ministers in Moscow at the end of April 1947 convinced not merely that Western Europe was heading for a crisis but that the Soviet Union was waiting for one to arrive. Molotov had in fact been a little less rude than usual in Moscow. He had even backed the setting up of a central government in Germany, to which Clay gave top priority, but as he had provided few details as to how this was to be done, he merely fed American suspicions that he wanted to get control of the entire country. He had reiterated the demand for $10 billion in reparations, including reparations from current production, which the Americans flatly refused to consider. The Russian stance may well have been intended as the start of a bargaining bout but the Americans did not believe that they could any longer afford the time which the protracted process of bargaining with the Russians involved, especially as they could not be sure that the intention of their opponents was serious. Better to run the risk of dividing Germany than that of seeing it united but Communist. Marshall sent for Kennan and gave him three weeks to find staff and work out a plan for saving the situation.

The answer which Kennan provided was not so much a plan for recovery as a plan for getting such a plan drawn up. (Nobody at that stage seems to have found it anomalous that the protagonist of free enterprise was calling for planning!) It was based on his conviction that the threat was economic and political, not military. The need was not to prevent the Russians conquering Western Europe but to prevent Western Europe from deciding that Communism was better able to bring prosperity than was private enterprise. The existing European economy had to be restored to the condition in which it was believed to have functioned so successfully in the nineteenth century. This had of course been the aim of the various plans for post-war reconstruction. They had failed because they had underestimated the scale of the dislocation which needed to be put right. That mistake must not be repeated. American money would be essential to the operation and the securing of the necessary consent from Congress would not be easy. But to make a single request for a large sum would be better than to ask for too little and have to go back again later. Congress must also be convinced that the money would achieve its purpose and not just be 'poured down a rat-hole'. The best assurance would lie in the willing co-operation of European governments, which could most easily be obtained by making the plan one formulated by Europeans instead of an American concoction thrust upon them readymade. Finally there must be only one co-ordinated plan for the whole area, not different ones for each individual country. The inter-governmental agreement needed to achieve such a plan might not be easy to reach, but a powerful inducement could be provided by making agreement a necessary condition to the grant of the dollars that were so widely and so keenly desired. Finally this approach would place German recovery in a framework of European co-operation and thus reduce the hesitation about reviving German power which was a natural feeling in countries so recently subjected to it.

Marshall next devised an opportunity for making a speech at Harvard University on 5 June. Having emphasised (not for the first time) the gravity of the crisis and the scale of help which would be needed, he not only appealed to the idealism of his countrymen but told them that it was against their material interest to let Europe collapse. He then told the Europeans that, while his country stood ready to help, the initiative must come from them.

> It would be neither fitting nor efficacious for this Government to draw up a programme designed to place Europe on its feet economically.... The programme should be a joint one, agreed to by a number of, if not all European nations.

No previews of this speech had been leaked beforehand, for fear unsympathetic commentators might try to prejudice the public against it in advance. But Dean Acheson had dropped hints to the British Embassy, which reported them to London, and to three British journalists including the correspondent of the BBC. He in his commentary emphasised not merely that the Harvard speech was important but that the success or failure of the proposal hung upon its receiving a prompt response from the other side of the Atlantic. Bevin, listening to the broadcast as he dressed next morning, 'grasped the opportunity with both hands'. He brushed aside suggestions from his officials that he should cable Washington to find out what Marshall really had in mind, and arranged to meet Bidault, the French Foreign Minister, in Paris eleven days later. They then invited Molotov to confer with them on 27 June.

Marshall's offer had been made to all European nations.

> Any Government that is willing to assist in the task of recovery will find full co-operation on the part of the United States Government. Any Government which manoeuvres to block the recovery of other countries cannot expect help from us. Furthermore governments, political parties or groups which seek to perpetuate human misery in order to profit therefrom politically or otherwise will encounter the opposition of the United States.

This was a calculated risk. Marshall and his advisers preferred incurring the danger that the Russians would join in and then obstruct to that of letting the United States be blamed for splitting Europe. If the Russians had been equally bold, they would have accepted the offer and by doing so would probably have killed all chance of Congress granting the necessary money. That some such calculation may have occurred to them is suggested by Molotov's willingness to meet Bevin and Bidault in Paris and the fact that he did not on arrival reject the American proposals out of hand. The plan did after all offer the Soviet Union a means of getting the financial help from outside for which they had been looking in vain for so long. But second thoughts soon prevailed; instructions were received, presumably from Stalin, to object to any terms which might 'prejudice the sovereignty of the European countries or infringe their economic independence'. Molotov proposed that each country should draw up a list of its needs and itself disburse the necessary money when that had been provided by the US. Such a

Would-be planners see a red light

In determining requirements of coal and steel, account should be taken of relative efficiencies of available plants and other related matters. The report on steel avoids this problem by assuming that all existing steel capacity in the 16 countries will be operated at its maximum, beginning in 1948, and that there will be sufficient coal and transportation for this purpose. Since realistic estimates of coal and coke supplies indicate that the committee's optimistic expectations will not be fulfilled, attention must be given to an initial selective utilisation of productive capacity, without regard to national boundaries.

Clayton (US Under-Secretary for Economic Affairs) to Secretary of State, from Paris, 31 August 1947

Any attempt to press further would so impair national sovereignty that many countries would rebel.

Ernest Bevin, as reported by US Ambassador in London, 9 September 1947

Some of the criticisms of the programme ... arise from the opinion held by a few that the European participating countries should designate, without regard to national frontiers, the productive facilities which should first be brought into production. This view sounds plausible at first sight but its implications are far-reaching. First, it inevitably requires an international organization to select the plants which will be given priority; second, it inevitably requires an international organization to allocate the necessary raw materials for the plants enjoying priority; third, it inevitably requires an international organization to allocate among several or all of the participating countries the products of the plant facilities to which priority has been given. The evidence is clear that the 16 participating countries would not accept this sort of system and organization. Moreover even if they were prepared to agree to such a system, interminable arguments would ensue among many of the participating countries as to which plants would be first brought into production, how raw materials and in what amounts should be allocated to them, and to which countries the products of these plants should be allocated. Finally such a procedure and organization would result in a planned economy to a dangerous degree. It is almost certain to lead to international cartels which would stimulate nationalism and frustrate the ultimate restoration of natural economic forces.

Clayton and US Ambassadors in Paris and London to State Department, 15 September 1947

procedure, however, was incompatible with the collective approach which Marshall regarded as essential. Each country taking part must disclose its needs to the rest for approval by them and inclusion in a consolidated demand. When this was insisted on, the Russians walked out. To their rooted dislike of outsiders gaining insight into their internal affairs was probably added fear of the disintegrating effect which contact with the West might have on their satellites. The Poles and Czechs were soon afterwards made, against their own inclinations, to keep out as well.

Next day Bevin and Bidault invited fourteen other countries, all outside the Russian ambit, to a further meeting on 12 July at which a Committee for European Economic Co-operation was set up, with the ex-philosopher Sir Oliver Franks as Chairman, to produce within ten weeks the collective estimate of needs called for by the Americans; the three Western Zones of Germany were to be represented by their Occupying Powers. The CEEC was expected to work out how much aid Western Europe would need in order to stand on its own feet by 1952. But when the calculations were made, it appeared likely that there would be a continuing deficit of some $5 billion after that date. The American negotiators objected that such a conclusion would make the plan unacceptable to Congress and complained both that too high a standard of life was being aimed at and that not enough was proposed as regards the pooling of resources. The European negotiators replied that modifications in those directions would be unacceptable to the Governments concerned and to their publics, while the Americans began to see that a thorough-going integration of the West European economies might call for a degree of planning and regulation which would hardly be compatible with free enterprise.

The CEEC Report said that $19.66 billion would be needed from the US, on a diminishing scale, in order to buy the fuel, food and materials which Europe did not possess and could not afford, yet without which the rest of the programme would be impracticable. The President in December 1947 asked for $17 billion spread over four years but Congress, although endorsing the plan in April 1948 by large majorities, decided only to authorise spending on a year-to-year basis. In practice, the total amount made available was about $13.15 billion; in the first year the aid given was equivalent to 1.6 per cent of the US gross national product, falling at the end to 0.3 per cent. The first year began on 1 July 1948 but, as action to meet the crisis could not have been delayed until then, stop-gap aid was arranged in the second half of 1947. Between the end of the war and the start of the plan, the US had already given $11.3 billion in various forms of aid.

The CEEC in May 1948 turned itself into the Organisation for European Economic Co-operation (OEEC), a continuing body based in

Paris with the task of assessing need, allocating aid, supervising its spending and planning for the future. The OEEC remained, in deference to British and Scandinavian insistence, an association of sovereign states, a sort of international conference in permanent session, in which each member had one vote and unanimity was required for all decisions of substance; delegates were however expected to be in a position to commit their governments, since the speed of action needed for success could not have been achieved if each decision had had to wait for subsequent ratification nationally. The countries represented had many similarities and common interests, particularly the need for dollars; the continuing character of the meetings meant that delegates got to know one another and could negotiate away from the limelight. As a result the OEEC proved able to perform with competence the functions assigned to it. But this was not evidence that its constitution would be equally successful in other circumstances, while even as things were certain delicate tasks like the first division of aid between the claimant members had to be handed over to a group of individuals, the 'four wise men' whose recommendations were then endorsed by the OEEC Council. In the US a matching organisation, the Economic Co-operation Administration (ECA), was set up under a businessman, Paul Hoffman, to act as the continuing link between the OEEC and Congress, authorising the one in detail to spend the money provided by the other. The actual purchasing of supplies bought with aid was done by representatives in the US of the recipient Governments who were in effect told by ECA that it would honour dollar cheques drawn on it and offered in payment.

Each country receiving aid signed with the US Government an agreement in terms reminiscent of those in Article VII of the Lend-Lease Agreements (p. 18); it involved promises to increase production, take steps against inflation and co-operate in mutual efforts to reduce trade barriers. The freeing of trade within the area from import quotas soon emerged as one of the OEEC's main aims but progress towards it depended upon establishing a multilateral payments system. For the object of imposing quotas had been to make sure that goods were paid for with goods and that the selling country did not accumulate from the buyer unlimited quantities of a currency which no other country was prepared to accept. The mere fear that this might happen, even where it had not actually done so, was enough to inhibit trade. In October 1948 American pressure led to an Agreement for Intra-European Payments being concluded under which debts between

OEEC members were registered with the Bank of International Settlements in Basel, and the overall position of each country was calculated at regular intervals, setting off debts against credits; a limited number of aid dollars were made available to smooth this process, on condition that members who were in the black agreed to extend credit to countries in the red.

The scheme, which ran for a year, had limitations and its successor was not much more extensive. Britain was a major obstacle to anything more ambitious, since the gold and dollar reserves held in London provided the financial basis not simply for the British economy but for all the countries (chiefly in the Commonwealth) between which sterling was convertible ('the rest of the Sterling Area'). For Britain to join a system in which sterling could be converted with little restriction into the currencies of all other OEEC members would mean bringing into the system the whole Sterling Area, thereby increasing considerably the scale of payments involved and the debts which might have to be met out of the London reserves. By 1949, however, it was becoming clear that the exchange rate of £1 = $4 which had been fixed at the end of the war did not take enough account of the effects of the war upon the British economy and its relative competitiveness with the US; as a result the ability of the Sterling Area to export was handicapped. The US authorities pressed, through the IMF, for devaluation and in September 1949 the rate was lowered to £1 = $2.80, a level chosen to prevent speculation that a further devaluation might be necessary. Most other West European currencies were devalued by varying amounts at the same time.

The change made the British Government readier to take risks and in July 1950 the European Payments Union was set up, a sort of IMF confined to members of OEEC and the Sterling Area, in which each country cleared its account with the Union as a whole instead of with each other member separately. The ECA at the outset boosted the Union's central fund by a grant of $350 million. That British fears had not been unfounded was shown by the fact that during the ten years of the EPU's existence a considerable debt was built up by the UK – and an even larger one by France. Progress in freeing payments made possible progress in removing quotas. In November 1949 the OEEC Council asked members to eliminate them on at least 50 per cent of their imports from inside the area; in October 1950 this was raised to 60 per cent and in February 1951 to 75 per cent. (Quotas to countries outside the OEEC remained unaffected.)

Britain was the country which did best out of Marshall Aid, receiving nearly a quarter of the total; France and Italy came next with 21.5 per cent and 11 per cent, and after them West Germany with 10.5 per cent. As each country was receiving goods without paying for them, the natural effect would have been deflationary (i.e. would have increased the proportion of goods to money in the economy). Moreover the goods were not kept by the recipient governments but passed on to manufacturers and traders for use; if some of these had got supplies free of charge while competitors were paying to buy them from normal sources, the result would clearly have been unfair. Each government was therefore required to set aside sums in its own currency equivalent to the value of the supplies paid for in dollars by the US. These 'counterpart funds' had to be spent, under the supervision of the ECA and OEEC, in ways which would forward the general purpose of the scheme, notably by investment to relieve particular shortages ('bottlenecks') which were holding up production in other industries (e.g. particular types of tools). In Britain, however, productive capacity was thought to be so fully stretched that any expenditure making further calls upon it was likely to be inflationary; 'counterpart' was therefore used to reduce debt and train personnel in ways of producing more efficiently (e.g. by trips to inspect US methods).

Industrial output in OEEC countries, which in 1947 had been at about 87 per cent of the pre-war level, climbed in 1948 to 98 per cent and in 1949 to 110 per cent. Trade inside the OEEC, which at the beginning of 1948 was only two-thirds of what it had been in 1938, had risen by the end of 1949 to 110 per cent of that level. Whereas between 1919 and 1939 international trade had scarcely expanded at all, it now began to grow faster than at any previous period in history, including the nineteenth century. There were a number of reasons for this success story. The world had been starved of goods since 1939 and had stagnated since 1914, building up a big backlog of demand which only needed to be made effective. Keynesian economics had made governments more willing to act in order deliberately to promote growth. There may have been a speeding up of the rate at which improvements in techniques of production were discovered and brought into use. But there can be little doubt that a significant share of the credit is deserved by the policy of the American Government. Of course America benefited in both wealth and security from a prosperous Western Europe. But no government can be expected to disregard its country's material interests. What should be applauded is action based on reasoned and long-term appreciation of those interests.

The success of Marshall Aid was not however unlimited. In 1949 Hoffman told the OEEC Council that the American Congress and people set great store by the development of European integration, a term increasingly used to denote the creation of a single large market like the United States themselves. He warned the Council that, unless substantial progress in this direction was made, the Americans might abandon the Marshall Plan. But although the quotas were reduced and convertibility extended, a group set up in 1947 to study the creation of a European Customs Union did not get beyond the formulation of a standardised customs nomenclature – an essential but hardly epoch-making preliminary. (Perhaps illogically, the US objection to schemes in which certain countries enjoyed preferential tariffs did not extend to schemes in which certain countries were freed from tariffs altogether.) An attempt was made to co-ordinate investment, so as to eliminate unnecessary duplication and the creation of capacity which might well prove surplus to requirements. But it was not easy to shake the confidence of governments and industrialists in the share of the market which any new plant of theirs was going to obtain, although the encouragement of better forecasting, based upon wider and fuller statistics, did something to kill off the less promising projects.

In any case the reduction of tariffs was considered, particularly by the British, to be the task of the International Trade Organisation. The ITO however never came into existence. The Conference convened at Havana (p. 50) duly met in the winter of 1948/9 and with some difficulty succeeded in agreeing on the text of an International Trade Charter. But this document, unlike the General Agreement on Tariffs and Trade, was in a form which required ratification by the US Congress. By April 1949, when the Truman Administration submitted it for this purpose, the temper of Congress had turned against such multilateral documents (even though the Communist countries were not going to join the Organisation). In December 1950 the lukewarm attempts which had been made to secure approval were finally abandoned as hopeless and in the circumstances no other country was prepared to ratify. The GATT thus acquired an importance which it had not been intended to have, both as a forum for discussing broad questions of trade policy and as the organiser of negotiations to reduce tariffs. In 1949 a second bargaining round took place at Annecy between the US and the members of the OEEC; the atmosphere was more confident than it had been at Geneva in 1947 and agreement was reached on some tariff reductions and on numerous undertakings to 'bind' (i.e. not to raise) the existing levels of duties. A third round at Torquay in 1950–1 prolonged till 1954 the concessions made at Geneva and Annecy but otherwise had limited results because Britain, Australia and New Zealand refused to abandon Imperial Preference except in return for concessions which the US were not prepared to make.

2   The Russian reaction

Hoffman more than once said that the Marshall Plan should not be regarded as a form of economic warfare against Russia, but a main objective had undeniably been to win the mouths and minds of the West European peoples so as to prevent them from turning Communist. The task of converting an America always inclined to isolation into a country which recognised its international responsibilities was not easy, in spite of the support which the Republican leader Senator Vandenberg gave to Truman's European policy. The money needed for the Plan would probably not have been granted unless a considerable amount of emphasis had been laid on the danger of Communism in Europe and on the significance of US aid as a protective device. In these circumstances the Russians could hardly be blamed if they interpreted the Plan as an attempt to halt their advance and limit their influence. Western capitalism, which had seemed to be on the point of justifying Marxist predictions by collapsing, was being resuscitated and given a prosperity highly alluring to the countries on the fringe of the USSR, held down as these were against their will by puppet governments backed by Soviet bayonets. Molotov at Paris had represented Marshall Aid as an attempt by American capitalists to capture additional markets and thus avoid depression. But although this became a stock line of propaganda, the Plan came later to be given a more military significance. Its intention was seen as being to recreate the military power of Western Europe, enable Britain and France to resume their roles as Great Powers and provide armies which would be strong enough, especially when backed by American atomic weapons, to recover the position which had been lost between 1944 and 1947.

One Russian reaction took the form of a series of trade treaties with the satellites, described as a Molotov Plan, but this merely demonstrated that 'there are some things you do which we can't'. For whereas the Americans were giving economic resources to Western Europe, the economic system in Eastern Europe was so organised as to enable the Russians to take resources away. The satellite countries were underpaid for the goods which they were forced to supply and overcharged for those which they were forced to accept in exchange. In January 1949 a Council for Mutual Economic Assistance (Comecon) was set up and portrayed as the equivalent of the OEEC. But not only was Russia in no position to spare resources for aid on the US scale. The concept underlying the Western policy could have no application in a group of planned economies. For inherent in the creed of free enterprise is the tenet that, if trade is left to private individuals, they will discover points where demand is unsatisfied and, lured by the prospect of profits, proceed to satisfy it. Thus the removal of barriers between countries inside Western Europe resulted in a great growth of trade within the area. But in a command economy, production does not happen unless it has been included in a plan; if an opening for sales suddenly presents itself, the goods needed for exploiting it may not be available. Moreover telling whether goods can be made cheaper elsewhere is only possible in an economy where the costs of making things are exactly calculated; in an economy where prices are fixed without relation to costs it is hard to know what imports are worthwhile. International trade tends therefore to be conducted by the very bilateral deals from which it was a main purpose of the Marshall Plan to escape.

A second slightly more impressive counter to Western developments (though one with only nine years of life ahead of it) was launched in September 1947 at a meeting of Communist Parties held in Silesia, ostensibly at Polish invitation. The Third International (Comintern) had been closed down in May 1943, at a time when the hope was that the chances of Communist Parties coming to power in various countries after the war would be enhanced if they did not seem to be mere units in a centrally-controlled international organisation. Now however Moscow, frightened by the anxiety of Poland and Czechoslovakia to accept the American invitation and by the possible attraction which Western prosperity might have for all the satellites, wanted to draw the reins tighter again. The time was over for talk about each nation having its own road to Communism. To have reconstituted the Comintern would have made this intention undesirably obvious, so what was set up was represented as being merely a centre for the exchange of views and information, or Cominform. Membership was confined to the Communist Parties of the USSR, the six satellites, France and Italy;

presumably the presence of Communists from Asia or the Americas would have introduced too many distracting influences. The intention was to centre the organisation in Belgrade though, as will be seen, it soon became necessary to substitute Bucharest. The first meeting was devoted to diatribes against Marshall and all his works, against Western Social Democrats and against the French and Italian parties for having collaborated with them – on Moscow's orders. These parties were now told that their job henceforward was to do all they could short of revolution to disrupt their countries and thus help to prevent Europe from recovering. The chief result was to lend support to American suspicions.

Among the satellites two gave particular cause for anxiety. Both Czechoslovakia and Yugoslavia were so located geographically as to have easy access to – and even a common frontier with – the West. The Red Army, though it had done more to liberate the Czechs than the Yugoslavs, was no longer stationed on the territory of either. The Czechs under President Beneš, one of the country's founders, with Jan Masaryk, son of the other founder, as Foreign Minister, had during the war pursued a more realistic policy than the Poles and a more anti-German one than the Hungarians, Rumanians and Bulgarians. Although a westernised and liberal country, with a developed middle class, their treatment by Britain and France in 1938 had left them with a certain antipathy to the West and they had taken pains to keep their fences with the Russians mended. The British and Americans thought that this showed a lack of courage and in 1946 Byrnes had refused them further credits. There were only nine Communists in a Cabinet of twenty-seven, but they included the Prime Minister (Gottwald) and those for the Interior and Information. In relatively free elections in 1946 the Communists got nearly 40 per cent of the votes. In February 1948 the Cabinet agreed that certain senior policemen who were Communists should be dismissed but the Minister of the Interior refused to carry out the decision. The Soviet Deputy Foreign Minister flew to Prague to support him. Twelve ministers from the moderate democratic parties, in an effort to force a decision against the Communists, sent their resignations to Beneš who refused to accept them. They were barred from the radio by the Minister of Information. The Communists organised mass demonstrations and 'Action Committees' which took over the Ministries not under Communist control. There was nobody among the democrats prepared to take a lead and the army remained neutral. Though there were American troops within ninety miles of Prague, the West does not seem to have even contemplated intervention. After a week, Beneš gave way – he had had two heart attacks and died six months later – and allowed a cabinet of Communists and fellow-travellers to take office. Masaryk remained Foreign Minister but a fortnight afterwards died by falling from a window. Whether he was pushed or killed himself to escape something worse will probably never be known. But his death, completing as it did the extinction of liberal democracy in Central and Eastern Europe, sent a wave of revulsion and alarm through the free world.

The more or less simultaneous attempt to bring Tito's Yugoslavia to heel had a different outcome. Trouble had been brewing behind the scenes for some time. The Yugoslav leaders, many of them peasants by origin, took to themselves most of the credit for driving out the Germans and laying with remarkable speed the foundations of a Communist state. While prepared to acknowledge the pre-eminence of the Soviet Union in World Communism, and the indispensable contribution which the Red Army had made to defeating Hitler, they were not prepared to accept orders unquestioningly. The Kremlin, unaccustomed to having its orders queried, was irritated at people who thought themselves entitled to make up their own minds. The Yugoslavs resented what they regarded as Russian failure to back them up in clashes with the Anglo-American imperialists over the possession of Trieste and other matters, whereas Stalin had been exasperated by their light-hearted disregard for the wider risks of local confrontation. Further disillusion resulted from the ruthless self-interest shown by Moscow in trade negotiations, and in particular by disagreement over Yugoslavia's economic role; Stalin wished this to consist in supplying raw materials to Russia whereas Leninist theory said that industrialisation was essential to the building of Communism. There was further trouble over a plan for bringing Albania and Bulgaria into the Yugoslav Federation, where Russian last-minute encouragement aroused almost as much suspicion as earlier obstruction. In March 1948 the Soviet Government removed all its military and civilian advisers, complaining that they were 'surrounded by unfriendliness and treated with hostility'.

There followed an exchange of letters in which Tito insisted that his country was being misjudged and suggested various remedies. Stalin brushed these aside and instead accused the Yugoslav Party not just of hostility but of thinking on wrong lines and working in wrong directions. Russian friendship and help were not to be looked for in future unless there was a complete change of mind. He ended by demanding that the dispute be submitted to the Cominform which, meeting in Bucharest in June, publicly condemned the Yugoslavs in their absence and called on the 'healthy elements' in the country to compel the leadership to recognise its mistakes openly and rectify them, to 'break with nationalism and return to internationalism'.

Stalin knew that inside Yugoslavia there was considerable opposition to Tito both among Communists and anti-Communists, not to speak of the traditional rivalry between the westernised Catholic Croats and the Balkan Orthodox Serbs. He believed the prestige of the Soviet Union was such that his mere call would be enough to secure Tito's overthrow; he was reputed (probably apocryphally) to have said 'I will shake my little finger and there will be no more Tito'. But Tito managed to present the quarrel as national rather than ideological and in July a Party Congress gave him a vote of confidence. Thereafter hardly a rat stirred and such as did found that no deviation had affected the secret police. There was however great reluctance on the Yugoslav side to believe that the break was final. Paradoxically its first effect was to produce a string of measures extending Communism, in a determined effort to prove how empty the Russian accusations were. But as the Russians did not relent, this policy had no future, since it greatly reduced the chances of getting help from the West, and help from somewhere was imperative. Yugoslav overconfidence had extended to their planning; the degree of self-sacrifice which the proposed scale of capital development demanded from the population was excessive once the support of that population became vital to the regime's continued existence. Incentives had to reinforce coercion and incentives could only be afforded with outside aid. Gradually the need to defend their course and to remedy a system which was failing to work drove the leaders to devise a new ideology and a novel society. For their refusal to renounce what they regarded as the essentials of Communism meant that their innovations became a determined search for a fresh way of reconciling individual self-expression with communal advantage. Surprisingly enough, Russia confined herself to proliferating abuse and promoting sedition and did not risk military action. Had she done so, the West would have been even less inclined to intervene than in Czechoslovakia. If, however, guerrilla resistance had developed, as against the Germans, the situation might have become delicate.

The escape of one fish made the Russians determined to see that no others got away. During the next years, purges were conducted in the Polish, Bulgarian, Hungarian and Czech parties. Anyone who had voiced criticisms of or was on bad terms with the local trusties, even anyone who had spent the war in or had links with the West, was imprisoned or liquidated, usually after a trial more sensational than convincing. Collectivisation of industry and agriculture was hurried forward.

Thus Marshall Aid had a dual rather than a single effect. It consolidated free enterprise and pluralist societies in the West of Europe, bringing in due course higher standards of life than the area had ever known. But at the same time it deepened the split between East and West, bringing in Eastern Europe a consolidation of Communism and Soviet power. It ended, at any rate for a time, any readiness of the leaders on each side to understand and work together with one another, setting them instead to frustrate what they imagined to be the sinister intentions of the opposite side. 'Cold' wars do not break out suddenly, as hot wars do. But if a date had to be named for the start of this one, Molotov's withdrawal from the Paris meeting on 2 July 1947 would be more appropriate than most. That withdrawal was of course itself a reaction; a Communist would no doubt prefer to name the Marshall speech at Harvard a month earlier. But that speech was in turn a reaction to earlier Russian behaviour. Thus in 1947 the American effort to establish a Free World reached a turning-point. In order to retain the possibility of keeping one half free, it had not merely to accept but even to precipitate a splitting of the world into halves. The history of the years down to 1962 is that of consolidating the split. There was however one country, Germany, which was both a main cause and a principal victim of the split. Its effect there must now be described.

3   The Berlin blockade

In December 1947 the Council of Foreign Ministers (p. 56) met in London for the last time. Most of the meeting was taken up in arguing about the Russian demand for $10 billion in reparations. If this amount was to be obtained from the Russian Zone alone, it would have to remain for a long time a bad advertisement for Communism. Molotov may therefore well have been in earnest when he told Bevin that what he wanted was a unified Germany. But the British and Americans were coming to the conclusion that a Germany which was divided but had two-thirds prospering was preferable to one which was unified but poverty-stricken. The French were coming to the same conclusion, though more reluctantly, spurred on by the discovery that their Zone would only receive Marshall Aid if it was merged with 'Bizonia' (p. 65). The result was that a breakdown in the Council's negotiations had lost its fears for the Western Powers and they agreed to adjourn rather than further aggravate relations between the Four Powers. Another conference was held in London two months later, this time with the French but without the Russians, at which arrangements for merging were agreed, as were the admission of the three western Zones to OEEC and the basis on which the area should become a political as well as an economic unit. In the Control Council Marshal Sokolovsky, the Russian representative, demanded information as to what was going on in London and on 20 March 1948 walked out, claiming that the answers were unsatisfactory; the experiment of running Germany by Four-Power agreement was at an end.

The economic recovery of the western Zones, though under way, was held up by one big obstacle. Thanks to a war-time financial policy which increased the money supply but used controls to hold down prices, followed by the demoralisation of defeat, the German public had completely lost confidence in the currency. The legal channels of trade were less and less used; goods were exchanged either by barter or on the black market. Everyone realised that a reform must come and, to avoid losing by it, sought to hold their wealth in solid form; such goods as had been manufactured were not sold on the market but stored away until they could get a meaningful price. The volume of money available had to be brought more into line with the volume of goods available, either by raising the price of the goods or by reducing the amount of the money.

But if Germany was to remain a unity, any reform had to be uniform throughout it. A central bank of issue was virtually essential to reform but there was little prospect of such a bank being able to operate on a quadripartite basis when one of the four had quite different economic aims from the others. Moreover any change of this kind is bound to hit some people harder than others and the judgment as to where the main loss ought to fall is bound to be coloured by views about the ethics of private profit-making. To wait any longer was therefore unlikely to result in agreement, yet likely to hold up recovery. On 20 June the old Reichsmark was made valueless in the three Western Zones and replaced by the new Deutsche Mark; for every hundred of the old marks turned in, 6.5 of the new ones were issued (though private debtors had to pay 10 per hundred, so that creditors came off well). The reform bore heavily on those who held their savings in money rather than goods, but they tended to be the people who had gained by the cost of the war being largely met by borrowing; if it had instead been met by higher taxation, the extent of the later devaluation could have been smaller. (For the effects of the reform, see below, pages 122–30).

Two days before the reform the Western Allies had expressed to the Russians their hope that a quadripartite measure uniform throughout Germany could still be agreed. But Sokolovsky turned the idea down, announcing that the new West German notes would not be allowed to circulate in the Russian Zone or in Berlin; a less drastic measure was hastily improvised for those areas with stamps stuck on the old notes to show the new values. The Russians clearly decided that they could not afford to overlook the first major Western departure from the Yalta-Potsdam principle of ruling Germany by agreement. The time had come for them to play the one strong card in their hand, the position of Berlin one hundred miles inside their Zone. That such an arrangement should ever have been accepted with apparent equanimity shows vividly how unrealistic statesmen had been in their expectations of what the world would be like after the war. All along the West had been irresponsibly oblivious of the risks involved in the situation, which had not been improved by the sketchy nature of the agreements about access accepted in June 1945 by their commanders as the price of getting into the city in time for the Potsdam Conference (p. 34). But the effect of this should not be exaggerated; in the last resort the Western presence in Berlin rested (and rests) not on written texts but on the degree of power deployed in its support.

The Western Powers were, however, vulnerable in Berlin not merely because they had to keep their own troops and staffs in the city supplied; they had also been induced in 1945 to accept responsibility for meeting the needs of the Germans living in their Sectors for food and fuel. Surface access to Berlin depended on one motorway and one railway. Already in March the Russians had begun to interfere with these; after the currency reform they clamped down on movements of freight as well as of people. They believed that this blockade presented the West with an ugly choice between (a) immediate withdrawal, (b) staying until starved out, and (c) dropping the plans for rebuilding their Zones as the price of continued access. Any of the three courses would have had far-reaching effects by suggesting to the world that the West could not or would not protect its friends. There was of course a fourth option, to force a way in, and this the American commander Clay wanted to do. A column of troops would have been more likely to be met by demolitions than by arms and might have had to end up by garrisoning the entire route so as to keep it open. But the matter was never put to the test because the three Governments preferred to explore a fifth solution.

For in the twentieth century land and water were no longer the only ways into the city; there was also the air. Here three corridors had been authorised in the Control Council. Nobody imagined at the start that a city of 2.25 million people could be kept supplied indefinitely by air and no plans had been made for attempting the feat; if the winter weather of 1947/8 had been worse, the expedient might have failed. But, begun originally as a stopgap to give time for negotiations, it was steadily expanded when the negotiations led nowhere; the world was combed for available planes until loads were being brought in at the rate of thirty an hour all round the clock. There was also however a limit to the risks which the Russians were prepared to take. After one of their fighters had caused a British airliner to crash, they did not persevere in harassing Western aircraft, though by slowing down the timetable they could have materially reduced the amount brought in. They never withdrew their representative in the quadripartite Air Control Centre regulating traffic to and from the city. And although one of the radio beacons used in guiding aircraft was situated in the Russian Sector, it was allowed to go on functioning. What may well have prompted this caution was the knowledge that, although they had atom bombs in the making, the first one would not be exploded till three or four months after the blockade ended. They had probably felt compelled to make their attempt to force the Western hand earlier than they would ideally have chosen.

By the spring of 1949 the attempt had clearly failed and a counter-blockade by the West was making itself felt in the Soviet Zone. Feelers were put out through the Russian representative at the United Nations and on 10 May the world learnt with some surprise that the blockade was to be lifted. An attempt was then made to agree on a permanent arrangement for Berlin but, after a month of fruitless argument, the position had to be left virtually as it had been before.

Apart from the humiliation of failure, the Russians lost in three ways by the blockade. The Berlin City Hall was in the Russian Sector, but when the councillors from the other Sectors found themselves prevented by Communist demonstrations from getting to it, they retaliated by shifting meetings to the British Sector. Those who stayed behind declared the old Lord Mayor and executive committee deposed, replacing them by people with their own views. Elections brought a sweeping majority to the Social Democrats in West Berlin, and an even more sweeping one to the Socialist Unity Party in East Berlin. The city thus acquired two governments, neither recognising the other.

By 1948 three years had passed since the war ended. The Germans had recovered even more psychologically than economically and were beginning to get restive under their alien and rather ineffective governors. Their unrest might easily have led to action if it had not been for the Russians. As things were, the need to meet what was seen as a general menace drew the two sides together. The blockade could not have been frustrated if the Germans of West Berlin had not been prepared to tolerate scarcities of food, heat and light. The British General Robertson talked openly about 'our common enemy' and ideas about the length and severity of the occupation began to be scaled down considerably.

In June 1948 the British Labour Government agreed to make British airfields available to American bombers along with the atomic weapons which these machines carried. The range of the bombers was insufficient for them to deliver such weapons behind the Iron Curtain direct from America; the moving of their base to Europe gave them this capacity and when the blockade ended, they were not withdrawn. To achieve parity, the Russians had not merely to equip themselves with bombs but with means of delivery; and they had no prospect of obtaining bases on the western side of the Atlantic. This disadvantage on the part of the Russians was not fully understood by the American public.

4 The Brussels Pact and NATO

Before 1914 and again before 1939 Britain (except in the Locarno Treaties) had firmly refused to promise military help to France in the event of a German attack. The uncertainty which resulted as to British action was thought to have contributed to making France suspicious and vindictive towards Germany and thus to poisoning the European atmosphere. Neither country wanted to see the same mistake made a third time and in March 1947 a Treaty was signed (appropriately at

Dunkirk) by which each of the two promised all possible military support and assistance if the other became involved in hostilities with Germany. In March 1948 a further Treaty was signed at Brussels which in effect extended the Dunkirk provisions to include Belgium, Holland and Luxembourg (although this time there was no actual mention of Germany). This however did not solve the real problem of European security.

For Germany was ceasing to be the menace, yet if the attack were to come from Russia, there were doubts as to whether the armed forces of the five Brussels countries would be able to resist it; not only were they too few but too many of them were tied up outside Europe. What was really needed to give the West Europeans confidence was a pledge that North America would continue to keep troops in Europe and regard the atomic bomb as a weapon of last resort in its defence. The mere fear that it *might* be used was adequate as a strategic deterrent. When the Brussels Treaty was signed, the Canadian Prime Minister suggested that it needed enlarging to cover both shores of the North Atlantic. A resolution in favour of US participation in such a system was proposed by the senior Republican on the Senate Foreign Relations Committee and overwhelmingly approved by the whole Senate thirteen days before the Russians tightened the noose round Berlin. The drafting of a Treaty was complicated by the fact that the American Constitution put the right to declare war in the hands of the Senate, making difficult an automatic commitment to do so. But on 4 April 1949 a Treaty was signed by the US, Canada, the five Brussels Powers, Denmark, Iceland, Italy, Norway and Portugal. The core lay in Article 5 which said that

> an armed attack against one or more of the Parties to the Treaty in
> Europe or North America shall be considered an attack against them
> all and consequently they agree that ... each of them ... will assist
> the Party or Parties so attacked by taking forthwith ... such action as
> it deems necessary, including the use of armed force.

Another Article said that the Treaty's provisions were to be carried out by the signatories in accordance with their respective constitutional arrangements. The Treaty was to cover French Algeria, islands in the North Atlantic, the signatories' ships and aircraft, and their occupation forces in Europe. It was to last for at least twenty years but could be reviewed after ten. In October 1951 Greece and Turkey were brought in. At this stage no machinery was provided for carrying out the undertakings made in the Treaty; it remained a mere commitment to take action, leaving the arrangements for action to be decided when an attack occurred.

Russian propaganda taunted the United States with having gone back on the principle, laid down by George Washington, of not making alliances in peacetime. The Americans could have replied that, in all but the actual shooting, the time was one of war. Nervous Europeans who had in the past reproached the United States for retreating into isolation and failing to assume responsibilities commensurate with its power now took to fearing that their own fate would be decided without their consent by some 'trigger-happy' character on the other side of the Atlantic. The real problem was rather different.

The Senate resolution had recommended US association with 'such regional and other collective arrangements as are based on continuous and effective self-help and mutual aid' – in other words, the American role was to back up local initiative. Countries which wanted to defend themselves should be helped to do so. In somewhat the same way Marshall Aid was being given not to transform the economic structure of an area but to enable facilities already in existence to be restored to a condition in which proper use could be made of them. On this basis these two manifestations of the policy of 'containment' were highly successful – though part of the success was due to the fact that the Communists did not need as much containing as was popularly supposed.

But Western Europe was exceptional in being an area which was both industrialised and governed by leaders broadly representative of the popular will. The Communist challenge was not however confined to Europe. It was likely to be even stronger in the many other parts of the world where standards of living were low, the popular will unformulated, governments unrepresentative and often corrupt. Did containment involve providing economic and military aid everywhere? Two answers were possible. The more cautious one was that outside Europe an active containment policy was unlikely to win the local co-operation without which it could not succeed; that the resources of the US, though great, were not infinite; and that what mattered was keeping out of Communist control the industrial centres of the US, Britain, the Rhine Valley and Japan. The more ambitious answer was that freedom is indivisible; and that even in Europe local co-operation had not been unlimited; that if the resources of the US were not infinite, neither were those of the Communists; and that if the US drew a line outside which it would not act to protect its friends, they would all in succession be lost to it (the so-called 'domino' theory). Those who saw the relations between the US and the USSR as the traditional ones between two Great Powers tended to give the first answer; those who saw anti-Communism as a crusade, the second.

5   The establishment of two German Republics

The Allied occupation of Germany had four main aims. The first was to disarm. This was done in the technical sense very thoroughly. The German Armed Forces were completely disbanded, installations like barracks closed or pulled down and factories making military equipment demolished. Less than had been intended was done to reduce the capacity of German heavy industry, in spite of the ease with which it could be converted to military uses, because its use for non-military purposes proved vital to prosperity. Much the same applied to reparations, which were accepted at Potsdam as a second main aim but soon afterwards scaled down considerably by the Western Powers (though demolitions continued till 1951). As regards denazification, which was the third aim, laws and institutions on which the National Socialists had stamped their distinctive character were done away with, as they probably would have been anyhow, and most people who had been prominent in the Third Reich were removed from public life, at any rate for a time; it proved impracticable however to rewrite all the laws passed since 1933 and dismiss all the trained personnel who had worked under Hitler. Something has already been said about the punishment of major offenders (pp. 39–42).

The fourth aim was that of reform: changing the institutions and even the ideas which were thought to have made the Germans willing to accept not merely the rule of the Nazis but an over-emphasis on military influence and on the warlike virtues. Linked with this was the intention on the part of some people to reduce the influence of the big industrialists and landowners who were widely considered to have encouraged expansive aggressive policies for their own private advantage. The Zone in which most progress was undeniably made in both these fields was the Soviet one, though the system substituted was in many ways closer to Nazi than to American ideas. In the Western Zones big landowners had been relatively few in number by comparison with the east, but there was a small land reform. The action of the

British Labour Government in taking the coal and steel industries into public ownership had to be put on ice at American insistence, as was the implementation of articles providing for socialisation which the Social Democratic majority had inserted in the new constitution for *Land* Hesse and which had been approved in a referendum. To many Americans there was little to choose between Socialism and Communism, so that if such measures had been carried out, Congress might have been provoked into refusing its approval to the Aid programme. In such fields as education and the civil service the kind of changes which the Western occupiers favoured met with almost universal opposition from those Germans who would have had to carry them out and as a result few were made. There was after all a paradox in the very idea of compelling people to be free.

All the same it should not be imagined that nothing was achieved. In the process of the occupation, much was altered and more new ideas made familiar than would have been likely if the Germans had been left to themselves. By no means all the alterations endured, by no means all the ideas were accepted. But some effort was made to forestall a defensive reaction by relying on reasoning and collaboration rather than on compulsion. There were many Germans who welcomed the opportunity of re-establishing contact with the outside world. There were also many who were as worried as their occupiers by the excesses of their nation and who, without accepting in full the outsiders' diagnosis of what was wrong, were concerned to find a remedy. A good deal was done to help such persons into positions of influence; to have done more might have been counter-productive.

Above all, the interval of external control gave the Germans time to sort themselves out. The Weimar Republic had been handicapped by the conditions under which it had to start work, with its leaders' attention continually diverted from the job of devising a satisfactory new system by the need to cope with urgent crises. Given world conditions between 1945 and 1949, no government in Germany could have satisfied the population, while one staffed by Germans would have got distinctly less attention in Washington than Clay and his assistants. A new German regime after 1945 could not wholly avoid the association with failure which had been one of the chronic handicaps of democracy in that country. But by postponing the assumption of responsibility for four years, the chances of fairly soon achieving a reasonably creditable record were much increased. The cards were stacked so heavily against the Occupation being satisfactory that a new German government did not need to be very successful in order to seem an improvement on its predecessor.

The Three-Power Conference in London in March 1948 (p. 96) authorised the convening in Germany of a 'Constituent Assembly' to draw up a 'constitution'. But when the Ministers-President of the eleven *Länder* already existing in the Western Zones met to consider this plan a fortnight after the Berlin blockade began, they turned the offer down, to the indignation of the Occupation authorities, on the ground that it might prejudice the chances of reuniting Germany. But after they had been begged to consider the European situation, they agreed to set up a 'Parliamentary Council' to draft a 'Basic Law' (*Grundgesetz*). The Council met at Bonn on 1 September and was composed of representatives of the political parties in proportion to their strength in the *Länder* Assemblies, which meant that the Christian Democrats and Social Democrats had twenty-seven members each, the Free Democrats five and the German Party, Centre and Communists two each. They elected as their Chairman a 72-year-old Christian Democrat who had been Lord Mayor of Cologne before 1933, called Konrad Adenauer. He had been too convinced a Catholic and too downright a personality to work with the Nazis; after being dismissed from his post, he retired to cultivate his roses and his taste for wine. In his new position, he saw to it that the Ministers-President were not allowed to take part in the Council's proceedings and that no particular attention was paid to a draft constitution which they submitted.

It was a foregone conclusion that the new State would have the form of a Federation. Although the Allies had given up the idea of dismembering Germany (except as a result of disagreement between themselves), they still set considerable store on devolution to prevent too strong a central government. The Americans naturally favoured a Federal system. The Christian Democrats did so too because that had been Germany's form in the days before 1918 when most of them had grown up, whereas their Social Democratic opponents wanted a central government strong enough to impose socialist institutions on the whole country. Finally the *Länder* were already operating and determined not to lose any of the powers which the Allies had already given them. The chief of these related to education, police, planning and local government.

The first draft of the *Grundgesetz*, presented to the Allied Commanders in February 1949, was referred back by them, largely because the Americans and French thought it over-centralised. But the

Socialists (who had brought this about by concessions on other matters) stood firm, the Occupying Powers gave way and the Law came into force eleven days after the Berlin blockade ended. By it West Germany was to be governed by a Chancellor chosen by the Federal Assembly (*Bundestag*), whose composition is decided by universal suffrage and proportional representation with an election every four years. Parties however get no seats unless they obtain 5 per cent of the votes cast throughout the country (so as to discourage the small parties which had been the bane of the Weimar Republic). The Chancellor, who chooses the other Ministers, can only lose office if the Assembly votes by a majority against him and in addition has already agreed on a successor. If the Chancellor asks the Assembly for a vote of confidence and fails to get one, he can then ask the Federal President to dissolve the *Bundestag* and hold fresh elections, which have to occur unless the Assembly before being dissolved can agree on an alternative Chancellor. The Upper House or Federal Council (*Bundesrat*) represents the *Länder* Governments which have votes roughly proportionate to their size; its consent is required to all laws in which the *Länder* have an interest and its rejection of a bill can only be overridden by the Assembly with a vote of at least equal proportions (i.e. a majority, if the Council has voted by a majority, a two-thirds majority if by a two-thirds majority). The President is elected every five years by a Convention composed of the *Bundestag* and an equal number of representatives chosen by the *Länder* Assemblies; he has relatively little power. There is a Supreme Constitutional Court in the American style to judge whether the *Grundgesetz* is being observed; its importance is enhanced by the fact that the first nineteen articles of that law define fundamental rights for the individual citizen and legislation which is held to infringe them is automatically invalid. (This account of the *Grundgesetz* has been slightly simplified in the interest of brevity.)

The first elections, held in August 1949, gave the Christian Democratic Union (CDU), along with its Bavarian counterpart the Christian Social Union (CSU), 139 seats, the Social Democratic Party (SPD) 131, the Free Democratic Party (FDP) 52, and others 80. The SPD and the left wing of the CDU would have liked to form a coalition government between their two parties, but Adenauer was too adroit for them, and secured the votes of the FDP for his own nomination as Chancellor by promising to support their leader Heuss as President. On 17 September his nomination was approved in the *Bundestag* by a single vote – and he admitted having voted for himself!

For some time after the war the general assumption had been that the first German Government to be set up would be dominated by Socialists. There were several reasons why this did not happen. Many of the areas in which support for them was strongest lay in the Russian Zone. Adenauer proved an abler politician than the Socialist leader Schumacher; the resolute faith which had enabled the latter to survive many years in concentration camps made him mentally inflexible, apt to act as though the situation was still the same as it had been in 1930. But undoubtedly a major cause was the fact that the election did not take place until 1949. The enthusiasm generated during the war for subordinating private interests to public ones had waned, especially as the policy pursued since the currency reform of freeing private enterprise from controls was having startling success (p. 123). There was something about the Federal Republic in its early years which recalled the days before 1933 – and even those before 1914. Some who think that a chance of making timely social changes was missed have recently begun to blame the Allies – and particularly the Americans – for deliberately putting off elections until the situation had become more stable and the readiness to accept reform less general. This they undeniably did; Clay wrote to his Deputy in October 1947 that if they could defer the issue of socialising industry until free enterprise had had time to bring economic improvement, it might cease to be a live political issue.

The answer to such criticism is that the ideas of the Socialists had not won anything like general acceptance and, if acted on, would have been widely opposed. The renewed attempt at liberal democracy, if it was to last, needed above all else to win the support of the bureaucracy and professional and managerial classes, instead of being cold-shouldered and even sabotaged by them as had happened after 1919. For this reason it was a considerable advantage that the first cabinet was far enough to the right to deprive any of the more reactionary groups of most of their allure. It was not easy to regard Adenauer as a traitor to the nation – though Schumacher bitterly reproached him with being the Chancellor of the Allies. Moreover as a Rhinelander and a Catholic he was predisposed in favour of integrating the new state with the rest of Western Europe. He always vigorously denied a lack of interest in German unity but he was certainly not prepared to give it overriding priority. If Schumacher and the Socialists had come to power in 1949 there would have been endless bickerings with the Americans and West Germany would have had a more divided society. Its progress to economic prosperity would probably have been slower and the integration of Western Europe might never have got as far as it has. The possiblity that as an alternative Germany would have been reunited is highly questionable.

In November 1947 the German authorities in the Russian Zone had convened a People's Congress for Unity and a Just Peace, with delegates drawn ostensibly from all over Germany, although few turned up from the other three Zones. A further Congress met in March 1948 and set up a People's Council (*Volksrat*) of 400 with sub-committees for economics and politics, the latter being given the task of drawing up a constitution. This was drafted in such a way as to be applicable, like the *Grundgesetz*, to the whole country and much resembled the old Weimar system, with a People's Chamber (*Volkskammer*) and a Chamber representing the *Land* Governments. It was finally approved by the *Volksrat* in March 1949, after the Bonn Parliamentary Council had submitted the *Grundgesetz* to the Occupation authorities but before they had given their approval; in May the *Volksrat*'s action was confirmed by a newly-elected People's Congress. In October 1949, a month after Adenauer's election as Chancellor, the *Volksrat* turned itself into a 'provisional *Volkskammer*', proclaimed the foundation of the German Democratic Republic (DDR) and authorised Grotewohl, chairman of the SED, to form a Government. Elections for a *Volkskammer* were not held until October 1950 when voters were presented with a single list of candidates which 99.7 per cent of them were said to have accepted. In theory the Chamber's powers were considerable; in practice it confined itself to endorsing without opposition or debate the proposals already decided on by the SED leadership.

Whereas in West Germany most of the police forces belonged to the *Länder* and the only federal force was that controlling the frontier, the authorities in the Russian Zone were allowed in June 1948 to form a centralised People's Police Force. In the autumn of 1949 this was increased in strength to 55,000, given tanks and artillery, and stationed in barracks.

6   The Council of Europe

There were some in Germany, particularly among the young, who were after 1945 so soured by the demonstration of what national patriotism could end in that they wanted to transfer their allegiance to a higher plane. In France, the Low Countries and Scandinavia the shared experience of being occupied by the Germans and the desire to prevent Europe from being ravaged again by war made many people sympathetic to the idea of bringing their countries together. The National Socialists had sought to get their rule accepted by talk of uniting Europe under German leadership; their opponents felt bound to offer an alternative road. The argument was often heard that Europe must combine in some way politically if it was to deal in future on level terms with the new superpowers of America and Russia. For all these reasons the enthusiasts for European unification who had been until 1939 a scanty band had by 1945 become an appreciable group. But the attention of the governments in France and Italy was absorbed by their pressing domestic problems while Germany was in no position to take an initiative. The smaller states looked for a leader. They thought that they had found one in Winston Churchill who, in a broadcast in 1943 and again in a speech in Zurich in September 1946, advocated the uniting of Europe. But if due care was taken to read what he said, he could be clearly seen to think of Britain as a friend rather than as a member of any closer association; in any case he lost office in 1945. The Labour Government was suspicious rather than encouraging; Bevin was said to have remarked: 'Don't you open that Pandora's box, you'll find it full of Trojan horses.'

Progress had therefore to depend on private individuals, though some of them were influential. In December 1947 the various groups came together in a Committee directed by Duncan Sandys, Churchill's son-in-law; this proceeded to organise a Congress of 663 delegates, including Churchill, from sixteen European countries at The Hague in the following May. A resolution was passed saying that it was the urgent duty of the nations of Europe to create an economic and political union to assure security and social progress. The time had come when the European states must merge some part of their sovereign rights to secure common political and economic action for the integration and proper development of their common resources. It called for the urgent convening of a European Assembly to advise on measures for these purposes.

The British Government reacted by suggesting that it would be enough if the Foreign Ministers of the countries concerned were to meet at intervals to consider questions of common interest. This was so grotesquely out of line with what the pro-Europeans were seeking as to

Churchill on European integration

The United States supports this grand design [of the United Nations]. We in Britain have our own Commonwealth of Nations. These do not weaken, on the contrary they strengthen the United Nations. Why then should there not be a European group, which could give a sense of enlarged patriotism and common citizenship to the downhearted people of this turbulent and mighty continent? Why should it not take its place with other great powers in shaping the destinies of men? Great Britain, the British Commonwealth, mighty America, and, I trust, Soviet Russia – for then indeed all would be well – must be the friends and sponsors of the new Europe.

Churchill at Zürich, September 1946

Mr Churchill gave his unfavourable view of Schuman's European Defence Community, which was to be repeated often. He pictured a bewildered French drill sergeant sweating over a platoon made up of a few Greeks, Italians, Germans, Turks and Dutchmen, all in utter confusion over the simplest orders. What he hoped to see were spirited and strong national armies marching to the defence of freedom singing their national anthems. No one could get up enthusiasm singing 'March, NATO, march on!'. Eden patiently explained, as he had doubtless done before, that the proposal did not contemplate any such heterogeneous mixing of nationalities, but a creation of national units in the form of divisions, or *groupements*, of approximately twelve thousand men. They might perhaps, where numbers permitted, be further combined into army corps of perhaps 3 or 4 *groupements*. A strong and spirited German army was what bothered the French. I added that General Eisenhower approved the proposal and found no language or other difficulty not already present in his united command and in the army that NATO would hope to put into the field in case of trouble.

These arguments seemed to win Mr Churchill's approval. But each time the subject came up, we went back to the baffled drill sergeant. The fact was that, although on occasion he could be brought to say a good word for the Defence Community, at heart he did not approve of it.

Dean Acheson

provoke some even of the other Governments into demanding more. The British were induced to sign reluctantly in May 1949 a Statute setting up a Council of Europe, with a Committee of Ministers drawn from the participating governments to meet in private, and a Consultative Assembly chosen (in most cases) by the participating parliaments to meet in public. But the aim of the Council was described as being merely 'a greater unity' – not 'union' – and when the Assembly met for the first time in August 1949, it became clear that the

British concession had been one of form rather than of substance. For the Assembly could only debate subjects placed before it by the Ministers who, when they received in reply the resolutions which it adopted, were under no other obligation than to pass them on to their governments for study. In addition the Council was debarred from discussing defence, since that was dealt with under the North Atlantic Treaty, while economics were usually left to OEEC. Proposals to bring greater uniformity into European tariffs were consistently disregarded. Moreover unanimity was required for all substantial decisions of the Committee of Ministers. Demands that the Council should be given 'limited functions but real powers' fell on deaf governmental ears, particularly in Britain and Scandinavia.

In later years the Council was freed from some of its restrictions and has done good work in co-ordinating official requirements throughout Western Europe in such matters as patents, passports, extradition, car headlamps and school-leaving certificates: it also drew up in 1950 a Convention for the Protection of Human Rights and Fundamental Freedoms, with a judicial machinery to operate it (but little sanction behind its decisions beyond goodwill and a sense of shame). It has provided a useful sounding-board for the expression of European opinion. The chief significance of its creation was the clear evidence it afforded that this was not the road to closer integration, and that any serious move in such a direction must go without Britain.

This is of course precisely the path which six countries in Western Europe were going to take, confronting Britain with an established organisation which she was to decide she could not afford not to join. She has often been criticised for missing a great chance at the end of the war, when her prestige was at its highest and when she could, by clearsighted leadership, have given to any organisation which really did something to unite Europe pretty well whatever form suited her best. There were many reasons for her apparent obtuseness besides obscurantism. Although most of her public realised that the war had weakened her, they did not realise by how much; she still had the third largest armed force in the world, with an atomic capacity, and her gross national product per head was still higher than that of any other country in Europe. At that time only a third of her trade was done with Europe. Unlike most of Europe she had not been humiliated by defeat and occupation between 1940 and 1945. Some people still feared that Europe might collapse economically or go Communist and were anxious to avoid being involved. The other members of the

Commonwealth had no particular enthusiasm for greater British involvement in Europe and if she wanted to make anything of the new idea of the Empire as an association of equal autonomous states, she had to pay some attention to what the others thought. Her wartime association with the United States had been overplayed, leaving a belief that the Americans were ready to go on according to her a special relationship which entry into Europe would impair. The influence of Christian Democrats in France, Italy and West Germany made the Labour Government fear that right-wingers would be predominant in West European councils and, if given authority to do so, might interfere with the pursuit of socialist policies in Britain. All in all, Britain would have needed to undergo a fundamental change of outlook if she was to become on entry anything but a difficult partner and an obstacle to progress.

7 The establishment of Israel

Another overseas responsibility which Britain shed during these years was the Mandate to govern Palestine which she had received from the League of Nations in 1920. It had throughout been a source of trouble. The promises which she had made during the First World War of self-government to the Arabs and of a National Home to the Jews probably were, and were certainly considered by both groups to be, in practice incompatible. During the 1930s persecution of the Jews in Germany and elsewhere increased the number anxious to enter the country; the Arabs grew increasingly alarmed. A Commission of Enquiry in 1937 declared the Mandate unworkable and recommended dividing the area (one and a half times the size of Yorkshire) into a Jewish and an Arab state, with Jerusalem to be international. Though history has done much to confirm the realism of this scheme, nobody would accept it at the time and in 1939, with war in the offing, the British Government limited to 75,000 the number of Jews who would be allowed entry during the next five years, and promised that immigration thereafter would be 'subject to Arab acquiescence'.

At the start of the war the Jews supported the West, while some Arabs intrigued for the Germans. But as victory came in sight the Jews began organising to force open the door for refugees from Europe, acquiring arms by all sorts of means and forming terrorist gangs, one of which murdered a British Minister in Cairo in November 1944.

In February 1945 Roosevelt, on his way back from Yalta, called various Arab rulers to meet him in Egypt. King Ibn Saud of Saudi Arabia was brought up the Red Sea on an American destroyer, accompanied by the royal astrologer, a coffee server and nine miscellaneous slaves, porters, cooks and scullions; for practically the whole voyage he sat on deck in a gilt armchair while his minions caused some alarm by choosing the vicinity of the ammunition hoist as the site for a brazier on which to make the coffee. Roosevelt, on meeting the King, opened by saying he hoped that the Arabs would modify their racial hostility to the Jews sufficiently to allow 10,000 who had been persecuted in Germany and Eastern Europe to settle in Palestine. Ibn Saud in reply denied that Arab hostility to the Jews was racial, for both groups were Semitic. The real cause of the antagonism was the immigration of people who were technically and culturally on a higher level than the Arabs and put them to economic disadvantage. When the President tried to justify his appeal by referring to all that the Jews had suffered under the Nazis, the King replied that he did not see why it should be the Arabs who had to expiate Hitler's sins when there were other countries in a better position to help. 'Arabs would choose to die rather than to yield their land to Jews.' The President promised that he would do nothing to assist the Jews against the Arabs and would make no move hostile to the Arab people; he told Congress that he had learnt more by talking with Ibn Saud for five minutes than he could have done in an exchange of two or three dozen letters.

Action on this illuminating experience was however complicated for his successor by the fact that there are as many Jews in the United States as in Palestine and almost as many in New York as in Jerusalem. They are strongly represented in the academic, legal and medical professions and in the information media. The states in which they are concentrated – New York, New Jersey, Massachusetts, Illinois, California and Florida – are among the ten with the most votes in the electoral college which chooses the President (and the holders of all the seats for any state in that college are bound to cast their votes in favour of the party which has received a majority in the state election, no matter how small that majority may be). Thus a candidate who carried the principal states containing Jews would already have 160 out of the 270 votes needed for victory. No wonder anti-Semitism in America has been equated with political suicide!

This helps to explain why Americans believed that attention must be paid to the wishes of the Jews regarding their form of government and in April 1946 Truman, disregarding his diplomatic and military advisers, accepted the proposal of a joint Anglo-American Commission that 100,000 Jews (the number estimated to have survived the death-camps) should be allowed to enter Palestine forthwith. He probably thereby contributed significantly to his unexpected re-election in 1948 but he certainly complicated considerably the task of the British Government as the body actually responsible on the spot. The Commission had recommended against partition and in favour of continuing the Mandate. But the British, faced with continuing Arab opposition and Jewish terrorism (exemplified by 91 officials killed by a bomb planted at the instigation of a future Israeli Prime Minister and 250 Arab villagers shot down by Jewish guerrillas in 1947) decided, after various abortive attempts at compromise, that they had had enough. Bevin was much criticised in America for his insistence on trying to hold the balance fairly between Arabs and Jews. The United Nations produced a plan for partition but, when the Arabs rejected it, took no steps to provide the force without which it could not be imposed. Britain, seeing no prospect of being able to do so single-handed, announced that she would stop acting as Mandatory Power and withdrew her forces in May 1948.

On her departure the violence intermittently current between the Jews and Arabs flared into open war. Israel declared its existence as a state and was immediately recognised by both the US and the USSR. In three bursts of fighting the Israelis, to most people's surprise, beat the Arab armies and secured a bigger area than the UN had proposed for them; in September Count Bernadotte, the Swede sent by the UN to mediate, was murdered by a Jewish gang. Half-a-million Arabs fled from Israel across the Jordan and into a narrow strip of land round Gaza on the coast; the Jews said afterwards that this had been unnecessary but enough unarmed Arab civilians had been killed in cold blood to make it intelligible. The Arab states, though defeated, refused to make peace, closed the Suez Canal to Israeli shipping and boycotted firms trading with Israel. The Israelis refused to consider readmitting the refugees until there was a change of Arab attitude; the rest of the world failed to find any room for the outcasts.

Helped by generous contributions from Jewish communities all over the world but particularly in the US, the Israelis succeeded in making their lands blossom as the Arabs had never done. They also declared that no Jew who wished to come to Israel should be denied entry, so that the population steadily rose. Their frontier remained indented and vulnerable; until 1967 Arab-held land came at one point within ten miles of the Mediterranean. But the arms which the US helped them to obtain and their superior abilities as soldiers made them more than a match for the Arabs and they felt confident that, in the last resort, the West would come to their aid rather than see them obliterated. Thus here again the US took over a British responsibility, although without any explicit political link.

The situation created by these developments would, in view of the possibility of super power involvement, have been quite dangerous enough. It was however aggravated by the speed with which after 1945 the world grew dependent on oil for energy, transport and petro-chemicals. The vast increase in consumption drew heavily on the reserves in many existing sources, notably the United States. By far the largest alternative stocks were in Arab hands (p. 116). Thus the world in general and Western Europe in particular put itself at the mercy of the Arabs at the same time as it exasperated them by protecting the Jews. The danger was belittled by the argument that 'the Arabs could not drink their oil'. To obtain benefit from it they had to get it distributed and sold to people who could use it. For this they in their turn were said to be dependent on and unable to risk antagonising the oil companies of the West. As events were to show, this was not the whole truth. But alternative technologies were not available for doing the things which oil made possible or cheap, so that the cost of renouncing Arab supplies would have been to forego many aids to comfortable living. Humanity yielded to temptation and trusted to luck.

The Jewish-Arab antagonism has a bearing on a tenet of considerable importance in regard to a free world. Advocates of such a world often talk as though it were unquestionably possible for groups of people differing in background, language and economic levels to live harmoniously together inside a single political community and that their failure to do so merely means that the appropriate political institutions and laws have not yet been found. Whether history justifies such a belief is extremely questionable. What is essential in such cases is the will to live together and that will is unlikely to be forthcoming on both sides if one or both suspect that the other is going to make it poorer or deprive it of some good which it enjoys (such as speaking a distinctive language or practising a distinctive religion). It is one thing for peoples of different backgrounds to come together of their own volition in a new territory like the US (though even there the negroes, the group which was both most distinctive and did not go of their own free will, have proved the hardest to assimilate). It is another matter where a distinctive group thrusts itself into an already inhabited territory without the consent of the inhabitants. Even when this occurred long ago, the desire to prevent any further loss of influence often causes distinguishing marks to be clung to when they might otherwise be abandoned. Once one group has used violence against the other, suspicions and fear are hard to erase. Even a strong and impartial government has great difficulty in compelling the two antagonised groups to co-operate. The most promising solution is to resettle the area so that the two groups are no longer in close contact, but even that course creates refugees who hope to recover their homelands unless, as with the Germans in Eastern Europe, the power situation is such as to make the hope slender.

Appendix: World production and consumption of oil 1938–77 (millions of tons)

Area	1938	1951	1955	1960	1965	1977
USA	162	298	334	350	431	408
	151	*341*	*409*	*468*	*549*	*867*
	+ 11	**− 43**	**− 75**	**− 118**	**− 118**	**− 459**
Rest of	45	120	160	221	286	315
Western Hemisphere	*23*	*63*	*91*	*125*	*156*	*277*
	+ 22	**+ 57**	**+ 69**	**+ 96**	**+ 130**	**+ 38**
Middle East	15	94	160	262	416	1104
	2	*7*	*15*	*32*	*33*	*79*
	+ 13	**+ 87**	**+ 145**	**+ 230**	**+ 383**	**+ 1025**
Western	1	5	10	15	22	70
Europe	*36*	*73*	*115*	*202*	*389*	*697*
	− 35	**− 68**	**− 105**	**− 187**	**− 367**	**− 627**
Eastern Europe,	35	47	84	167	268	641
USSR and China	*25*	*49*	*79*	*142*	*221*	*568*
	+ 10	**− 2**	**+ 5**	**+ 25**	**+ 47**	**+ 73**
Rest of	10	16	21	41	141	446
world	*18*	*41*	*54*	*91*	*183*	*484*
	− 8	**− 25**	**− 33**	**− 50**	**− 42**	**− 38**
Total	268	580	769	1056	1564	2984
	255	*574*	*763*	*1060*	*1531*	*2972*
	+ 13	**+ 6**	**+ 6**	**− 4**	**+ 33**	**+ 12**

Roman figures: production
Italic figures: consumption
Bold figures: balance

CHAPTER 4

1950-2

1 The Korean War

The Americans believed that in Chiang Kai-shek they had found a doughty fighter for democracy who would make China into a pillar of the Free World. As time went on and their envoys observed him at close quarters, they discovered that he was not much of a fighter and little of a democrat. Indeed he constituted the first notable case where opposing Communism meant backing a government which was corrupt, incompetent and unpopular. Misled by some skilful Russian misrepresentation, they did not take the Communism of Mao Tse-tung too seriously and thought that he could be induced to work with Chiang. China was notoriously a large country in which they were loath to get involved, an attitude which caused Mao to describe the US as a 'paper tiger'. Probably against Russia's advice he launched an attack on Chiang, who was only given arms by America and not men. By mid-1949, to the surprise of everyone including himself, he succeeded in driving Chiang and the Nationalists off the entire mainland to Formosa (Taiwan). This was perhaps one of the most far-reaching events recorded in this book, though its full implications took time to emerge. When it occurred, with the wave of anti-Communist feeling in the US coming to a crest (pp. 75), there were bitter recriminations and accusations of treachery. But it was then too late to do more than hope that in due course the profound civilisation and the democratic individualism of China would reassert themselves, and that she would throw off the Soviet yoke. For the time being, the US took the view that what must not be could not be and refused to recognise diplomatically the existence of the Mao regime. One consequence was that they vetoed Communist China's admission to the United Nations which led early in 1950 to the Soviet Union's temporary withdrawal from that body in protest.

This proved a miscalculation when on 25 June 1950 North Korean forces invaded South Korea, especially as it had been the Russians rather than the Chinese who instigated them to do so. Korea, like Germany, had been entered at the end of the war by American forces from one direction and Russian from the other; the local commanders had fixed a zonal boundary at the 38th Parallel and this had remained effective after the Great Powers had withdrawn their troops. The Russians had some grounds for thinking that the Americans would not intervene in Korea when they had refrained from doing so in China, especially as US spokesmen had more than once talked in ways which suggested that South Korea was not regarded as a vital American interest. The calculation seems to have been that the Communist conquest of yet another area would either lead the Americans to cut their losses and evacuate Japan (which might then have turned Communist too) or involve themselves more deeply there, in which case they would have fewer resources to spare for Europe while Mao would be made more dependent on Soviet support.

What the US in fact did was to convene the UN Security Council and within two days obtain from it a resolution (which the Russians owing to their absence could not veto) condemning the aggression and ordering all UN members to help South Korea. By the end of September, thirty were doing so. American naval and air units were sent in immediately (followed later by ground forces) while the 7th Fleet was sent to protect Formosa from the mainland (and also, though less urgently, the mainland from Formosa). These reinforcements reversed the early successes which the North Koreans had won and by October the line was back at the 38th Parallel. The Russians, chary of risking a confrontation, lived up to their self-bestowed epithet of 'peace-loving' and gave no help. But when the American General MacArthur, as UN Commander, sent his forces (85 per cent of which were American) northwards over the Parallel, the Chinese were induced – or ordered – to pull the chestnuts out of a fire which was none of their making. In November volunteers arrived from China to help the North Koreans, followed soon afterwards by regular troops; back went the front south of the Parallel. The swashbuckling MacArthur wanted to attack China but once again Washington fought shy of such a large commitment (much as Moscow was doing); when the General made a direct approach to Congress over the President's head, he was sacked. Although 69 per cent of the public supported him he failed to exploit their backing. In July 1951 peace negotiations began which led two years later to an armistice leaving things much as they had been at the outset. It was only in 1955 that all non-Korean forces were finally withdrawn. The war cost the United Nations 36,700 dead of whom 33,500 were American.

2 The impact of the Korean War in Europe

The Korean War had almost more impact on Europe than on Asia. If the Russians could miscalculate in one continent, why not in another? Hitherto the easy assumption had been that they would not want the extra liability of a Western Europe conquered against its will and of an America made more hostile than ever. Today's knowledge suggests strongly that this appreciation was correct. But the fact remained that, should they become unable to resist trying to pick the ripe plum, there were only about twelve divisions in the way and these incompletely equipped; a NATO staff officer, asked what the Russians would need to reach the Pyrenees, is said to have answered 'Shoes'. It might be true that many of the 175 Soviet divisions in Eastern Europe were required for police purposes and that a Soviet division was smaller than a Western one, but the discrepancy was still uncomfortably large and the Russians, reversing the rundown of their forces, were in the process of raising them from the 2.9 million of 1948 towards the 5.8 million which they were to attain in 1955. The West had lost its monopoly of atomic weapons; although the Russian stock was still small and could not be delivered in North America, the mere possibility of retaliation anywhere inclined planners to look on the use of such weapons as a last resort. The feeling had been growing for some time that, as long as the West remained so vulnerable militarily, its diplomatic bargaining position would be dangerously weak.

The first step was to carry through the conversion of the North Atlantic system from an alliance to an organisation, with a hierarchy of committees, an American Supreme Commander (in the first instance, General Eisenhower), and an elaborate multinational command structure. Previous plans only to set up such machinery after hostilities began were clearly seen to overestimate the amount of time which might be available. Another precaution was the American decision to proceed from the fission atomic to the more powerful (though smaller) fusion bomb; when the question of doing so was put to Truman, he is said merely to have asked 'Can they make it? If so, how can we not?' But although the Americans were nine months ahead of the Russians in producing an explosion, they were seven months behind in producing a droppable bomb. Neither of these two steps remedied the need for more 'conventional' forces, i.e. fighting men. The plans of the Brussels Powers had called for 80 to 85 divisions; the North American Treaty Organisation, meeting at Rome in November 1951, more modestly decided to aim at an increase from 15 to 43 over the next two years.

But where were the men to come from? America could only finance the rearmament of others as long as she was prosperous herself, which was thought to preclude taking men away from peacetime industry. The British and French economies were fully stretched, while many of their troops were required for commitments outside Europe. It might be true that the original NATO members represented some 350 million people whereas the Soviet bloc only represented 260 million. But there were limits to the extent to which the free peoples of the world were prepared to impoverish themselves deliberately by diverting resources from industry and welfare to defence. As a Frenchman put it

> With you Americans, the big problem is the immediate threat of Russia to our collective security. With us the big problem is the immediate threat to our standards of living which cannot be depressed significantly without endangering public support for the rearmament programme you are demanding of us.

The only way of obtaining appreciable (though by no means complete) relief was to rearm the German Federal Republic, which still had half-a-million of its population unemployed. At this stage its productive capacity or technical skills were of secondary interest, except for the need to keep them out of Russian control. The War Department in Washington had for some time been pressing for such a policy; now at last they succeeded in overcoming the political hesitations of the State Department. At a meeting of Foreign Ministers in New York in September 1950 Acheson (who had just succeeded Marshall as Secretary of State) made clear that his Government's willingness to remain in Europe depended on agreement to rearm West Germany as a matter of urgency.

The proposal met on all sides with considerably less than enthusiasm. Many Europeans were deeply disturbed at the thought of giving arms back to a nation which had in the past put them to such brutal and destructive purposes. A Germany equipped with nuclear weapons was a particularly distasteful thought. A wave of pacifist revulsion, partly spontaneous, partly the outcome of Allied indoctrination, swept through West Germany itself. There was little eagerness to provide the West with cannon fodder; the catch phrase of the time was '*ohne mich*' or 'include me out'. Rearmament would imperil the economic revival, increase the risk of Germany becoming the first theatre of any East–West clash and above all reduce the likelihood of the country being reunited. Yet these dangers would not necessarily be avoided by remaining disarmed. And the plain fact remained that the rearming of West Germany was the price demanded by the Americans for continuing to act as the protectors of Western Europe.

Since 1947 recovery had continued to forge ahead. For OEEC countries generally, industrial output in the second half of 1950 was some 25 per cent above 1938. Production of refined oil products was 200 per cent above pre-war levels and electric power generated 75 per cent; coal in contrast was still slightly below the pre-war figure. Agricultural output was 14 per cent higher, thus outpacing a population rise of 11 per cent. Trade within the OEEC was up by 69 per cent on 1938 and exports to outside countries were 48 per cent higher in real terms than in 1938. The adverse balance with North America had (thanks partly to the 1949 devaluations) fallen from $6.1 billion in 1947 to $1.75 billion.

At this point however progress was interrupted by the need to respond to the Korean challenge. Existing forces had to be re-equipped with more modern (and more expensive) weapons; additional arms were required for new units. A big programme of armament production had therefore to be imposed on economies which were already at or approaching full stretch; the theory that rearmament was needed to revive a flagging economy is the reverse of the truth. Could the necessary resources be made available without seriously checking the growth in civilian production and living standards? The most immediate effect of the new programmes was a sharp rise in demand for raw materials, production of which had not increased much in the preceding years. Not only were they needed to make extra weapons, but fear of war breaking out and interfering with supplies leads people to build up stocks as a precaution. In this field the margin between glut and scarcity is always narrow, so that any rise in demand is apt to produce a big rise in prices. Consequently OEEC's balance of payments with the rest of the world, and particularly with the dollar area, began to deteriorate again. Britain gained at first through large increases in exports by the rest of the sterling area but later got into difficulties when she had to pay for her own raw material purchases. The attempt to rearm painlessly inevitably meant an attempt to get too much out of resources which (as always) were limited and hence a general revival of inflation, bringing with it more budgetary complications.

To meet the situation American aid was continued at a higher level than had been intended, being rechristened 'Mutual Security' from the end of 1951. Much of it went to pay for the extra supplies of raw materials, some to enlarge the facilities for the production of such materials, outside Europe as well as inside it. Considerable attention was given to improving European machinery, production methods, labour relations and management, with a view to getting more out of existing resources; the word 'productivity', which had begun to be heard in 1948, became generally current. To the Americans, the Europeans were inefficient, over-enamoured of established ways, over-reluctant to innovate. Vested interests and sacred cows had too much influence. What was needed above all was the stimulus of free competition, brought about by the removal of barriers, restrictions and agreements. By no means all the Europeans were convinced about the advantages of unrestricted competition or indeed about the urgency of the Soviet military threat. There was however one country which had not only embraced free competition with enthusiasm but was beginning to show spectacular results.

3   West Germany's 'Economic Miracle' *(Wirtschaftswunder)*

On the Sunday in June 1948 on which the West German Currency Reform was introduced (see p. 96), the German Director of the Economic Administrative Office for Bizonia had gone to the microphone and promised his public the removal of all but a handful of the multifarious controls existing on prices and supplies. The name of the man taking this step was Ludwig Erhard. He was not being quite as rash as he seemed, for the handful retained covered such essentials as bread, milk, meat, electricity, coal and steel, which influenced much of the rest of the economy, while control over wages was kept until the autumn. To cut in this manner through the whole complex of restrictions which the Occupying Powers had inherited from the Nazis was enough to unnerve many of the Control officials and strength of mind was needed to push the change through. But the Americans had a soft spot for anyone who, not content with arguing in favour of free enterprise, was actually prepared to practise it, while the idea commended itself to the Germans because it promised to reduce the opportunities for Allied interference.

The derestriction, taken together with the Currency Reform, came at exactly the right moment. The initial issue of the new currency was small enough to leave everyone short of money and therefore reversed the previous situation by making cash more desirable than stocks. Goods which had been hoarded were unloaded, the shops filled up their shelves and the black market disappeared overnight. The pipeline of supplies to the factories (p. 72) had been refilled with American aid so that the capacity was available to restock the shelves as soon as they were emptied. For some time past the German people had been ready to exert their habitual industry but had lacked any incentive to do so; they now set to work with a will. Much of the credit for the amazing change which ensued has with considerable justice been given to this response and to the population's readiness to trust the new currency. Less spectacular but equally important was the part played by the Allies, and particularly the Americans, in re-establishing supply lines, and paying out of their own pockets for many of the goods which went into them. It was not, as accounts often suggest, the Currency Reform alone which did the trick; had it come earlier, before the other preparations had had time to take effect, its success would have been less dramatic.

In the second half of 1948 West German industrial production rose by 50 per cent, and in the following year by a further 25 per cent. By 1953 average living standards were higher than in 1938, while in the fourteen years following 1950 the gross national product trebled. In 1958 the Federal Republic overtook Britain to become the world's second largest exporter and by 1961 was the third largest industrial producer. What is more surprising is that Germany's net balance of foreign trade on current account showed from 1951 to 1964 an uninterrupted surplus, occasionally of high proportions. No wonder that people talked about a 'miracle' and that Erhard's prestige soared. In reality however the phenomenon was due to the happy coincidence of various identifiable factors, not all of them likely to last. The euphoria of the moment often caused this fact to be overlooked, and the assumption was too easily made that the 'Free Market Economy' was the permanent cure for all the world's ills. For this reason the main factors at work merit description.

(a)   As has been mentioned (p. 88), West Germany was the fourth largest recipient of Marshall Aid. Moreover Marshall Aid meant that the Federal Republic was recovering in the middle of a continent doing the same, and each part stimulated the others.

(b)   Although Germany's industrial areas appeared at the end of the war to have been completely devastated, much of the damage to plant was superficial; only 15 to 20 per cent was wrecked beyond repair. Dismantling for disarmament and reparations only affected 5 per cent of total industrial capacity and fell mainly on industries which had expanded during the war. Both processes literally cleared the ground for re-equipment, often with the help of a government subsidy which in other circumstances would have broken the GATT rules of fair competition. Some firms which might not otherwise have modernised their plant and products were driven to do so.

(c)   The loss of the lands east of the Oder–Neisse as a source of food-supply has often been considered a great disadvantage for the rest of Germany. But in fact these areas were relatively expensive producers by comparison with many extra-European sources. As soon as Germany could find the exports with which to pay for substitute imports of food from overseas, she stood to gain by the switch.

(d)   In the years following 1945, many people had been unable to see how West Germany could ever support the vast addition to her population caused by the inflow of refugees from areas east of the Oder–Neisse, from the Sudeten districts of Czechoslovakia, from East Germany and from even further afield. And indeed, as soon as many nominal jobs were made uneconomic by the Currency Reform, unemployment rose to 2 million and did not fall below half a million until 1955, while the provision of housing for the newcomers (on top of the need to replace the destroyed and damaged pre-war houses) did constitute a heavy burden. On the other hand the presence of a plentiful supply of labour (and one which was being constantly replenished as more people left East Germany) removed what was to prove a major hindrance to growth in other more settled countries. Moreover the additional labour, having left its roots behind, could easily move to where it was needed.

(e)   West Germany is often considered to have gained because her economy was not burdened till the mid-1950s by any defence expenditure of her own but only by the costs of her Occupiers (which until 1952 were fixed without any reference to her). For some time these took up a proportion of her resources comparable to the defence outlays of many countries; it was only after the expansion of the economy got under way, in 1953–4, that the proportion fell appreciably. But this burden was counterbalanced by the considerable amount of military expenditure made directly or indirectly in Germany by foreign governments which was *not* charged to occupation costs.

(f) The German people as a whole are hard-working and methodical by tradition and training. Their standard of education has long been high so that they make an admirable labour force for an industrial country. Supplies of skilled managers were ample, not least from the highly trained General Staff officers forced to seek civilian jobs as a result of disarmament.

(g) Patriotism, extensive unemployment, lack of funds (as a result of Currency Reform) and the fact that in Germany their membership had never been anything like complete all combined to keep trade unions from making exorbitant demands. Union structure had been reorganised after the war (with British encouragement) in such a way as to reduce inter-union rivalry and demarcation disputes, while German labour has never been able to establish the principle of the 'closed shop' (which would probably violate the 'human rights' clauses of the *Grundgesetz* (p. 104) so that a law in favour of it passed by the *Bundestag* would be unenforceable). In 1946 the Control Council re-established the Works Councils which had flourished between 1920 and 1933. Every firm of any size had to have such a Council, elected by the workers, with a right of co-decision with management in many matters which affected working conditions (though not wages). In the coal and steel industries the British authorities, in response to a trade union demand, required all firms in their Zone to give the workers equal representation with the shareholders on the Supervisory Board (the body which meets four or five times a year, approves the balance sheet, authorises major investments and appoints the smaller Managing Committee which takes the day-to-day decisions). The Board was to have a chairman chosen by agreement between the two sides. In addition the Managing Committee had to include a Labour Director who had been approved by the workers' representatives on the Supervisory Board and who could not be removed without their consent. The extension of this principle to the rest of industry, and to the rest of West Germany, remained for some time at issue and was finally settled in 1951 on the basis of one-third representation for the workers; the desire to get some such arrangement accepted acted as a restraining influence on the trade unions in the interval. Opinions differ as to the exact effect of 'co-determination' (*Mitbestimmung*) but there is no doubt that the demands of the workers were moderated by the knowledge that their views were being voiced at the top and by the insights which their representatives gained into the problems of their firms.

For all these reasons demands for wage increases remained moderate, while production was not interrupted by strikes. The failure of a 24-hour general strike in November 1948 reinforced the trend.

(h) Almost everyone in Germany had suffered material loss and come down in the world. Consequently almost everyone was prepared to work hard and anxious to make money in order to rebuild his capital and possessions and provide himself with fresh security. German society, like Germany itself, was starting again from zero and could use all its resources to build up instead of facing the British problem of having to make reduced resources stretch to maintain an established position. Sacred cows were comparatively rare and vested interests on the defensive.

(i) Thanks to the restraint of the unions, wages remained at a relatively low level and salaries did the same, amounting (1950–60) to only 47 per cent GNP as compared with 58 per cent in Britain. Although both showed a steady rise over the years, the rates were for long slower than the growth in output. Thanks to the desire to rebuild personal positions, the propensity to consume was the lowest in Western Europe. The rate of saving was high, while the profits of firms were mostly ploughed back in fresh investment instead of being distributed in wages and dividends. Private consumption only accounted for 59 per cent of GNP, as against 65 per cent in Britain.

(j) The Government exempted overtime from tax and gave considerable premiums to savers. The tax rate on higher incomes was not much heavier than on lower ones. Considerable inequalities in income were tolerated and even encouraged while the ability of the successful to save was increased.

(k) The new political system quickly established itself on a firm basis and the growing prosperity combined with the relative stability of prices to create confidence in the future, in spite of the Communist threat on the very boundary of the country. Political and economic success went hand in hand, each stimulating the other.

(l) Thanks to all the factors mentioned, the rate of investment was high. Gross domestic capital formation rose between 1950 and 1960 by 157 per cent in real terms, as compared with 46 per cent in Britain.

Total fixed investment at home during the same period absorbed 22 per cent of GNP, as compared with a British figure of 16.6 per cent. But as saving was also high, this rate of investment did not lead to serious inflation or price rises.

(m) A frequent result of high investment is a bigger demand for equipment than can be met by home production, thus creating an increase in imports so that the national trade figures are thrown into deficit. Why did this not happen in West Germany? One answer is that at the start it did. Until March 1951 the Federal Republic was in serious deficit, especially in the European Payments Union (p. 87) where it exhausted its credit quota by December 1950 and had to be granted a further $120 million of which it used three-quarters in the next two months. The situation was aggravated by the rapid rise in world prices resulting from the Korean War and the action of German private importers who rushed to buy large quantities immediately. The position was also aggravated by the cuts in import quotas ('liberalisation') which OEEC had called on all its members to make. For a time the Republic's position led to considerable criticism in OEEC, where the Germans were accused of making other people pay their way for them in order to avoid damaging their own interests by slowing down their expansion. Great pressure was put on Erhard to reimpose import quotas and tighten credit. His view was that such measures would merely check production just as it was getting under way and invite retaliation against German exports. He also argued that at a time of rising prices it was better to hold goods than money. At the end of February 1951 he was driven to halt liberalisation and put up interest rates, but just at that moment his standpoint was vindicated by West Germany's balance of payments taking a sharp turn for the better. By the end of May she had repaid the $120 million special credit and some of her previous debts. From that time forward she moved steadily into a stronger creditor position and Erhard's reputation became higher than ever. The explanation for the turn seems to be threefold:

(i) The heavy German purchases of raw materials at the start of the boom meant that stocks were accumulated, reducing the need to buy at the peak (as the British found themselves having to do). By the time it became necessary to replenish the stocks again, the peak had passed and prices were coming down again.

(ii) In spite of the large amount of plant and other goods needing to be replaced in West Germany, factors already described kept consumer demand within limits, and consequently also limited the imports to which such demand gave rise. The extensive efforts made by the Nazis to render Germany more nearly self-sufficient had some permanent effect in reducing the need for imports.

(iii) The rearmament programme set going throughout the world by the Korean War called above all for finished manufactures, and particularly for modern types of machinery. As these were just the types of machinery which the Federal Republic's reconstructed industry was well equipped to supply, external demand for West German goods soared. Even apart from Korea, the world had still not satisfied its need for goods to catch up on the failure to replace obsolete and worn-out equipment between 1939 and 1945, while the steady liberalisation of trade, the pursuit by governments of policies of full employment and the requirements of backward countries for development all combined to keep world demand for manufactures high. The part which armaments had played in the German economy down to 1945 was taken over by engineering exports.

In an economy such as West Germany's, in which foreign trade absorbs a relatively high proportion of output, buoyant exports are particularly important since it is they which principally make manufacturers confident that future demand will be high enough to keep their order-books full. But the view taken about future levels of demand is the chief factor influencing readiness to invest and thereby increase productive capacity; adequate investment is essential to rapid growth. If output is expanding quickly, productivity is also likely to rise, thanks to economies of scale and generally improved organisation, thereby reducing costs and increasing still further competitiveness on foreign markets. In addition, the return available on investment is likely to rise, making it more attractive in comparison to other uses for money, and hence stimulating it.

The essence of the Federal Republic's 'miracle' was that, at a time when world demand was high, its industry had spare capacity, the right products and relatively low costs, so that exporting was easy and profitable and hence popular. The West German share of world trade in manufactures rose from 7 per cent in 1950 to nearly 19 per cent in 1959 which had been approximately its level (allowing for partition) in 1913, whereas in 1937 the figure had only been 16.4 per cent. Once this export-led expansion got under way, the prospect of making profits attracted investment into export industries whose growing earnings made it easy to pay for all the imports which increasing manufacture for export involved. The pool of unemployed, continually refilled by migrants from East Germany, prevented shortage of labour from constricting output. Thanks to the high level of investment, production grew at a rate which allowed for ample increases in prices and wages without inflation. The exchange rate remained favourable (in spite of being devalued less than most other European currencies in 1949) and the costs of most of West Germany's competitors rose faster than hers did, so that she could afford increases without pricing herself out of the market. All in all, she was in the exceptional position of a 'virtuous spiral'. So far from needing to conduct an 'export drive', the Government was under permanent pressure to get the favourable balances reduced since their accumulation inside the country could not but have an inflationary effect.

(n) Neither the old Reichsmark nor the new Deutsche Mark was a currency in which other countries held their reserves, and the Federal Republic was under no obligation to provide them with capital. Indeed the authorities put up interest rates so as to check home demand with the result that, in spite of the big export surplus, capital for a time flowed in rather than out. Owing to the lack of institutions to make foreign investment easy, not to mention the caution engendered by having her holdings abroad twice confiscated for reparations, West Germany was slow in burdening her balance of payments by transfers of capital abroad. Even in the mid-1960s her total foreign investments were still only about one-twentieth the size of Britain's. A relatively generous agreement made by her creditors in 1953, before the full extent of her prosperity became evident, enabled her to pay off by moderate instalments the debts inherited from the Weimar Republic and those incurred since 1945.

(o) In times of slump, governments are blamed for much that is not their fault; in times of prosperity, the reverse occurs. For this reason, the part played by official policy in producing West Germany's success story has been left to the end so as to emphasise the number of other factors involved. But undoubtedly government actions contributed in many ways to the total result. Some have already been mentioned such as the provision of subsidies to help replace bombed or dismantled equipment and the exemption of overtime earnings from tax. Between 1950 and 1955 exports were stimulated, in violation of GATT rules, by certain taxes being refunded in respect of them. The abolition of import quotas was originally imposed on the Federal Republic by OEEC but in the mid-1950s its Government went further and deliberately made unilateral cuts in a number of tariffs with the double object of encouraging imports and depriving inefficient manufacturers of a sheltered life in the home market.

These however are not the government actions commonly given credit for the miracle. Many, particularly in circles where official interference with industry is disliked, have attributed this achievement first and foremost to Erhard's courage in removing controls and giving freedom to private enterprise. There is undoubtedly justification for this. Thanks to cartels and other restrictive agreements, as well as the chronic itch of an authoritarian government to regulate, Germany even before 1933 had never known an economy in which market forces were really allowed free play. And by 1948 the controlled economy had got into a straitjacket which distorted its natural shape. Initiative was being held back and resources used unprofitably. Their more rational allocation was unlikely ever to have been achieved by central government direction. Nobody knew which way the horse would naturally choose to go and, in order to discover the answer, it had for a time to be given its head. But without the incentives to work hard, save and invest which have been described in this section, the results of freedom might have been very different.

The second government policy for which much credit has been claimed is the deflationary policy of the Finance Ministry and Central Bank in restricting credit and holding down the supply of money in a world where desire for full employment was producing a steady trend to inflation. Undoubtedly this policy did help to check home demand and encourage exports. A tendency of retail prices to rise during the early months was also nipped in the bud. But when so many other powerful factors were working in the same direction, a contribution from monetary policy may have been superfluous. During the earlier years however the West German leaders may well be excused for lacking confidence that non-monetary forces would do the trick; the importance of the new state earning its way in the world was great enough to justify them in making assurance doubly sure.

Thus the background to the West Germany of the 1950s was one of great and growing prosperity, a situation all the more gratifying because in 1945 nobody would have believed it possible. For the first time in German history democratic government came to be associated with success. It was the best possible advertisement for the kind of world which the Americans had been seeking to create and appeared to vindicate their views.

4   Britain in the 1950s

In December 1950 the British Government announced that it could thenceforward manage without Marshall Aid dollars. As has already been said (p. 46) the Attlee Cabinet had succeeded over the previous five years in securing a steady growth in GNP and, by holding down consumption, had channelled most of the increase into exports and productive home investment. Inflation had been brought down by the end of the period to 3 per cent. Exports, which had faltered in 1949, had picked up again after the devaluation of the pound. Although the Government was still spending far more abroad than had been done before 1939, the balance of payments was in healthy surplus, while the gold and dollar reserves were rising.

This solid achievement was halted by the post-Korean drive for rearmament. Defence expenditure was increased by 50 per cent. Most of the extra money was to be spent on weapons, which made calls on the engineering, motor, aircraft and electrical industries; as these had been fully extended already, their ability to produce for exports and home investment was impaired. But the major problem was caused by the rise in world prices and the consequent extra cost of imports. Although higher prices at first benefited the raw material producers in the sterling area, many of them proceeded to spend their additional income in purchases from outside the area, while manufacturers at home had to replenish their stocks; the overall balance of payments became unfavourable and the reserves were still too small to last out till the corner had been turned. The country's deficit in 1951 was clearly going to be considerable.

An election in February 1950 had left the Labour Government with a very narrow majority. In April 1951 three Ministers, Aneurin Bevan, Harold Wilson and John Freeman resigned in protest against the scale of rearmament (and in particular against the introduction of charges in the National Health Service as one way of paying for it). In October Attlee decided that his parliamentary position was too weak for him to carry through the measures needed to balance the external accounts. The result of the ensuing election was an interesting commentary on the British parliamentary system. Labour won 700,000 more votes than it had done twenty months earlier and over 200,000 more votes than the Conservatives, a higher total than it has ever reached before or since. Yet owing to the way in which votes were distributed between constituencies, a Labour majority of eight seats was converted into a Conservative one of sixteen.

The mere return of the Conservatives helped to restore confidence in the pound. They proceeded to make drastic cuts in imports, which involved reimposing a number of the 'quotas' removed under the OEEC programme (p. 86). The scheme for allocating steel, relaxed in 1950, was tightened up again. The rearmament programme was scaled down and spread over a longer period (partly because it proved physically impossible to turn out the arms as quickly as had been planned). A more typical Conservative action was resort to higher interest rates in order to check demand, as contrasted with Labour's preference for direct controls.

By the end of 1952 not only had imports been reduced but their prices had begun to fall; payments were back in balance and the reserves were rising again. The Government proceeded to dismantle nearly all the controls, including food rationing and building licensing, and stopped official buying of foodstuffs in bulk; quotas were almost completely removed. Trade and industry were set free in the conviction that private enterprise was best qualified to find a solution to the country's problems. Many, including the Bank of England, wanted to extend decontrol to money by making the pound convertible into dollars and (in violation of the rules of the IMF) leaving it to 'float' – at any rate for a time. A majority of the Cabinet, however, remembering what had happened in 1947 (p. 73), fought shy of making such a 'dash for freedom'.

Import costs did not merely fall back to their previous level once the Korean crisis was over. The relative scarcity of raw materials and foodstuffs, as compared with manufactures (the so-called 'terms of trade'), which had been a feature of the world since 1945, was reversed. Over the next few years a 12 per cent price change in Britain's favour meant that her exports of goods and services became perfectly adequate to pay for imports and leave a fair surplus. This change is often treated as a piece of pure luck for the Conservatives which they did nothing to bring about. The major cause of it probably was the stimulus which the Korean War gave to investment, expanding the world's production of raw materials. But in raw material supplies the margin between scarcity and glut is surprisingly narrow, so that a small change in quantities available can bring a big change in prices. Britain was one of the world's biggest buyers, so that, if she cut down her purchases, the effect was considerable. The Conservative tightening of credit not only reduced the amount of money available for buying, but led industrialists to expect a fall in demand and therefore to let their stocks go unreplenished.

From 1953 to 1955 the economy was allowed to expand and for the first time since the war consumers were permitted to share in the growth; their expenditure rose by some 4 per cent a year. The Chancellor of the Exchequer, R. A. Butler, talked of doubling the British standard of life in twenty-five years and in fact the gross national product did nearly double during the 1950s (though this did not mean that everybody became twice as well off). The number of houses built was raised by 50 per cent. The danger in this policy was that too high a proportion of resources would go to consumption (including housing) at home, to the disadvantage of exports and manufacturing investment, with the result that Britain's ability to compete would be weakened if conditions in the world became less favourable to her.

This danger was aggravated by other features of the Government's policies:

(a) Loyalty to the principle of free trade and payments meant that, when adverse trends set in, any remedy which involved the reimposition of direct controls or import restrictions was regarded as out of the question. Thus when in 1955 the expansion of demand not only helped the Government to increase its majority in an election but caused imports to soar, the official reaction was not to pick and choose between them by imposing quotas but to damp down demand generally by increasing the rate of interest, asking the banks to restrict credit and raising taxes on consumer goods. As a result the economy remained virtually stationary for the next two years. The hope was that a higher proportion of output, unable to find an outlet in the home market, would go into exports. But this only happened to a limited extent; manufacturers also reacted by producing less and dropping their plans for installing machinery to produce more. In 1958-9 the Government again managed to get an expansion under way; the result was a rise in imports not only of raw materials but also of machinery and manufactures which Britain could not make in sufficient quantities herself until she had carried the expansion through. Once again the remedy adopted was an undiscriminating clamp-down on activity at home by altering interest rates and taxes. Payments were put back into balance but expansion was slowed down and Britain was no nearer a solution to the problem of producing enough manufactures for her own needs as well as for export. The repeated changes between 'go' and 'stop' exasperated industrialists and made them think twice about investing.

(b) Combined with the commitment to freedom of trade went an overriding priority to maintaining the value of the pound and in consequence an insistence on quick action if for any reason the balance of payments became unfavourable. There were many reasons for this. Britain was the banker for the whole sterling area but could not hope to remain so for long if the pound was often devalued. The position brought her undoubted benefits which she was loath to lose (though no longer perhaps quite so many as was generally supposed). Her overseas liabilities (which she could not repudiate) were not far short of her assets so that it was considered essential for her to maintain the confidence of her creditors. Devaluation would increase the amount of interest which she had to pay on her debts. Moreover she had from time immemorial made a practice of importing more goods than she exported and making up the gap by 'invisible' exports, i.e. services such as banking, shipping and insurance. For these to flourish a relatively stable currency and a minimum of restriction on payments were important, if not essential. But though there were times when the rest of the sterling area as a whole was in surplus and the reserves rose as a result, there were other times when it or parts of it were in deficit and the drain thus caused had repercussions on internal policy. The most notable example occurred in 1957 when a run on the pound was attributed to inflation at home, in spite of the fact that the UK's own account was in comfortable balance. The Bank rate was raised to the unprecedented level of 7 per cent and internal expansion checked as a result. Only afterwards did it emerge that excessive spending through Kuwait and by India had been at least equally to blame.

(c) Britain's surplus on current account (i.e. the amount by which visible and invisible exports exceeded imports) had to defray two further outlays. One, already mentioned (p. 64) was government expenditure overseas, mainly on defence; in spite of attempts at economy, this showed a disturbing tendency to rise. The other outlay was on investment overseas. To have cut either form of expenditure would have affected Britain's position as a world power. Moreover both expenditures indirectly produced or safeguarded income. The rebuilding of some of the overseas investment which had been sold during the war was also regarded as an essential element in recovery. The question however was not whether such outlays were beneficial but the relative benefit to be obtained by using the surplus for these purposes instead of using it to improve the country's productive equipment or strengthening the reserves of gold and dollars (and thereby making it less urgent to worry about the balance of payments). None of these objectives could be wholly disregarded; the vital issue was how much importance to attach to each. Some critics consider that, in determining priorities, enough attention was not paid to the way the world and Britain's position in it had changed since 1939 – or even 1914.

(d)   The two chief instruments on which the Government relied for stimulating industrial investment at home were (i) the allowances by which money spent for such a purpose was exempted from income tax; (ii) reductions in the standard rate of income tax. The allowances were only introduced in 1954 and then cancelled again between 1956 and 1959 (as part of the programme for restricting expansion) so that, although effective when in operation, they did not operate for long. The chief effect of the reductions in rate was to put more money into the pockets of consumers and thereby encourage industry to produce more for them to buy. Both were blunt instruments. They did not ensure that the money to be invested went to the points at which it could do most good; higher sales and consumption at home are not necessarily the best way of strengthening a country's competitive position abroad. But then it was a fundamental tenet of Conservatism that private enterprise was a better judge than governments of what the best way to spend might be.

By the end of the 1950s the record of achievement during the decade was not at first sight bad. Although in 1958–60 unemployment rose to just over 2 per cent (half-a-million), that was still a figure which in any peacetime year prior to 1940 would have been regarded as gratifyingly low. As has been said, GNP had doubled. Prices of goods and services had risen since 1952 by an average of 3.25 per cent per year, but wage earnings had gone up by nearly twice as much (the difference being accounted for by higher productivity). The exchange value of the pound had been maintained and its convertibility into dollars had been made easier. Overseas investments had been increased by more than £1,500 million. Thus full employment had been combined with reasonably stable prices, rising productivity and a sound currency, the four targets often taken as the most important ones for a government to aim at.

The picture however became less satisfactory when viewed in relation to Britain's competitors on the Continent and to Japan; they were all growing much faster. It is true that they had had more leeway to make up since the war but the leaders among them at any rate had done so and achieved a GNP per head which was higher than the British. This may have been merely the continuation of a trend which had started before 1900 but it was a trend which, unless interrupted, would render it increasingly difficult for Britain to flourish or make ends meet. The incentives to hard work, thrift and investment were far weaker than in West Germany. The share of GNP which was going to investment, though higher than for many years, was the lowest in Western Europe. The country was not using her existing equipment efficiently enough, she was not replacing it fast enough and she was not doing enough to devise or adopt new techniques.

This was not entirely for want of trying. Expenditure on research and development was higher than in any other European country and little below that in the US. Britain was the first country to put into service a passenger jet airliner (the Comet) and an atomic power station, but the former proved unsafe and the latter of a type which was not suitable elsewhere. The trouble does not seem to have been so much a question of finding the money as of finding ways of spending it which looked like being profitable (profit having been taken as the acid test). Management may have been unenterprising but the vacillating policies of government and the narrow-minded attitudes of workers did not give them much encouragement. In 1962 government concern at the situation led to a National Economic Development Council being set up. But though it was fairly easy to see things which were wrong, the way to set about remedying them proved harder to find.

5 The Schuman Plan

Since the war, France had done little to make herself loved in Germany. Not for the first time, she had tried to go her own way without having the resources to succeed. America had forced her to join in a co-operative Western Europe, in which a restored West Germany was to be an equal partner, but she had done so with a bad grace, and made repeated efforts to keep the new state weak. There were, however, a certain number of Frenchmen, particularly ex-members of the Resistance, who felt strongly that steps must be taken to end the Franco–German antagonism which had over three centuries done so much damage to Europe. They looked to European integration as a way of bringing the two countries together. Prominent among them was Jean Monnet, the man in charge of France's Planning Commission (p. 54).

In that position he saw clearly that France was going in future to depend on Germany for over 10 per cent of her coal supplies but, thanks to his Plan, would have surplus steel needing a market. He conceived the idea of pooling the French and German coal and steel industries and in the spring of 1950 sold it to the Foreign Minister Robert Schuman, a native of Lorraine who spoke German as well as he did French. This 'functional' approach to the problem of European integration had been voiced for some time in the Council of Europe and various pressure groups.

On 9 May 1950 Schuman announced to the world that the French Government proposed that Franco-German production of coal and steel should be placed under a common High Authority, within an organisation open to the participation of other countries of Europe. He made clear his hope that the proposal would lead to the realisation of the first concrete foundation of a European Federation. Any other countries interested were invited to a conference for working out details but were required as a precondition for attendance to accept the principle of the scheme. The British were only told of the proposal a few minutes before it was publicly announced. As Monnet was well aware, it ran counter to their ideas about international and European co-operation, since they did not believe that supranational institutions would work and were not prepared to surrender to such bodies final decisions about any aspects of their affairs. They could also say with some justice that the problems of their nationalised coal and steel industries were different from those on the continent, making membership of the proposed pool inappropriate for them. In fact Monnet did not want British participation at that stage, foreseeing that if Britain joined in, she would bend her energies to watering down the proposals and robbing them of the novel significance which lay behind them. When asked whether France would go ahead even if Britain kept out, Monnet replied that 'with her traditional realism, Britain will adjust herself to the facts once she finds that the enterprise is a success'.

Adenauer on the other hand had been given a day's warning, not to mention previous informal soundings, and immediately expressed German sympathy for the Plan. It appealed to the Catholic Rhinelander all the more because it was a first step towards integrating Europe and reconciling France with Germany. It would help to recover for his country her equality of status in international affairs. It would also help to get rid of the International Authority which the British, Americans and French had set up to control the Ruhr (largely to give France a say in the allocation of German coal as well as to soothe her fears about security) and which was much resented by the Germans. It would also nullify the main advantages of another arrangement disliked by them, the Customs Union which France had established with the Saar in the hope of being able thereafter to annex that area, with its valuable coal and steel resources. Before long, the Allied Governments promised that, as soon as Schuman's High Authority was in being, they would abolish the limit which was still placed on German steel production. The SPD leader Schumacher attacked the Plan on the grounds that integration with the West meant sacrificing the reunification of Germany and that it would deprive the German people of the right to decide for themselves on the ownership of heavy industry. But in general the Schuman Plan fitted in admirably with West German aims – in fact it was more popular there than it was with French industry. Italy and the Benelux countries also expressed readiness to join.

Detailed negotiations began in June 1950 and took nine months. The fundamental aim was to establish a free and common market in coal and steel and to draw up general rules enabling the price system to provide free competition. To satisfy the Italians, freedom of movement was granted to workers in the industries. But Monnet looked further. He had chosen coal and steel as the two most basic industries. He believed that, if a real common market free of barriers could be established there, it would create pressure to take similar action in related fields, such as oil, electricity and transport, and would end by spreading to the whole of industry. It would be like putting a man on a bicycle – he would find himself compelled to choose between falling off and going on.

The Coal and Steel Community was given four institutions. Two resembled those found in many international organisations, such as the Council of Europe – a Council of six Ministers (not officials) representing the six participating Governments and an Assembly chosen by the national Parliaments. A third was a Court of Justice, to interpret and enforce the Treaty. But the fourth was a novelty and attempted to bridge the gulf between a secretariat, which only does what it is told to do by the body running the institution and has no initiative of its own, and a fullblown executive like a national cabinet. This 'High Authority' consisted of nine individuals, chosen as such and expressly forbidden to accept instructions from any national government, although eight of them were proposed by those governments (the ninth being nominated by the eight). They were to hold office for six years. Within strictly defined limits they could take decisions and issue directives which would be binding on coal and steel firms throughout the six countries, without the national Governments having any right to interfere. The Authority was to be financed by a levy paid to it direct by the firms within its sphere. The Authority was however required to submit proposals in certain fields to the Council of Ministers before putting them into operation while in others the Council itself was given power to decide. The Treaty foresaw that free competition might drive some firms out of business and therefore included provisions to help owners to invest elsewhere and workers to train for new jobs.

Opinion in Europe was divided between those (like most of the British) who did not believe that the sovereignty of individual states could or should be restricted and those who believed that progress towards a more orderly world was dependent on such limitation being achieved. In deference to the former, the powers of both OEEC and the Council of Europe had been limited so as to prevent them going over the heads of national governments. In both cases experience had shown that, as a result, their effectiveness was also limited. The European Coal and Steel Community (ECSC) was a start upon another road. It only got going by being proposed at a moment when no less than six Governments were exceptionally ready to make the concessions involved in membership, as well as by adroit manoeuvring to keep out of the negotiations other Governments who were not thus ready. But there was another way in which it represented a new departure. Hitherto proposals for transcending state sovereignty had assumed, in the light of experience in the United States and elsewhere, that the first step would have to be a deliberate decision by participating states to create a political federation with its own executive and legislature. But there was justified doubt as to whether the countries of Europe with their varying histories, institutions and languages would ever be willing to take so big a step, except perhaps under extreme external danger (and it was hard to see what danger could be thought greater than that threatened by Russia). The constitution of the ECSC suggested an alternative and easier, since more modest, approach.

The Treaty of Paris setting up the ECSC was signed in April 1951; when Adenauer attended the ceremony, it was the first time he had left the Federal Republic as Chancellor. It came into force in July 1952 and the common markets were established in the following year. But by then there had been other more important developments regarding European integration.

6   The European Defence Community

The negotiations to establish the Coal and Steel Community had only been going for five days when the Communist attack on South Korea occurred. As has been said (p. 118), suggestions about rearming West Germany soon began to be heard. The advocates of European integration saw in this an opportunity to advance their cause further, though one which had presented itself sooner than some could have wished. The objections to giving arms back to Germans would be much reduced if instead they were given to Europeans, in a common army under the same sort of common control as coal and steel. When the Assembly of the Council of Europe met in August 1950 Churchill (who was still out of office) called on it to declare itself in favour of a single European Army 'in which we shall all play a worthy and honourable part'; a motion in this sense was carried by 89 votes to 5 (with 27 abstentions including significantly the representatives of the British Labour Party). Two months later Jean Monnet, using as his mouthpiece the French Prime Minister René Pleven, told the French National Assembly that France would only agree to German rearmament within the framework of a completely integrated Western European army, under a European Minister of Defence.

Adenauer exploited his opportunity with skill. He had repeatedly assured the Allies that he did not want to see Germany rearmed, though he also lost no opportunity of emphasising to them how insecure and exposed he considered the Federal Republic to be. When the talk about a Western European army began, he indicated (without consulting his colleagues) that he would be ready to contribute a contingent. But at the same time he made clear that the price of this contribution would approximate to the complete restoration of sovereignty to West Germany; her troops must be on a footing of equality with those of other countries.

This time no attempt was made to bypass the British who at a meeting with the Americans and French in December 1950 agreed to the practical implications of the Pleven Plan being explored. That did not however mean being prepared themselves to join in a common army. The six Governments which were so prepared (being those in the ECSC) worked out a scheme not unlike that Community, with a Council of Ministers, a Board of nine Defence Commissioners (replacing the original idea of a single Defence Minister), an Assembly and a Court. The Board would draw up a common budget which would require approval from the Council (unanimously) and the Assembly; each member state would then be legally bound to pay its contribution. The maximum size of a unit which men of a single nationality would compose was fixed at a division of about 13,000 men; anything larger would be multinational. West Germany was to provide the largest contingent, twelve divisions, but these were to be placed under non-German commanders, while she was to be the only member forbidden to have forces outside the European Army. A scheme was worked out for bringing that Army into NATO which West Germany however was not to join.

A certain amount of rather hilarious criticism focused on the question of how an army speaking different languages would understand what its commanders told it to do. But this was neither an unprecedented (e.g. airliner pilots and controllers) nor an insoluble problem. A more serious one was the question of who was to give the commanders their orders. A single army implies a common foreign policy. But it raises an even deeper issue. There are two basic points about any political system — who has the right to raise money and who controls the monopoly of organised force. They go closely together and, to be a government, a body needs both. Equally, any body which possesses both is a government and any body which possesses one is well on the way to being a government. The sphere of the ECSC had been cleverly chosen as looking less important than it was; the national Governments which joined it need not feel that they were giving away undue power. The European Defence Community (EDC) was a much more fundamental challenge which presupposed a higher degree of integration. The British were certainly justified in doubting whether such a degree had been reached, less certainly so in doubting whether in the probable conditions of an East–West conflict a higher degree was desirable. In September 1952 the Foreign Ministers of the ECSC states instructed the ECSC Assembly to co-opt the additional members which it was to receive under the EDC scheme and work out a plan for a European Political Community. But when such a plan was presented six months later, it became evident that too much was being taken for granted.

After the EDC framework had been formulated, agreement about it was held up by arguments between France and Germany over debts and over the Saar; months were lost which were possibly vital. During them the three Occupying Powers worked out with Adenauer the terms of another agreement restoring sovereignty to the Federal Republic and bringing the occupation to an end (except in Berlin where the Russian unreadiness to leave made it necessary for the other three to stay). Henceforward American, British and French troops would be in West Germany only in the interests of mutual security against the East, and not in order to control Germans. An important article provided that America, Britain, France and the Federal Republic would all aim at 'a peace settlement freely negotiated between Germany and her former enemies'. The final delimitation of the boundaries of Germany must await such a settlement. (The DDR had in 1950 recognised the Oder–Neisse frontier as permanent.) Pending its conclusion, all four states would co-operate to achieve, by peaceful means, their common aim of a unified Germany enjoying a liberal-democratic constitution like that of the Federal Republic and integrated within the European Community.

A Treaty embodying these arrangements was signed in Bonn on 25 May 1952 and on the following day another embodying those for the EDC was signed in Paris. The first was only to come into force when the second did. Both required ratification by the Parliaments of the countries concerned. That of Paris was resolutely opposed in West Germany by the Social Democrats whose objections were not based solely on dislike of rearmament and fear of a militarist revival but also on the belief that the best hope of reuniting the country lay in co-operating with the East rather than in combating it. To this Adenauer, to American applause, answered that the only way to get concessions from the Russians was to negotiate from strength. The opposition claimed that the Treaty was incompatible with the *Grundgesetz* but failed to convince the Constitutional Court and in March 1954 Adenauer obtained a majority in the *Bundestag* for ratification. By that time Holland, Belgium and Luxemburg had ratified and in Italy De Gasperi (p. 54) looked like being able to do so once it was certain that the French would accept. Much disappointment had been caused in Europe by the failure of Churchill, after his return to power in 1951, to make any change in the British attitude of friendly aloofness.

Between the time that Pleven proposed his Plan and the signature of the Treaty of Paris, four French Prime Ministers came and went, as did another three before the Treaty was finally put to a vote in the National Assembly in August 1954. What was perhaps more serious was that in January 1953 Schuman ceased to be Foreign Minister. France was torn internally over the question of withdrawing from Indo-China, over the policy to be adopted towards Arab unrest in Algeria and over financial difficulties. But she was also in several minds as to whether the sacrifice

Impatient negotiators

At a Press Conference ... in Paris ... Dulles was severely heckled ... I could see that his temper was beginning to get the better of him. ... The public relations adviser sitting next to him kept tugging at his sleeve in the hope of preventing an explosion. He failed.

When Dulles began to explain the aims of US policy in the Cold War, and of American hopes for European unity, he was interrupted by Harold King, Reuter's correspondent in Paris. Would the US Government be prepared, King asked, to guarantee the presence of American troops in Europe for the next twenty years? Dulles replied abruptly that no statesman could commit himself for that length of time. King realised at once that he had uncovered a weak spot in the American position and attacked with a supplementary question. 'Why then', he asked, 'do you expect France to commit herself for fifty years under the proposed Treaty for a European Defence Community?' Dulles took it badly. If France did not adopt the European Defence Treaty, he growled, the US would have to subject her foreign policy to an 'agonizing reappraisal'. It was a clear threat and, to make matters worse, it was made in public.

Thomas Barman

Some say we were brought to the verge of war. Of course we were brought to the verge of war. The ability to get to the verge without getting into war is a necessary art. If you try to run away from it, if you are scared to go to the brink, you are lost.

John Foster Dulles, January 1956

Each of the delegations at the [1955 Geneva Heads of Government] Conference had got into the habit of inviting the senior members of another delegation to dinner after the day's work. ... On the night Khrushchev dined with the French, he worked himself up into yet another emotional outburst. ... When the party left the table for cognac and cigars, he seized the French Foreign Minister by the lapel of his jacket and shook him. 'We will never, never change our minds about the German problem,' he shouted. 'Never. Do you understand?'

Thomas Barman

of sovereignty involved in joining the EDC was or was not a price worth paying to get some control over the rearming of Germany. For many Frenchmen the issue was clouded by a refusal to realise that France was not in a position to stop German rearmament and that rejection of the EDC would only mean having later to accept an alternative which gave even less control. The Gaullists and other right-wing parties, whose votes were needed for measures to balance the budget, beat the national drum; the Communists would not support a measure unwelcome to Russia. Even some enthusiasts for European integration opposed a proposal which was limited to six countries and made what they regarded as excessive concessions to national interests! Resentment was strong against America for forcing the issue by insisting on Germany being rearmed; Dulles (pp. 58, 148) achieved the opposite of what he intended by threatening that a French 'No' would lead the US to make an 'agonising reappraisal' of their whole European policy. Attempts were made to pin the blame for France's rejection on Britain's refusal to join. These were unfair in that at a late stage Eden, as Churchill's Foreign Secretary, did consider doing so but was dissuaded by President Eisenhower (p. 148) who was afraid that such a move would cause further delay. Thereafter the British had gone so far as to promise that they would keep troops on the Continent as long as there was any threat to the security of Western Europe and the EDC. The step between such a commitment and full membership may seem small and might have been taken had it not been for the fact that logically a common army must mean a common political system, and indeed was intended by some people to achieve just that – the very issue of sovereignty which was sticking in French throats.

A series of attempts to reduce opposition to the Treaty by amending or interpreting it either failed to do so or were rejected by the other signatories. When in August 1954 Mendès-France, the then Prime Minister, finally took the plunge of putting the matter to the Assembly (without showing any enthusiasm for the proposal himself, since if he had he would have brought down his own Cabinet!), that body evaded taking a clear decision by voting instead to go on to the next subject on its agenda. Instead of advancing the cause of European integration, the EDC project appeared to have wrecked it. Resentments between France and Germany, instead of being mollified, had been inflamed.

7 Communist reactions to the EDC

There can be little doubt that the Russians saw the development of events in Western Europe with profound misgiving. Exactly what they had feared was coming to pass; the considerable resources of the area were, as it seemed to them, being rebuilt to strengthen capitalism and facilitate an assault upon the communist world. In their nervousness they tended to overlook their own indisputable superiority in conventional weapons and the difficulty of using nuclear weapons as a means of extorting political concessions. They hankered after a return to the Potsdam policy of keeping Germany united, weak and neutral, but the Western Powers demanded as a precondition the holding of free elections throughout the country and as time passed the prospect of such elections resulting in anything but an anti-communist government grew increasingly dim. The Russians set no particular store by the East German Government; they were always afraid of it involving them in an intra-German clash which would escalate into full-scale war. They would have been quite prepared to jettison it, and with it the hope of keeping any part of Germany communist, if they could have been sure that a reunited but non-communist Germany could have been kept genuinely neutral. But such a state could hardly be denied freedom of choice in its foreign policy indefinitely and all the indications were that it would then choose the West.

The Western standpoint was almost diametrically opposite. A neutral Germany would not only rule out all idea of using German divisions to bring NATO up to the minimum strength needed to withstand an attack from the East. Policy-makers were haunted by a suspicion that the Russians would in one way or another contrive to undermine Germany's neutrality and thereafter align her with the East. With her large, skilled and disciplined population she was too big a weight in the balance of power for either side to run a risk of her falling into the other basket of the scales. But there was a further difficulty. Desire for reunification was almost universal in the BRD and few people were prepared to accept that it was, for the time being at any rate, incapable of achievement on tolerable terms. Accordingly Adenauer's policy of integration with the West could not be advocated as a second-best alternative to reunification but had to be presented as the only way of achieving reunification in freedom. In other words reunification was not to be negotiated on compromise terms but was to be imposed, which logically implied advancing from a strategy of containment to one of negotiating from strength. Such an advance meant disregarding the problem of how the West was to acquire not merely parity but superiority in conventional forces, as well as disregarding the loss by the West of its monopoly of nuclear weapons. The economic and strategic recovery programmes of OEEC and NATO were misread as destined to produce a steady improvement in the West's relative strength. In fact that strength is now thought to have been at its most advantageous point between 1951 and 1953 yet no attempt to negotiate from it was then made, partly because of the belief that time was on the West's side, partly because anti-Communist fervour in the US ruled out the compromises which negotiation needs for success.

In March 1952 the Russians, faced with the imminent (if fallacious) prospect of EDC coming into being, offered their three former Allies a settlement which went further than any previous proposal. Germany within the Potsdam frontiers was to be reunited and allowed to become self-governing, with a limited measure of rearmament. 'Democratic' parties were to be allowed but 'organisations inimical to freedom and to the maintenance of peace' would be forbidden (as parties 'seeking to influence or set aside the free democratic order' already were in the *Grundgesetz*). The reunited state was however to promise not to join any kind of coalition or military alliance directed against any state which had fought Germany between 1939 and 1945. The Western Powers, convinced that the offer was primarily a ruse to hold up the EDC and afraid of getting into long arguments about details, replied that free elections, supervised by a UN Commission, were an indispensable preliminary to the signature of any Treaty on the lines proposed. The Russians stuck to their view that a Treaty and with it the establishment of a Government must precede elections; as a result negotiations came to a deadlock. Wishful thinkers took the Russian offer as proof that Western policy was having the desired results and only had to be pursued further to elicit better offers in future. As Adenauer said at the time:

> The aim of German policy today as yesterday is that the West should
> become strong enough to conduct reasonable conversations with the
> Soviet Union. We are firmly convinced that if we continue in this
> path the moment will not be too far distant when Soviet Russia
> declares itself ready for reasonable negotiations.

The leaders of the DDR were well aware that the Russians regarded them as expendable; one of them said later that if the West had accepted the 1952 proposals 'the position of the Party and state would have been in serious danger'. They therefore set out to make themselves more valuable. In the first place the SED was changed into something of an elite cadre, on the traditional Communist model; members with Social Democratic, bourgeois or Western connections were weeded out and even put on trial. The other political parties, though allowed to continue, were treated more than ever as puppets.

The prime mover in this development was Walther Ulbricht, a life-long Communist of sixty, who had spent most of the Nazi years in Russia and come back in 1945 as First Secretary of the Party. His influence now became predominant. He exerted it not only against capitalists and Social Democrats, but also against the Russians.

He it was who initiated a five-year plan of industralisation, to fill the gaps where the Russians had depended on the other Zones. Metal-working was to rise by 250 per cent, machine-tool production by 200 per cent; mining, energy and chemicals were all to expand. Coming as it did on top of continuing Russian exactions in reparations, it implied many austere years for consumers. Although in line with orthodox ideas about building socialism, it was not particularly welcome to the Russians who, as in Yugoslavia, preferred an economy which would leave the Germans weaker and more dependent. Socialisation was speeded up, differentiating the DDR from the BRD and thus making reunification harder – another policy not entirely to Russian liking.

When the Communists found that their offers were not going to deflect the West, they decided to safeguard themselves in other ways. On the night after the EDC Treaty was signed in Paris, a 'protective belt' was established across Germany, stretching five kilometres back from the boundary separating the Russian from the British and US Zones. A continuous wire fence was built, road surfaces were torn up and ground cleared, so that anyone who tried to cross could be seen – and shot at. Only on one or two main roads, on the railway and in Berlin was passage allowed. But through these a stream of refugees continued to pour westwards; in the twelve years between 1949 and 1961 they numbered almost two million, or approximately one every three minutes.

CHAPTER 5

1953-6

1 The death of Stalin

In 1953 there were two big changes of cast on the international stage. In the US the Republicans, by hitching to their campaign the personal prestige of General Eisenhower, succeeded in ending the twenty years' tenure of the Presidency by the Democrats. As his Secretary of State the new President appointed John Foster Dulles, whose grandfather and uncle had held that post in the past but who also inherited from his father firm Presbyterian faith and missionary zeal. The new brooms ostensibly stood for a refusal to accept the limits which experience had placed on Hull's aims. In their election campaign, they proclaimed that containment was not enough and that the US should aim at restoring liberty to the Moscow-dominated nations of Europe and Asia. Dulles in particular believed that, by continually emphasising their desire to bring about liberation, the United States could create unrest among the Communist satellites and thereby achieve disintegration and a change of regime. As events were to show, this belief rested on a mistaken appreciation of the relative power of the two sides and the fact that Dulles's long and intimate experience of international affairs did not prevent him from making such a mistake proves (if further proof were needed) that knowledge and energy are less important in a Foreign Minister than good judgment.

The very moment of introducing a change of policy proved inopportune. For on 6 March Stalin died – in his bed – at the age of seventy-three. Only two months earlier the announcement of a plot by eminent doctors, mainly Jewish, to kill a number of Soviet leaders had seemed the signal for another blood purge. The moment had come for which political observers all over the world had been waiting. Could the machine of authoritarian dictatorship handle the succession without civil war? A stepping-up of the threat from outside could only increase its chances of doing so. Churchill's idea of a meeting with the new leaders was better conceived but nothing came of it because Washington objected and he had a stroke. The biggest share of the inheritance appeared at first to have fallen to a pudgy 51-year-old intellectual of middle-class origins, Georgi Malenkov, whom Stalin seemed to have been grooming as successor, albeit carefully rationing his share of power. But within a week he was foiled in his bid to do as Stalin had done by uniting in his person the top Party post with the top administrative one (see Appendix at end of chapter). The nine other members of the Presidium insisted on the two jobs being separated and he was made to join in a 'collective leadership', described afterwards as 'a period when all opinions clashed'.

Stalin had tended in his later years to work through the state administration rather than the Party. Malenkov decided that this was likely to become the permanent shape of things and chose to stay Chairman of the Council of Ministers, leaving the leadership of the Party Secretariat to Nikita Khrushchev, a Ukrainian peasant of fifty-nine. The two other most prominent personalities were Molotov, still Foreign Minister, and Beria, a Georgian (like Stalin) who had consolidated power as Minister of the Interior in charge of the security police. At the end of June Beria was detected in what seemed to be preparations for a coup; he was shot without trial and his fall meant a loss of influence by the police. Malenkov and Khrushchev had long been rivals and it was only a question of time before one of them eliminated the other. Malenkov started with the advantage that there were no other Party representatives in the Presidium to back Khrushchev up (although most of the other members had worked in the Party before being posted to administrative jobs). Khrushchev however had spent more time outside Moscow, was in touch with the local Party secretaries (who provided many of the members of the Central Committee) and had first-hand knowledge of the country's problems, particularly in agriculture. Stalin had despised the peasants who provided the labour for the collective farms and had demanded big deliveries of foodstuffs from them in the belief that they would then work hard to increase the residue which they were allowed to keep. This system in fact proved a disincentive and, as the prices which the state paid for the deliveries were very low, many collective farms were heavily in debt and unable to afford improvements. Russian farm output per head of population in 1952 was lower than it had been in 1913. Khrushchev not only proposed higher prices for deliveries (as did Malenkov), but also grouping the farms into bigger units and giving them more freedom to decide what they grew. This decentralisation decreased the power of the Ministries but increased that of the local Party officials. To get a quick increase in production Khrushchev also organised the bringing into immediate production of thirteen million virgin acres in Central Asia.

There was general agreement led by Malenkov that, to prevent Stalin's death being used as a signal for popular unrest, consumers must be given more to buy. Not only had priority hitherto been taken by heavy industry; the system of planning production centrally worked less well with light industry, and the shops had inadequate stocks, or too many unwanted goods and much of poor quality. Here again Khrushchev encouraged decentralisation, again at the expense of the Ministries and to the benefit of the Party. But diverting more resources to agriculture and light industry meant taking them away from somewhere else; the obvious 'somewhere else' was heavy industry and defence – to some extent interdependent. Russia's explosion of a hydrogen bomb, which Malenkov announced in August 1953, could be seen as making an attack by America less likely, and thus reducing the need for spending on conventional weapons. Naturally the conventional soldiers did not agree; Khrushchev exploited their fears and Molotov's objections to any relaxation in foreign policy, not so much because he disagreed with Malenkov's aims as because he wanted allies against Malenkov. Finally Khrushchev brought home a charge that Malenkov had worked hand in glove with Beria, particularly over a purge in Leningrad in 1948. Early in 1955 Malenkov was forced to hand over the chairmanship of the Council of Ministers to Bulganin, a supporter of Khrushchev, though he kept his place in the Presidium.

The tension in Moscow quickly spread to East Germany. Malenkov and Beria seem to have been, even before Stalin's death, the main advocates of jettisoning the DDR on the ground that it was more a liability than an asset (p. 146). In the DDR their chief allies were Zaisser, the Minister of State Security, a former member of the General Staff who had played a major part in building up the People's Police (p. 107), and Herrnstadt, an able Jew who before 1933 had worked on the liberal *Berliner Tageblatt* and was now the top Communist publicist. On 11 June *Neues Deutschland*, of which Herrnstadt was editor, published an admission that mistakes had been made, accompanied by a programme of relaxation in many directions which had been called for by Moscow and corresponded to the trends in the Soviet Union. Such changes remained anathema to Ulbricht, who stood to lose his position if they were carried through. He had already as a precaution put out of action his chief rival Dahlem by accusing him of 'total blindness to attempts by imperialist agents to infiltrate the Party'. He had also, in pursuance of his policy of building socialism by intensified industrialisation, announced that, as from 30 June, all workers would have to increase their output by 10 per cent without getting any more pay. He managed to prevent this decision from being rescinded as part of the new policy of conciliation and when *Neues Deutschland* said that it should not have been announced until the workers had been convinced of the need for it, caused an article to be published in another paper ruling out the possibility of it being changed.

Lack of food and bad living conditions had already soured the workers. When the disagreement inside the Government became obvious, a number employed on building sites in East Berlin marched to the main government offices and called for free elections. Next day something approaching a general strike followed throughout the Republic. The People's Police could not or would not cope with the situation and two Russian armoured divisions had to come to the rescue. Though they behaved with restraint, twenty-one people were killed. The rising collapsed, as it might have done in any case for lack of organisation. Zaisser, Herrnstadt and others were deprived of power on the same day as Beria. Though persons variously described as 'interested spectators' and *agents provocateurs* came from West Berlin to see what was going on, the whole affair was over before Western governments had had time to decide how to react. The hostile mood of the workers told in favour of those who argued that jettisoning the DDR would mean losing East Germany to the West. Either by luck, or by deliberately provoking a crisis, Ulbricht had survived.

2   Western European Union

The failure of the French National Assembly to vote on the EDC Treaty (p. 144) created a situation which could not be left as it was. Not merely did it remove the agreed basis for the rearmament of West Germany, to which the US attached such importance. The Bonn Treaty (p. 142), restoring sovereignty to the Federal Republic, had been in existence for two years and, although technically it had not come into force (since that was conditional on the ratification of the EDC Treaty), most other Governments had, as the interval dragged itself out to a totally unexpected length, been behaving in many ways as though it were already operating. To revert to the previous situation was out of the question. A means had to be found of regulating matters, including the creation of West German Armed Forces (*Bundeswehr*), for which many preparations had been made even though the calling up of conscripts had not actually begun. Adenauer, who had staked his political life on the wisdom of combining rearmament with integration into the West, was particularly insistent on action.

Eden lit upon the answer in his bath, though Macmillan later claimed to have already thought of it without such assistance. The Treaty signed in Brussels in March 1948 between Britain, France and Benelux (p. 100) was still in force although the machinery connected with it was being less and less used. This it was now proposed to expand into a Western European Union, which is best described as a Defence Community without supranational elements. Germany and Italy were to join it, and accept much the same limitations on their arming as had been contemplated under EDC. Britain promised to keep four divisions and a Tactical Air Force on the Continent (though there was an escape clause of which she took advantage within three years). Germany was to contribute 500,000 men to NATO (the size of the *Reichswehr* when Hitler reoccupied the Rhineland in 1936) but would not maintain a separate General Staff. A Secretariat replaced the proposed Commission and the Assembly (though empowered to take certain decisions by a two-thirds majority) was only allowed consultative powers. Various functions outside the sphere of defence were given to the Union in the hope of making it look more like an organ of integration than a mere alliance, but none of these came to much.

West Germany for her part renounced the right to manufacture on her territory (though not to acquire or control) atomic, bacteriological or chemical weapons, as well as guided missiles and bombers. Moreover she undertook never to have recourse to force to achieve reunification or changes in her frontiers. In return the Americans, British and French recognised the Government of the Federal Republic as the only German one 'freely and legitimately constituted and therefore entitled to speak for Germany as the representative of the German people in international affairs'. They went on to reaffirm that a peace settlement for the whole of Germany, freely negotiated between Germany and her former enemies, which would lay the foundations of a lasting peace, remained an essential aim of their policy. The final delimitation of the frontiers of Germany must await such a settlement. The Bonn

Government would have preferred an open declaration that, in the absence of such delimitation, the legal frontiers were those of 1937 and these were certainly the frontiers which that Government (with technical justification) continued to claim. Whether, in view of what had been said at Yalta and Potsdam, the Americans and British could consistently have supported such a claim was fortunately never put to a test.

These substitute arrangements were worked out in October 1954, within two months of EDC's demise, but it remained to be seen whether even they would be acceptable to the French Assembly. For, as the French had been repeatedly warned, the alternative to EDC was a big German contingent in NATO rather than lots of smaller German units distributed through a European army. In fact on 24 December the Assembly rejected the first article, dealing with the establishment of WEU and the admission of West Germany to NATO. The British in reply let it be known that the question was no longer whether West Germany would rearm but of how she should rearm and that the British offer to keep forces on the Continent depended on the new Treaty being ratified. Dulles had only reluctantly agreed to the disappearance of the supranational provisions and it was clear that any further French recalcitrance would lead to a reduction in the American commitment to Europe. After Christmas the Assembly bowed to what had become inevitable.

But in the five years which had passed since West German rearmament was first discussed, the 'Economic Miracle' had forged ahead until the country had few unemployed left and not much productive capacity to spare. Industry became afraid that if a labour shortage were artifically induced as a result of conscription, wage claims would become impossible to hold in check. In 1956 the Christian Social Union (p. 105) began to make difficulties in the *Bundestag* about the rearmament programme. Adenauer's reply was to appoint as Defence Minister Franz Josef Strauss, an exceptionally bright butcher's son and ex-bicycling champion who was working his passage to the top of the CSU. He immediately cut down the numbers to be raised, until it gradually emerged that the total would be only 350,000 and then only in 1961. At the same time both the US and Britain were coming to the conclusion that they could no longer afford the full cost of both nuclear and conventional defence and that the best way to make economies was to cut down their conventional forces.

These developments made clear that even the reduced NATO target of forty-three divisions was unlikely to be attained; in practice the

Organisation was by 1960 only to reach on the central part of its front twenty-one and a third divisions, instead of thirty. It was however argued that these could be made adequate for purposes of defence (though not attack) by raising their fire-power. As it happened, technological advances in the use of atomic weapons indicated the possibility of using them in small sizes as artillery. NATO's leaders argued that the employment of such 'tactical' weapons offered the only means short of full-scale atomic war by which the West could hope to offset Communist superiority in men and conventional weapons. Strauss on occasion argued that, as West Germany had been put on a footing of complete equality with her NATO allies, her army must be equipped with such weapons. The Americans however, though willing to see all NATO troops trained in their use, insisted that the actual warheads must remain under US control – and local American commanders were required to get authorisation from the President himself before ordering them to be fired. The paradox was that the case for rearming West Germany had rested on the need to match up to the Communists in conventional weapons – as things worked out, German rearmament was accompanied by a decision to abandon for all practical purposes the idea of defending the West entirely by conventional means. Meanwhile a glaring contradiction existed between the professed desire of the new US administration to roll back the Iron Curtain and the means available for doing so, with the result that the actual behaviour of Eisenhower and Dulles did not differ much from that of their predecessors.

The Eastern reply to WEU was a conference on European security held in Moscow in November 1954, which led in May of the following year to the Warsaw Pact, a defensive alliance of European Communist States to act as a formal counterbalance to NATO. The DDR was allowed to rechristen its armed police an army and to join the Pact. The new machinery of joint command meant less change than WEU, since the satellites had all along been under Russian orders. But their armies were strengthened in numbers and equipment while the bogey of another German occupation may have made the reality of a Russian one less irksome.

3 The path towards détente

(a) In January 1955 the Soviet Government made another try at securing a reunited but neutral Germany. In return for the abandonment of 'remilitarisation' (i.e. WEU), free all-German elections 'under appropriate international supervision' were proposed, as the West had demanded. The Germany so created would be forbidden to join any military alliance. When the West insisted that WEU must go ahead, an interparliamentary conference on the German question, held in Warsaw, ended with a resolution supported by the Soviet delegates, proposing the withdrawal of occupation armies to their respective frontiers, the holding of free all-German elections on the basis proposed by the West and the guarantee of a neutralised Germany by Europe and the US. Before the West could reply, Malenkov was replaced by Bulganin and nothing more was heard of the proposal. The suggestion has been made that these two offers represented Malenkov's last attempt to carry out a policy of conciliation and that the West's failure to show interest sealed his downfall. The decision to remove him seems however to have been taken before the end of 1954. On the other hand, the Soviet Government showed no subsequent interest in reunification.

(b)   After saying for years that they would only sign a Peace Treaty for Austria after the German problem had been settled, the Russians suddenly changed their minds and in April 1954 offered to join in a quadripartite withdrawal from the country in return for an international guarantee that it would remain neutral. Austria was easier for them to leave than Germany because a (non-Communist) central government had been in existence since 1945 so that no question arose of how it should be set up. They may have wanted to keep the Western-occupied Zones of Austria from being included in NATO and probably also hoped that the example would stimulate a demand in Germany for similar treatment. Indeed it did do so but without practical result; the Great Powers were prepared to take risks with a country of seven million inhabitants which they would not run with one of seventy million.

(c)   Ten years had elapsed since the heads of government had met in a 'summit' conference and voices were increasingly heard arguing that only a meeting at such a level offered any hope of settling East–West differences. The hope was put to the test at Geneva in July 1955. The deductions which both sides drew from the conference were more important than the decisions which they announced at the end of it. In effect both showed themselves willing to rest content with the *status quo* in Germany. The Russians no longer talked about reunification but displayed confidence about their ability to resist

Western attempts at change, presumably contrasting NATO's failure to reach its targets with their own progress in nuclear weapons. On the other hand they clearly realised that a military attack on the West would incur such retaliation as to make its cost in lives prohibitive. As Eden wrote later, 'Each country present learnt that no country present wanted war and each understood why.' The danger was thus not so much one of deliberate attack but of misunderstanding or of minor incidents, perhaps in smaller countries, getting out of control. The Summit therefore did something to reduce tension.

(d)   In August Adenauer, who had been afraid of the West giving too much away at Geneva, decided to try his own hand at negotiating and, against the advice of his officials, accepted an invitation to visit Moscow. It was now the turn of Ulbricht to fear that his patron would give too much away. Two subjects were proposed for discussion – reunification and the return of German prisoners-of-war still in Russian hands. The Kremlin yielded no ground on the first and in return for a limited verbal agreement on the second secured the establishment of diplomatic relations with the Federal Republic. To prevent such relations from being interpreted as implying West German recognition of the 1945 territorial arrangements, Adenauer insisted on the Russians accepting a note stating that this was not so, to which the Russians added counter-arguments in a footnote. The prisoners – or some of them – in due course came back but two days after Adenauer left a DDR delegation arrived to conclude a Treaty which matched the one establishing WEU in that the Soviet Union formally restored sovereignty to the East German Government and authorised it to establish diplomatic relations with other states. To counter this the Bonn Government in December 1955 enunciated the 'Hallstein' doctrine according to which recognition of the DDR by any state would be regarded by the BRD as an 'unfriendly act' since it would involve recognition of the division of Germany into two states for which there was (according to the Bonn thesis) no legal justification. The most notable case of the policy being applied was against Yugoslavia between 1957 and 1968 when the number of German tourists in the one country and of Yugoslav workers in the other made their inability to negotiate directly highly inconvenient to both.

4 The transient triumph of Tito

The rift with the Soviet Union sent the Yugoslav leaders back to their holy writ, the writings of Marx and Lenin. As they were not prepared to admit the charge that they had betrayed the gospel of Socialism by 'revisionist deviations', they had to explain to themselves as well as to their followers how it could be that two professedly Socialist states could interpret the same events in diametrically opposite ways. The answer which they formulated was that it was the Russians who had gone astray by stopping the Revolution at the stage of State Capitalism, when all property was owned centrally. The doctrine of 'democratic centralism' had then been invoked by the Communist Party, claiming without justification to embody a fictitious 'will of the proletariat', to direct state and economy from the top downwards. The result was the creation of a vast bureaucracy to the detriment of local initiative and enthusiasm, while the rulers at the centre, inevitably corrupted by the possession of unchecked power, degenerated into tyrants. It was an attempt to apply the same procedure internationally and insist that all other Socialist states adopt unquestioningly the standpoint of Moscow which had produced the clash with Belgrade.

The revolution, in the view of the Yugoslavs, had to be saved from its bureaucrats. This was to be done by establishing political and social self-management, with ownership and the right of taking decisions transferred to the level of the local factory and district council. The ultimate end of this process was held to be that the state would become unnecessary and wither away. An integral part of the transition would be a change from a command to a market economy, in which decisions at local level would be taken on a basis of profit and loss in the light of supply and demand as expressed in prices. The state was to withdraw from attempts at planning the conduct of individual enterprises in detail and restrict itself to indicative planning of overall targets for such things as investment and savings. Between May 1949 and 1953, tentatively at first but with growing confidence, a series of measures were enacted to introduce such a system. And while in industry ownership remained in collective hands, in agriculture the drive for collectivisation was almost completely abandoned and land given back to peasants, with only the safeguard that no holding should exceed twenty-five acres.

This drastic decentralisation was to be accompanied by a radical change in the function of the Communist Party. The reformers were not prepared to re-establish a multi-party system since they believed that in current conditions it would only play into the hands of people hostile to the system, whether anti-Communist or pro-Russian. When the leading ideologist Djilas declared in 1953–4 that the monopoly of a single party was incompatible with individual freedom, he was expelled. The problem of how to reconcile monopoly with freedom was instead solved by calling for free discussion of current issues within the Party which was in addition required to divorce itself from the State and become primarily an educational body whose members set themselves to influence events, much as Christians are expected to do, by the role which they play in the world around them.

The glaring weakness of the whole theory is of course that it is bound to end in chaos and waste, particularly in a world of good communications when the actions of each unit so rapidly impinge on those of many others. It assumes too easily that people only need to be good Socialists in order to see eye to eye so that a fully socialised society will not require a state to reconcile differences and impose solutions. Moreover the devolution of the making of decisions to the parochial level leads to their being taken by people whose vision is often narrow in both space and time, who not merely give priority to their own interests at the expense of the wider community but who also prefer immediate advantage to long-term benefits (as in choosing to devote profits to consumption rather than investment). Yugoslavia as a country was particularly vulnerable to such failings not merely because its six constituent republics had not co-existed in a single state long enough for a central loyalty to override local ones, but also because the greater wealth of the northern ones tempted them to spend their money on themselves rather than to make it available through the centre for raising standards in the south. Between 1919 and 1941 centralisation had meant the dominance of the Orthodox Serbs over the more advanced Catholic Croats who bitterly resented their subordination; one of the achievements of Tito (himself a Croat) had been to reduce the antagonism between these two groups. The emphasis on low-level decision-taking has continually threatened to reverse this process and weaken the bonds which held the country together.

Yugoslav heads are however too hard for them to be carried away by an excess of theory, and in practice the State did not wither away nor did the Party confine its role to that of a ginger group. Workers' councils might be set up in the factories but many decisions on vital issues like investment and wages long continued to be taken at the centre. The country's history since 1949 has as a result been one of oscillation between devolution and centralisation, with groups remarkably like conservative and liberal parties developing informally inside the monolithic Communist structure. Some critics maintain that the theory is merely a charade to justify the leadership in defying Moscow and to aid them in getting help from the West, that the decisions which matter are still taken centrally and that the supposed changes have made little difference to the ordinary worker. If this is true, the charade is a remarkably elaborate one, a great deal of time has been devoted to playing it, and it has undoubtedly succeeded in mobilising more goodwill towards the regime than is evident in most Communist countries, which in addition allow the individual considerably less freedom of speech, reading and travelling. A more charitable view would be that the Yugoslavs have embarked, a trifle naïvely, on an original solution to a fundamental social problem and that, even if their answer is not wholly satisfactory, either in theory or practice, the answers offered elsewhere in the world nowadays all leave something to be desired.

After four very lean years, aggravated by a couple of droughts, in which national income declined, a boom started in 1953 which lasted with almost no interruption until 1961. Considerable amounts of aid were obtained from the West and the increasing integration of the country with Western Europe meant that it benefited from that area's prosperity. A high rate of investment led to an exceptionally high rate of growth – though also to a chronic tendency towards inflation. The Yugoslavs were therefore in no mood to behave as penitents towards Stalin's successors and it was Moscow which took the initiative in reconciliation. Khrushchev argued that if the Soviet Union were to bury the hatchet, its image would be improved in the world generally. Diplomatic relations were re-established in 1954 and in May 1955 Khrushchev, after surmounting objections by Molotov, led a delegation on an eight-day visit which opened with his admission that the Soviet regime now sincerely regretted what had happened and ended with a joint pledge of

> mutual respect and non-interference in internal affairs for any reason, whether of an economic, political or ideological nature, since questions of the internal structure, differences of social systems and differences of concrete form in developing socialism are exclusively a matter for the peoples of the different countries.

The Russians were not merely admitting that there might be different roads to socialism in different countries, a view which Stalin had tried to stamp out as a heresy in 1948. Internal developments in Russia for a while made it look as though that country itself might be going to move down the road which Yugoslavia had pioneered. In April 1956 the Cominform (p. 91) was dissolved.

5 The European Economic Community

During the winter of 1954/5 some of the more determined advocates of European integration discussed how best to 'relaunch' their cause after the fiasco of the EDC. As a result the Benelux governments put a memorandum on the agenda of the Foreign Ministers of the ECSC members when the Italian Government, a strong supporter of integration, invited them to meet at Messina in June 1955. Three possible lines of advance were suggested. One was to extend the ECSC arrangements to the field of transport. The second was to set up a body similar to ECSC to deal with energy, and in particular the possibilities of atomic power. The third was to proceed straight away with the creation of a European Common Market. The Ministers agreed that 'we must work towards the establishment of a united Europe, through the development of common institutions, the gradual merger of national economies, the creation of a common market and increasing harmonisation of social policies'. They decided to set up a committee of officials, chaired by a 'political personality' (who proved to be the Belgian Foreign Minister, Paul-Henri Spaak, a convinced European), and gave it the job of working out methods of realising all three objectives, though in the course of the exercise the first got absorbed by the third.

A British official sat with this committee for the first stage of its work but, as his Government had repeatedly made clear that they would not join in a Customs Union, it was tactfully hinted to him that he should withdraw when the Committee began to draft a report favourable to such an idea. The report, largely the work of Spaak, was considered by the six Foreign Ministers at Venice in May 1956. They called for treaties to be drawn up on the basis of the recommendations and these documents, setting up the European Economic Community (EEC) and the European Atomic Energy Community (Euratom), were signed on Rome's Capitol Hill on 25 March 1957. Within nine months they had been ratified by all the countries concerned and they came into force on

1 January 1958. (In 1967 ECSC and Euratom were absorbed into the EEC, but it has so far proved impossible to get agreement on a law harmonising their three constitutions, which differ in various minor ways.)

The Euratom project was based on the belief that in the following years uranium would be scarce (so that there would be advantages in collective procurement of it) and that a continuing programme of expensive research (making the pooling of costs attractive) would be needed to harness atomic fission to the task of generating electricity. Neither assumption proved correct and the Community also ran into serious obstruction from the French who wanted to handle their own show. It has therefore achieved less than was originally hoped.

The EEC by contrast has remained a centre of political interest. Although it is charged with the duty of taking positive action in numerous directions, the underlying approach is liberal rather than authoritarian. The aim of action is to remove hindrances and establish common standards so that individual private enterprises can compete on level terms and goods produced in one member country be sold freely in all the others. It is thus in accord with the American ideal of a free-trading world and, in its initial stages at any rate, received warm US support. While it can accommodate itself to national monopolies such as State Railways, a thorough-going National Socialist or Communist state would be incompatible with it.

The Treaty was appropriately named. For its object was to establish an Economic Community or Common Market, and not just a Customs Union (i.e. an area having a single tariff with the outside world and no tariffs at all between its members). For, once tariffs had been removed, the ability of a producer in one country to compete with rivals elsewhere would depend largely on the level of his costs other than those of raw materials; many of these costs (e.g. taxes, social security payments) would be affected by government regulations, and others (e.g. cost of borrowing money, level of wages) by the general economic set-up in the country. The French in particular were nervous that, unless there was a steady movement towards the harmonising of these influences, their prices would not be competitive and their manufacturers would then insist on tariffs being restored. The removal of tariffs was however given to the Community as its first task, a timetable for doing so within twelve or fifteen years having been written into the Treaty.

The institutions of the EEC were to be essentially those of the ECSC (p. 138), that is to say an Assembly (common to all three

Communities), a Council of Ministers, a Commission and a Court of Justice. The Commission was in some cases required by the Treaty to put forward proposals to the Council; in other cases it was empowered to do so while in others again it could be called on to do so by the Council. When the Council receives a proposal from the Commission, it has three choices: to accept the proposal as it stands, to reject it or to agree unanimously on an amendment (though it has subsequently devised a fourth – to do nothing at all). If the Council is unable to agree on any of these, the project goes back to the Commission for reconsideration. The Commission takes its decisions by plain majority, and in some cases of minor importance (e.g. procedure) the Council does the same. In other more important ones the Treaty provided that, once the 'transitional period' was over (i.e. once tariffs were completely abolished), the Council could take decisions by a 'qualified majority', i.e. twelve votes out of seventeen (the bigger states having more votes than the smaller). In the most important cases of all the Council was only to act unanimously while in one or two the proposals (e.g. for admitting extra members) were to require ratification by the six Parliaments. (The exact composition of the Council has in practice varied with the agenda. Usually it is the Foreign Ministers who represent their countries but it can be those for Agriculture or Finance or Transport, etc.)

At the start the Community was to be financed by contributions from the Governments, according to a stated scale. But the Commission was required to submit to the Council proposals for replacing these contributions by the Community's 'own resources', especially the proceeds of the common customs duties and of certain types of taxation. The Assembly was given the right of proposing amendments to the annual budget but neither Council nor Commission were required to accept them. The Assembly was also given the power to dismiss the Commission by passing a vote of censure with a two-thirds majority, but the value of this provision turned out to be somewhat diminished by the lack of any say over who was appointed instead; the Governments, which were responsible for nominating the Commissioners, were free to put back the same men. The Assembly was required to draw up proposals for its own election by direct universal suffrage in a uniform way in all member states. A common investment fund was provided to finance ambitious projects while an adaptation fund was intended to ease the shift of resources out of activities made uncompetitive by the removal of protective barriers.

Member states were required to develop a common agricultural policy, five objectives of which were named. To effect it, common rules about competition were to be agreed, or the various national marketing organisations were to be co-ordinated or a common one set up. To satisfy the French, explicit permission was given for fixing minimum import prices and making long-term marketing agreements. But the Treaty itself did not call for the present Common Agricultural Policy and it was not until December 1960 that the system of levies on imports was approved. The principle of guaranteed target prices followed in January 1962 and the first actual prices (for cereals) were only fixed in December 1964.

The Commission was authorised to refer to the Court of Justice any Member State which was considered to have failed to fulfil its obligations under the Treaty. If the Court found the charge justified, the Member would be 'bound to take the measures required for the implementation of the judgment of the Court'. Nothing was said about what would happen if the Member refused; once matters had reached such a pass, the recalcitrant Member would presumably be on the verge of expulsion. There is however no provision in the Treaty for expulsion or withdrawal. The Treaty has no time limit, on the theory that if it succeeded in its object of integrating the economies of its members, withdrawal would become steadily less attractive or even feasible. The Treaty could only be amended by agreement of all the Parliaments of all Members, making the process a difficult one. Any European state could apply for membership; the conditions of admission were to be decided on by the Council, after consulting the Commission, and required the consent of all existing members. Association agreements could be worked out with any third country, a provision primarily intended to meet France's demand that her overseas territories be brought in.

Those responsible for founding the EEC and Euratom profited from the EDC experience. They kept the negotiations moving with what was, given the nature of the task, remarkable speed. They played supranationalism down. They went out of their way to make concessions, particularly to the French over agriculture, over the association of overseas territories and over the balancing of tariff removal by social harmonisation, so as to reduce the danger of opposition in the National Assembly. The French realised that their behaviour over EDC had got them a bad name and were reluctant to make it worse. Several unforeseen turns of fortune eased the path of the founders – the current atmosphere of prosperity, the success which

ECSC began to show, a change of leadership which made the German Social Democrats better disposed towards integration, the success of the French Socialists in the elections of 1956 which gave them a decisive voice in the Assembly and the country a convinced European, Guy Mollet, as Prime Minister. But if any single statesman deserves the credit for the acceptance of the Community, it is Adenauer. His Economics Minister Erhard was highly dubious of the advantage to Germany and the doubts were shared in industry, despite the attractiveness of the markets which integration might throw open. But to Adenauer political considerations took precedence over economic ones and he adroitly managed affairs so that the final document was acceptable to all six Parliaments. At the same time a hostile critic would have some justification for saying that the Treaty of Rome was hustled through by skilled handling in exceptional circumstances without obtaining wholehearted acceptance – or even comprehension – of its implications by the peoples who were going to live under it; this was probably inescapable but helps to explain subsequent troubles. Yet its opponents were so various that they could not possibly have agreed on any alternative.

Officially the British attitude towards the project of a Common Market was one of aloof benevolence; it was something in which others were welcome to indulge, with which Britain might well associate herself later (as she had in February 1955 with the ECSC) but to which she could not possibly belong (p. 137). So different was her thinking on the whole subject that, had she remained in the negotiations, they might never have ended in agreement. The more private attitude recalled the two cartoon characters 'Taint Necessary' and 'Twont Work'; all that it was desirable to do could perfectly well be done by existing institutions like OEEC (at a loss for work as there was no more aid to administer) or GATT (making slow progress in tariff reduction). To imagine however that states would part with control over their economies to the extent implied by the project seemed to the British with some reason to be an illusion; accordingly they thought it unlikely to come to much. But once the six would-be members got to the stage of actually drafting a Treaty, alarm bells began to ring in certain parts of Whitehall and notably in the mind of the Chancellor of the Exchequer Macmillan (who was to succeed Eden as Prime Minister in January 1957). If tariffs were to disappear across the Channel, Britain stood to lose sales which, though still less than those to the rest of the world, were both appreciable and increasing. Moreover if the Six began to speak with one voice in international councils, they might well carry more weight than Britain. She wanted to go on having the best of both the European and the non-European worlds; her instinctive reaction was to look for a compromise but the story of her unsuccessful attempt to do so can more appropriately be told later on (pp. 189–93).

6   The Suez crisis

In July 1952 King Farouk was turned off the throne of Egypt by a nationalist revolution with General Neguib as its figurehead and the 36-year-old Colonel Nasser as its driving force. Two years later Nasser supplanted Neguib as President of the new Republic. A major aim of the movement was to drive Britain out of the Suez Canal Zone to which she had withdrawn her forces at the end of the war. Although Egypt and the Canal were by tradition vital to Britain's imperial communications and her oil supplies, she had agreed to evacuate the Zone even before Nasser took control, partly to relieve the strain on her resources, partly because of doubts as to whether the Egyptians could be resisted indefinitely, partly under pressure from the Americans who wanted a friendly Egypt. Both Britain and America hoped to enlist that country in the anti-Communist front, but the past behaviour of the one and the present patronage of Israel by the other had left Nasser with little love for either. He preferred to remain non-committed, so as to play off one set of Cold War antagonists against the other and gain concessions from both. In 1955 he seemed to be doing nicely; the Czechs, at Russia's prompting, agreed to fit him out with modern arms while negotiations started for a loan of $400 million from the World Bank, the US and Britain to enable a high dam for irrigation to be built at Aswan on the Nile.

In 1956, however, a number of things increased American and British distrust of Nasser until in July John Foster Dulles broke the news that the money for the dam would not be forthcoming. A week later Nasser retaliated by seizing (and offering to give compensation for) the Suez Canal, so as to pay for the dam with its profits. This waterway was owned by an international company registered in Egypt but with its headquarters in Paris whose shareholders included (since 1875) the British Government and a number of private Frenchmen; its rights over the Canal were due to expire in 1968. It was widely forecast that, as Egyptians could not possibly possess the skills needed to operate the

Canal, they would soon be in breach of the Convention and justify international action against them. This expectation was questionable in law and soon proved unjustified in fact.

The British Government and more particularly the Prime Minister were anyhow in no mood to wait for it to be tested. The strain of the Second World War had imposed such a burden on Anthony Eden that his life was said to have been saved only by loss of office in 1945. Three-and-a-half more years as Foreign Secretary after 1951 and fifteen months as Prime Minister had made him once again a tired irritable man whose health (as events showed) would soon force him to leave public life. His patience had been further taxed by the long years of waiting for the decrepit Churchill to retire. Obsessed by memories of the 1930s, he insisted on regarding Nasser as a second edition of Hitler who was in addition opening the African gate to Communism; his conviction that it was never too early to resist a dictator illustrated only too well how much care has to be taken in drawing lessons from history. His desire to strike quickly and hard, however, was frustrated by the discovery that it would take Britain's forces several weeks to mount an attack. As a result Dulles, who had resented Eden's refusal two years earlier to take a strong line against the Communists in Indo-China (p. 142), had time to urge caution and to investigate a series of attempts at finding a peaceful solution. The British and French were led to think that each of these would bring them satisfaction or, by failing, justify resort to force. But though none of them did the former, the Americans never became willing to countenance the latter. Exasperation mounted and relations between Eden and Dulles went from bad to worse. The British and French official attitude, however, won little support from the rest of the world.

If Nasser had got arms from the Czechs and Russians, the Israelis in April 1956 got up-to-the-minute fighter aircraft from the French, whom Nasser had angered by supporting the Arab rebellion in Algeria. Israel was afraid that, if he went unpunished for his seizure of the Canal, his next step might be against her. The Franco–Israeli contacts led on to a plan for Israel to attack Egypt, both to improve her own security and to provide a pretext for an Anglo-French descent on the Canal Zone, camouflaged as a police action to separate the two belligerents. The Israeli conditions for starting the operation included not only French but also British air aid against the Egyptians to prevent them with their Russian bombers devastating Israel's cities. At meetings near Paris in October such support was promised. But considerable opposition to a course of this kind was to be expected inside Britain; and if the Americans came to know of it for certain, they would have demanded its abandonment. Knowledge was therefore confined to a very small circle which (as with Churchill in the war) did not include the majority of the Cabinet. On the other hand those Ministers who were excluded did not insist on being told, while the Minister of Defence, who knew and resigned, allowed his opposition to be concealed by accepting another post instead.

Israel attacked on 29 October. Next day Britain and France called on both sides to withdraw ten miles from the Canal; the Israelis, who had not got as close, complied, the Egyptians refused. On 31 October British planes from Cyprus bombed Egyptian airfields (although this had become unnecessary as the Russians had withdrawn their bombers). By 2 November Israel had achieved her objectives, which might have been expected to make further action unnecessary. But the forces to seize the Canal had to come from Malta and the pretence used to justify the action meant that they could not start until the Anglo-French demand had been rejected. Moving thereafter by sea at the speed of the slowest unit, the convoy did not reach Port Said until 6 November. Parachute troops had been dropped the previous day but the idea of using them at the outset, long before they could be backed up on the surface, had been rejected as too dangerous. On 7 November the British, although already in control of about half the Canal, halted the operation and the French reluctantly followed suit.

For the United Nations had been holding a series of frenzied meetings throughout the eight days. After the Security Council had been kept from reaching a decision by British and French vetoes, an emergency session of the Assembly was convened. At this the Anglo-French action was overwhelmingly condemned and an immediate cease-fire called for; the demand would have fallen on deaf ears if it had not been for American action. The US presidential election took place on 6 November and the hope had been that preoccupation with it would prevent Eisenhower and Dulles from intervening until after the Canal had been seized. Instead, the fear of losing votes by inaction led them not merely to give the UN full support but also to start a run on the pound which, if continued, would soon have exhausted Britain's reserves without there being any chance of the IMF coming to the rescue. The French were not vulnerable in this way but decided to their great chagrin that they were not in a position to succeed single-handed. The UN sent in a force to restore normality and clear the Canal; the

British and French were humiliated by being forbidden to take part.

It is tempting to argue that the only thing wrong with the Suez operation was its failure, that with American support it could have succeeded and that, if the Americans had backed it, they would have spared themselves much of the trouble which the Middle East has caused them since. But this assumes that Egyptian politicians could have been found who would both have taken on the job of running the country on lines approved by the West and also have succeeded in retaining office in spite of the stimulus to nationalism which a Western victory would have given. It also assumes that America could have afforded to incur even greater hatred in the Arab world. For Britain to launch the Suez venture with a vulnerable currency was foolhardy, to say the least, while a proper examination of the logistics would have shown how unlikely the operation was to achieve the speed needed for success. What was even more regrettable was that her attempt to defy world opinion invalidated her ability to pursue the policy which realism recommended, of working in close conjunction with the United States, the Commonwealth and other free countries to uphold international institutions and thereby to replace her waning physical power by increasing the moral respect in which she was held. Those of her inhabitants who still cherished illusions about her power received a salutary shock but the outburst of public indignation which occurred may have done something to reduce the damage caused to her relations with the rest of the English-speaking world (though the polls suggested that Eden had considerable support among workers).

On 5 November the Russians, who had previously had their attention absorbed by Poland and Hungary and whose action in withdrawing their bombers has been mentioned, invited the Americans to join them in action against the British and French. When this was rejected as 'unthinkable', Khrushchev threatened to bombard the two countries with missiles of an unspecified character. That this had any influence on the outcome of the West's crisis is almost as certainly untrue as the theory that, if the West had not been distracted, they would have intervened in the East's crisis. But not only did the Soviet image in the Middle East derive considerable benefit from the belief that it was the threat which had brought about the climb-down; Khrushchev himself emerged convinced that he had made the West give way. He was thereby encouraged to think that, if occasion ever arose, he could do the same again.

7   The Twentieth Party Congress: Poland and Hungary

In February 1956 the Russian leadership called a Party Congress for the first time since the death of Stalin (who had himself held such events with decreasing frequency). They were then brought up against the problem of what to say at it about the dead leader. Beria, before his arrest in 1953, had liberated a few prisoners whom he had not himself been responsible for arresting. His act, combined with the disappearance of the tyrant, precipitated a flood of appeals for release by or on behalf of political prisoners. With Khrushchev's encouragement, commissions were set up to investigate their cases and the upshot was not only the freeing in the years up to 1957 of some 7 to 8 million prisoners but also the realisation by the Presidium that the scale of previous terror had been even greater than they themselves had appreciated. The facts had become so widely known in Russia that complete silence about Stalin at the Congress, when his policies were being abandoned or modified, would have been almost as significant as a positive statement. There seems however to have been considerable argument over the best line to take. Khrushchev's speech at the beginning, presumably agreed with his colleagues, kept to generalities. But at the end he took advantage of a moment, between being himself renominated as First Secretary and nominating the rest of the Presidium, when he had in effect no colleagues; he called the delegates back at midnight and delivered his famous 4-hour 'secret' speech. To this day it has never been published in Russia but texts were quickly distributed to branches of the Party and soon leaked abroad.

The main theme of the speech was the virtue of collective leadership in contrast to the 'cult of the individual'. Whereas Lenin had always stressed the role of the Party and the need for its leaders to take advice before acting, Stalin had come to ignore it, to cease convening its organs and to take decisions on his own. The result had been not only numerous mistakes at home and abroad, both in peace and in war, but also wilful abuse of power. Many honest Russians and faithful Communists had been sentenced to death or imprisonment merely because they criticised Stalin or made him suspicious; often the only evidence for the verdicts had come from confessions obtained by torture. The Party must be restored to its old pre-eminence and individuals learn to behave with greater modesty.

Such a speech was obviously in the interest of the man who stood at the head of the Party rather than of the Government. But there were two obvious dangers in saying so much. The first was that many of those at the top (though Khrushchev less than his opponents in the Presidium) had risen to eminence under Stalin and been closely associated with him. How could they escape all share of blame for his crimes? One answer was found in placing much of the responsibility for carrying out Stalin's orders on the conveniently dead Beria. Another was to explain how, when a man sat beside Stalin, he did not know whether his next destination was home or jail. Individuals who raised objections in the tyrant's circle did so at risk of their lives, while the failure to take decisions collectively meant that there had been no opportunities for several individuals to join together in objecting. (Other evidence as well as Khrushchev's has made clear the extent to which Stalin did intimidate all his associates.) Moreover his decisions and actions had not all been unjustified. Particularly in his earlier years, drastic measures were said to have been necessary to preserve the pure gospel of the Revolution against deviationists and bourgeois nationalists. Stalin's followers could therefore be excused for having failed to spot the point at which high-handedness became criminal.

The second danger was that the reform movement might get out of control. If the leadership of the single Party could so easily degenerate into tyranny, was it right for the Party to remain single? The Yugoslavs had answered this question by locating the root of the trouble, not so much in the 'cult of the individual' but in 'democratic centralism', i.e. the whole principle of dictatorship from the centre, irrespective of whether it was exercised by one man or a group. They had sought to solve the problem by their measures of internal devolution, corresponding to which in the international sphere was the doctrine of several roads to socialism. Tito visited Moscow in June 1956 and induced Khrushchev to sign a joint declaration that

> the conditions of socialist development are different in different
> countries, the wealth of the forms of socialist development
> contributes to their strengthening and ... any tendency to impose
> one's own views in determining the needs and forms of socialist
> development are alien to both [the Soviet Union and Yugoslavia].

But even if Khrushchev had himself been prepared to accept the Yugoslav standpoint in full (which is questionable), his position in the Presidium was not Stalin's and he had no hope of carrying his colleagues with him. Tito had no sooner left Moscow than the leaders of the satellites were called there to be briefed about the visit; the declaration went unmentioned. Inevitably however the Secret Speech and the Yugoslav example had set off stirrings against the Stalinist regimes elsewhere, notably in Poland and Hungary. The Russian leadership saw that concessions might have to be made. Could they manage to relax the reins and yet prevent the horses from bolting?

Divergences in destalinisation

The Russians want to carry out a policy of de-Stalinization, but at the same time they want to keep their camp firmly under control – just as it had been under Stalin. ... If they find themselves in a dilemma and something has to go, it will be de-Stalinization. In this question, there are no Stalinists or anti-Stalinists in Russia. ... They would all rather go to war than let somebody take away from them the main prize of their historic victory in the Second World War – Eastern Europe.

Diary of Veljko Mićunović, Yugoslav Ambassador in Moscow, 22 March 1956

So much for all the kissing which had gone on at Brioni [Tito's holiday home on the Adriatic where Khrushchev had visited him in September 1956]. While making this entry, I can almost feel Malenkov's round fat face into whose cheek, which was like a half-blown balloon, the front half of my face was buried, while we were exchanging artificial and altogether unexpected kisses.

Mićunović, diary, 4 November 1956

One can always forgive young people many things but life forgives nothing, not even youth's thoughtless acts.

Gomulka, in advising Polish students to temper their ardour, 1956

Since 1944 Poland had been run by Poles who had spent the previous years in Moscow and were trusty Stalinists. They learnt of the Secret Speech with consternation and their chief Bierut, who heard it delivered, died of shock before he got home; Khrushchev took a hand in choosing another Stalinist, Ochab, as successor. The reputation of the new leadership was shaken when in June a workers' strike in Poznan, called in protest against living conditions, led to the local offices of the Party and secret police being sacked; the troops brought in to restore order showed considerable sympathy with the rioters. The Polish Central Committee, at a meeting which Bulganin and Marshal Zhukov sought but were not allowed to attend, decided that the only trustworthy Communist popular enough to satisfy national demands was Wladislaw Gomulka, who had spent the war in the Polish underground, had thereafter become Secretary-General of the Party, and had then been imprisoned on a charge of sympathising with Tito. But Gomulka's conditions for returning were his own appointment as First Secretary and the removal from the post of Defence Minister of Marshal Rokossovsky who, though born a Pole, had made his career in the Red Army. A minority of hard-liners in Warsaw wanted Russian intervention to prevent this but Moscow hesitated, uncomfortably aware that Gomulka had Polish workers, soldiers and peasants behind him. They were still hesitating in mid-October when news came that Gomulka's appointment was imminent. A carefully mixed delegation of hawks and doves went uninvited to Warsaw on 19 October for a stormy meeting, at which Khrushchev is said to have addressed Gomulka as 'an agent of Wall Street and the Zionists'. They got little or no change from the Poles and Gomulka's appointment followed two days later but assurances were given that it did not mean the abandonment of Communism or the Russian alliance.

What would have happened thereafter if Poland had been the only crisis is hard to tell. But news of what was going on there led on 23 October to the Stalinist leader in Hungary Gerö (installed by Moscow only three months earlier in place of the ham-fisted Rákosi) being replaced as Premier by Imre Nagy. Nagy had already shown signs of liberal views and now gave official posts to a number of non-Communists. Initially Moscow thought it prudent to run before the wind and issued a declaration that 'the principles of full equality, respect for territorial integrity, state independence and sovereignty and non-interference in each other's domestic affairs' must obtain between members of the 'great commonwealth of socialist nations'. The relatively few Russian troops in Hungary were withdrawn to their bases. But when popular agitation continued, Nagy announced that Hungary would cease to be a one-party state and would quit the Warsaw Pact. This was too much for the Russian leaders, who may also have counted on the Suez crisis to distract international attention; they poured reinforcements into the country and in ten days fighting ruthlessly smashed the resistance of the Hungarian troops and workers. A 'Revolutionary Worker-Peasant Government' was installed under Kádár, a Communist colleague of Nagy who saw more clearly the limits to the freedom which the Soviet Union would allow. Nagy took refuge in the Yugoslav Embassy, was persuaded by Kádár to come out on the strength of a promise that he would not be molested, was none the less arrested by the Russians and taken to Rumania where he was executed twenty months later. Although Tito admitted that Nagy had gone too far too fast and condoned the final Russian intervention as 'a lesser evil', he made clear his view that, if his moderating advice had been followed at earlier stages, the situation could have been kept in hand. The episode had put paid to his hopes that, through influence on Khrushchev, he could lead the Soviet Union down the Yugoslav road. Not only was there too much opposition to drastic internal change and in particular to any step which might weaken the monopoly control of the Party. The Kremlin might be prepared to treat its satellites less high-handedly but it was not prepared in the last resort to let them pass out of its control, as Yugoslavia had done. Tito was unable to prevent this but was not prepared to fall into line. Both sides emerged disillusioned and started to abuse one another again.

In the following years considerable concessions were made to the satellites. The existence of the Warsaw Pact was invoked to excuse the presence of Russian troops in Poland, Hungary and the German Democratic Republic in the same way as the existence of NATO justified the presence of American, British and French troops in the German Federal Republic. The collectivisation of peasants' smallholdings in Poland was reversed and considerable latitude given to the Catholic Church (which has as much influence in the country as the Communist Party). Debts were cancelled, loans were granted and Comecon (p. 91) dressed up to look like a mutual benefit scheme, though the Russians continued to drive hard bargains with the other members. Gomulka, who had not taken advantage of Russian difficulties in Hungary to demand further concessions, proved so faithful an ally that after fourteen years he was to exhaust his credit with his own people. Kádár on the other hand lived down his inauspicious start by getting Russian consent to various reforms, particularly as regards the restoration of prices and monetary incentives, so that the country's standard of life doubled within sixteen years. Khrushchev thus managed to achieve a certain amount of reform without incurring catastrophe.

The repression of the Hungarians disillusioned many Communists in the West and did much damage to the Soviet Union's reputation in the Third World. But the failure of the West to give any effective help disillusioned many non-Communists in Eastern Europe. Radio Free Europe, a broadcasting station in Munich run by ostensibly private Americans, had been particularly active in raising expectations which could not be fulfilled. For the West had no land access to Poland and could only reach Hungary by violating Austria's recent neutrality. Had there been more time, indirect aid might have been organised but the revolt was almost over before its scale was fully recognised. In any case intervention would have set going a conflict which it would have been difficult to keep limited. The episode bore out the lesson of 1953 that, if the exponents of free enterprise and of communism wanted to go on living, they must learn to do so side by side without seeking to interfere overmuch in one another's affairs. The next six years were to bring further experience in spelling out the conditions necessary for such co-existence.

Appendix: The Russian system of government

The Union of Soviet Socialist Republics contains fifteen Republics, of which the Russian Federal Republic is by far the largest, with over half the total population.

The organisation of the Communist Party exists side by side with the organisation of the State, which is itself divided into executive and legislature.

The supreme organ of the Party is the Congress which is supposed to meet every three years. This elects the Central Committee of some 200 members, meeting for several sessions each year. Between meetings, decisions on party affairs are made by the Politbureau (called from 1952 to 1964 the Presidium) of some twelve members, with additional 'candidate members'. Nominally the Politbureau is appointed by the Central Committee but in practice its members seem to decide for themselves on the changes to be made in their ranks, which has proved an obstacle to the introduction of new blood. All members of the Politbureau are nominally equal. If the First Secretary of the Party establishes himself as Chairman, it is a sign that his power is growing.

The executive of the State consists of some thirty Ministries or Committees, brought together in a Council of Ministers (called till 1946 Commissars). The Chairman of the Council (who is always a member of the Politbureau) is the equivalent of a Prime Minister (though in many ways he corresponds more closely to the Head of the Civil Service). Each constituent Republic has its own Council and Ministers. Detailed economic co-ordination between the Ministries is the responsibility of the State Planning Commission (Gosplan).

The legislature consists of Soviets ranging up from local level to the Supreme Soviet, which has two Houses, one elected by popular vote on a geographical basis, the other representing the various nationalities. The Supreme Soviet meets several times a year and has a Presidium to act for it between sessions. The President of the Presidium is the Head of State. The Supreme Soviet nominally appoints the Ministers but, as in all elections, the voter is presented with a list of candidates and given no alternative choice.

CHAPTER 6

1957-60

1   The Sputnik

On 21 August 1957 the Soviet Government announced that it had successfully tested an intercontinental ballistic missile. Though few people were in a position to realise the irony of the situation, Stalin was being vindicated at much the same time as he was being discredited. For when the war ended he had decided that, in view of Russia's lack of bases in the Western hemisphere, of the unlikelihood of quickly building an aeroplane which could fly to America and back without a stop and of the probability that a plane on such a long flight would be intercepted before arrival, Soviet resources would be better devoted to developing missiles than long-range bombers. The weakness of the policy had been that fission atomic bombs were too heavy to be used as warheads of missiles, while conventional high-explosive was unlikely to do enough damage to justify such an expensive means of delivery. The successful development of the fusion hydrogen bomb however had provided an escape from the dilemma since it was light enough for a missile to carry.

Forty-four days later, on 4 October, came a further Soviet announcement that an earth satellite, circling the globe every hour and thirty-five minutes at a height varying between 170 and 570 miles, had been successfully launched into orbit. Although this 'Sputnik' (i.e. traveller) was designed for making scientific observations, the two announcements taken together implied that the Soviet Union would soon be in a position to launch a missile with a nuclear warhead capable of travelling 5,000 miles in twenty minutes with sufficient accuracy of aim to destroy a target as limited as the Capitol in Washington. As the United States had made no similar claim, this was putting an outsize cat among the pigeons – and even more among the hawks. Not only did it destroy the assumption that in matters of weapons the West was comfortably in the lead. It threw doubt on the further assumptions that an open society offered a more favourable climate for scientific research than a closed one and that the greater wealth of the free economies would ensure that they kept ahead of the closed ones. The truth is that even though a closely regulated society may have scantier resources, its tight controls enable it to concentrate them on anything to which it gives priority, at the expense of everything to which it does not. Hence the contrast between Soviet ability to land on the moon and apparent inability to keep the population supplied with eggs! That the priority is enforced with little regard to risk is suggested by the fact that the world's worst nuclear accident occurred at a reactor in the Urals some time in 1957.

But the Sputnik had wider implications still. Until the first Russian fission bomb was exploded in August 1949, Western security had rested on the prospect that, if the Russians launched an attack with conventional forces, which the West owing to its inferiority in such forces could not withstand, the Americans would retaliate with an airborne nuclear attack from European bases on Russian cities, and the knowledge of this would deter the Russians from moving. In case the Russians were to seek to forestall this by a surprise 'pre-emptive' strike with conventional bombers on American bases in Europe, no moment was left in the whole twenty-four hours at which the entire American force of nuclear bombers was on the ground simultaneously. Thus even if the enemy did succeed in penetrating the elaborate radar screens unobserved and achieve surprise, enough planes would survive to deliver a strong counter-strike.

The Russian acquisition first of fission and then of fusion bombs changed this situation in that it increased the severity of the reply which they could give to an American nuclear strike, but that reply would still be directed primarily at European cities rather than at America itself. It was true that, if one of Russia's relatively few long-range bombers could cross the Atlantic (maybe without returning) and penetrate the US defences, the devastation caused by even a single fusion bomb would be such as to make this a threat which no US government could regard lightly. But broadly speaking the US remained less accessible to a Russian attack than Russia was to an American one, though the American public as a whole did not realise this.

The Sputnik altered this position in three ways. First, it gave Russia a weapon which not only could reach America but could do so much faster than a bomber, reducing the amount of warning likely to be available and making almost impossible (with technology as it then was) the task of interception. Second, it could be aimed more accurately, making it more advantageous to attack the enemies' bases (and thus his power of retaliation) rather than his cities. Third, intercontinental missiles were incapable of being kept waiting in the air like bombers. All three aspects combined gave added attraction to the strategy of a sudden surprise strike, with the aim of knocking the enemy out at one blow and winning the war at the outset with minimum damage to one's own people. For a country governed like the US to embark on such a venture was virtually impossible and it may well be that the Russians never considered it seriously either. But some of Khrushchev's remarks gave a different impression and in any case each Government was in duty bound to take the possibility seriously. If of course ways could be found (as in time they duly were, with heavily protected holes in the ground and submarines capable of firing nuclear weapons) which made it impossible for one side to be sure of knocking out all the other's weapons at one go, so that neither could strike first without a strong probability of receiving a nuclear attack in return, a 'balance of terror' would be achieved which was perhaps the most stable situation to be hoped for.

The exposure of the United States to direct risk had repercussions on the problem of defending Western Europe. Hitherto Europeans had often feared that the Americans would decide on all-out nuclear war, perhaps in Korea or South-East Asia, and thereby unleash destruction on Western Europe without its inhabitants being allowed any say in the decision. The new developments made this fear less acute though it began to be replaced by a fear, particularly strong in France, that the Americans and Russians would make some nuclear bargain without consulting anybody else. The main new fear however was that the Americans would be unwilling to use nuclear weapons except to ward off a direct threat to themselves and would not be prepared to expose their cities to the risk of devastation simply to achieve ends which West Europeans thought vital or to protect them against Soviet invasion. This was the consideration which led the British and then the French to insist on having their own nuclear weapons. The West Germans were the most nervous about invasion, since theirs was likely to be the first country invaded and yet in the WEU Treaty they had renounced the right to make their own nuclear weapons. The obvious solution was for Western Europe to acquire nuclear arms of its own. But if this was to be done on a national basis, not only would the WEU limitation have to be lifted; the Russians feared Germany so much that they might react to such a modification by an immediate conventional attack. To acquire the weapons on a collective basis would however only make sense if Britain and France were ready to contribute to the pool and this they showed no disposition to do.

In fact, Khrushchev's references to missiles were partly bluff. Russia certainly possessed intercontinental ones – but not many. Moreover they were extremely expensive; his original plan to put them into quantity production was overruled by his colleagues for that reason and effort was instead concentrated on ones with shorter range capable of reaching Western Europe but not the United States and thus making the first area in effect a hostage for the second's good behaviour. The American Intelligence Services soon acquired a picture of the situation which events proved to be reasonably accurate, though there was always a fear that it might be incomplete. Its conclusions were only known to a few people in Washington, just as only a few people in the Soviet Union knew what the real strength of that country was. As a result most people in high places in both countries – and outside them – thought that Russia was stronger and America weaker than was really the case. The Democrats in particular in the election campaigns of 1958 and 1960 accused the Republicans of having been so keen to save money and balance the budget that a 'missile gap' had been allowed to arise. On taking office in 1961 they discovered their error, which was all the greater because by then the false alarm had led to redoubled and ultimately successful American efforts to perfect their own long-range missiles – and in due course put a man on the moon. In the interval before that happened the American bomber force retained something of its effect as a deterrent.

While the launching of the Sputnik posed the problems which have been described, the arguments and answers were only gradually formulated over the ensuing years. In the military field therefore it marked the transition to a new period which has not ended yet. It also stimulated a number of proposals for the creation of neutral or nuclear-free zones, particularly in Central Europe, for the mutual withdrawal of troops, for agreed reduction or limitation of arms and for restrictions on the proliferation of nuclear weapons and their acquisition by countries which did not already possess them. Most of these proposals came to nothing; the most notable exception, already outside the range of this book, was the Anglo-American-Russian Treaty of 1963 banning tests of nuclear weapons (except underground). But the absence of any agreement underlined how important it was to avoid action which might provoke large-scale war.

2 Khrushchev and Berlin

Although Khrushchev's Secret Speech had not quite led to disaster, a majority of his colleagues in the Presidium had qualms about the course which he was taking. In the autumn of 1956 Molotov was made Minister of State Control, a position which gave him power over the whole state apparatus, and soon afterwards at a meeting of the Central Committee a new state body was set up to supervise the running of that apparatus. Both steps involved a loss of power by the Party – and Khrushchev. Two months later however the latter succeeded in persuading the Central Committee to go into reverse, decentralise the control of the economy to a multitude of local bodies and abolish many of the Ministries in Moscow. Like the Yugoslav reforms, this was directed against 'bureaucratic centralism' but instead of the Party being supposedly reduced to little more than a ginger group, as it had been there, the authority of the local Party leaders was enhanced. Trying to control too much from the centre was undoubtedly a weakness of the Stalinist system but, as both Yugoslavia and the Soviet Union were to find, leaving the provinces to their own devices is apt to result in chaos. For the moment however Khrushchev's interest in forms of organisation owed more to their possibilities as a political weapon than to a search for the ideal means of government.

For the change was a declaration of war against the people whom he later aptly described as the 'anti-Party group'. They laid plans for revenge when he was on a visit to Finland in June and, at a special Presidium meeting called immediately after his return, launched an attack on him and all his ways. Finding himself in a minority, he argued that, as he had been appointed by the Central Committee, only that body could kick him out. He managed to get word from the meeting to some of his supporters in the Committee, whose reaction left his enemies with no alternative but to convene it. The members, nominated by the branches all over the Soviet Union, were hurried to Moscow by military aircraft, since Khrushchev's close connection with the Army, dating back to the war, now paid off and it was not he but Molotov and Malenkov who lost their posts, the first being sent as Ambassador to Outer Mongolia and the latter to run power stations in Central Asia (a more civilised means of disposal than the firing squad). Four months later prudence got the upper hand over gratitude when Marshal Zhukov, the war hero who had personified the Army's attitude in the crisis, was abruptly replaced by Malinovsky who came like Khrushchev from the Ukraine and had fought with him at Stalingrad. Finally in March 1958 a further purge of the Party's opponents included Bulganin, and Khrushchev became Chairman of the Council of Ministers as well as First Party Secretary and member of the Presidium. He never however was to dominate his colleagues as Stalin had done. He could not change the composition of the Presidium without the consent of his fellow-members and he needed at least acquiescence from them in any policies on which he embarked.

Sayings of Khrushchev

What sort of Communist society is it that has no sausage?

Foreign Ministers cannot settle anything because they do not have the power which only heads of Government possess. If I were to ask Gromyko to take off his trousers and sit on a block of ice, he would have to comply.

We are in favour of a détente but if anybody thinks that for this reason we shall forget Marx, Engels and Lenin, he is mistaken. This will happen when shrimps learn to whistle. We are for coexistence because there is in the world a capitalist and a Socialist system but we shall always adhere to the building of Socialism. We don't believe that war is necessary to that end. Peaceful competition will be enough.

If anyone hit me on the left cheek, I would hit him on the right one and so hard it would knock his head off.

If certain Western Powers do not wish to respect the sovereignty of the German Democratic Republic and if, for this reason, they believe they have the right to resort to force, that is the right of the highwayman and prayers will not save anyone from him. A highwayman can only be beaten off with a stick.

Do you consider it a free election when the voters of New York State have a choice only between a Harriman and a Rockefeller?

There are absurd rumours about alleged differences between the Communist Party of the USSR and that of China. Just as you cannot see your nose, so you will not see these differences.

Political success combined with the prestige of the Sputnik to strengthen his natural ebullience. But he knew well that his critics, both at home and in China, had been silenced rather than eliminated. When in the summer of 1958 the US sent marines to the Lebanon and assurances of protection to Nationalist China, he seized on the openings thus provided to make truculent threats. On 10 November he said that the time had come for the signatories of the Potsdam Agreement (p. 34) to 'renounce the remnants of the Occupation regime in Berlin' (which had not in fact been mentioned in the Agreement at all) and thereby 'make it possible to create a normal situation in the capital of the German Democratic Republic' (a description incompatible with the agreements which had actually been made as regards Berlin). Seventeen days later his underlings followed this up by a more accurate but equally sinister note saying that the Russians regarded the pre-surrender agreements regulating the status of Berlin as obsolete. It then proposed that West Berlin should be made into a demilitarised free city under Four-Power guarantee and threatened that, unless the West accepted such a solution within six months, control over communications between the city and West Germany would be handed over to the DDR authorities. Apart from the fact that access to the city thereafter would involve the Western Powers in granting to the DDR in practice the recognition which they had rigidly withheld, the DDR authorities could be expected to act more provocatively than the Russians so that the chances of an armed clash would grow.

The events of 1956, particularly in Poland, had underlined the importance to Russia of keeping East Germany Communist. For the loyalty of most Poles to that doctrine was obviously only skin-deep, so that easier contact between them and the West was a thing to be avoided. But this made the tail able to wag the bear. Most of the Yugoslav ideas had found expression in the DDR and in 1956 Ulbricht had spent some anxious months. He might even have been overthrown if the intellectuals had had popular support. But the workers had learnt a lesson in 1953 and remained inactive; many potential troublemakers preferred to escape to the West. By midsummer 1958 all the dissident elements in the Party had been weeded out and Ulbricht was again secure. But just as Adenauer could use NATO's need of West Germany to get equal status with the rest of the Alliance, so Ulbricht could demand Russian help in making life in East Germany more attractive. A certain amount had already been done. Reparations had been stopped in 1954 (by which time the Russians were calculated to have extracted in one way or another close on the $10 billion which they had asked for at Yalta). Food rationing ended in 1958, in which year personal consumption per head rose above the pre-war level. But no marked improvement could be hoped for unless something was done about West Berlin.

The Americans and British (and to a lesser extent the French) used their two-thirds of the city as a show-window, to display to the crowds flocking in from the East the good things of the affluent society; as a gigantic transmitter, radiating out programmes which, if they were to be well-received in the Western sectors, had to be audible in many other areas as well; as a listening-post and paradise for secret agents; and finally as a conduit through which those who wished to leave the East could get to the West. The rate of this drain has already been mentioned (p. 147); the failure of the reform movement in the DDR helped to maintain it. Those who left were primarily the young, the active and the skilled; the DDR was not merely enabling the BRD to overcome its manpower shortage but was training technicians for it! Instead of 'containing' Communism or 'rolling it back', the West was using the prospect of good living as a magnet to draw away the weight-bearing girders. If as a result the edifice collapsed, it might shake in its fall many other structures throughout the Communist lands.

The Western reply to Khrushchev's ultimatum was that all four Powers were in the city on the basis of a multilateral agreement which could not be ended by unilateral repudiation; the use of force to give effect to such a repudiation would be met by force. They offered however to talk about modifications. For six months notes were exchanged, in the course of which the Russian time-limit gradually got forgotten. In May 1959 the four Foreign Ministers met in Geneva to bargain and, much to Adenauer's concern, came within sight of agreement. Rather than assault the remaining obstacles however they decided to wait until Khrushchev had paid an impending visit to America in case mutual confidence was strengthened as a result. But although his final meeting with Eisenhower at Camp David oozed bonhomie, the chief decision which emerged was that a Summit conference would be a good idea and pending this all other discussions were shelved.

Delaying tactics by Germany and France put off the Summit until May 1960. Ten days before it was due to begin, Khrushchev announced that the Russians had just shot down an American reconnaissance plane, the U2, over Central Asia. They had known of the flights of such planes for most of the five years during which these had been taking place but presumably it was only now that they had got a missile high enough to hit one. The State Department at first pretended that a weather-research plane had strayed off course, but was made to look foolish when the Russians revealed that they had captured the pilot alive with his equipment. Khrushchev then gave Eisenhower an opportunity for a dignified retreat by suggesting that the flights had been made without his knowledge but the President insisted on accepting responsibility and claiming that Russia's secrecy made such invasions of her airspace essential to America's security. Though Khrushchev came to Paris for the conference, he made an apology by Eisenhower a condition of attending it and, when none was forthcoming, went home again. On the way he stopped in Berlin and announced that he was going to postpone for the time being signature of the Peace Treaty which he had promised the Democratic Republic.

There is evidence that at this time he was under pressure from his rivals and opponents at home not only over his foreign policy but also over his proposals to cut conventional forces by a third (1,200,000 men), to reduce the priority given to heavy industry, to decentralise industrial management and to increase the size of farms. During the following months the execution of all these policies was in fact slowed down. Eisenhower's honesty in admitting responsibility is sometimes said to have played into the hands of the Soviet opposition by making it impossible for Khrushchev to go on negotiating without an unacceptable loss of face, but it may equally well be that Khrushchev had realised that he could not get what he wanted out of the Conference and grasped the opportunity to call it off. By the time that the commotion had died down, Eisenhower's term of office was almost over and further negotiations were put off until his successor was installed.

The Chinese had been prominent among Khrushchev's critics and personal relations between him and Mao had been deteriorating for some time. An agreement signed in 1957 about atomic co-operation was broken off by the Russians in 1959. In June 1960 the First Secretary, while attending the Party Congress of the Rumanian Communists, launched a violent attack on China and her Chairman which, although nominally confidential, soon leaked out. Later that summer all Russian technical advisers in China were withdrawn. Khrushchev and his colleagues may not have seen eye to eye as to how far provocation from a capitalist adversary should be tolerated but they gave every sign of being agreed that provocation from a Communist rival should receive short shrift.

3 Algeria and de Gaulle

After the Japanese defeat in 1945 the French, under de Gaulle, in contrast to Britain's example in India and in disregard of American wishes, resumed control of their colonies in Indo-China. As a result they brought themselves into collision with nationalist movements for independence and, after eight years of unsuccessful struggle, were persuaded by their allies in 1954 to pull out. The armistices arranged under Eden's aegis to make this possible might have led to the whole area falling to the Communists had it not been for the decision of the Americans, whose dislike of Communism had superseded their dislike of colonialism, to prop up the weak regime in South Vietnam. That however is another story which does not belong to this book.

Besides evacuating Indo-China the French in the same year decided to make Tunis independent and to give up their protectorate in Morocco, processes which were completed in 1956. In that year they also abandoned their policy of trying to assimilate to France their various colonies throughout the world and began instead to grant them self-government in a loose association (and seek an economic association for them with the Common Market). The only overseas territory then remaining was Algeria, a more difficult problem because it was nearer to France, a tenth of its population of ten million were French (including most of the leading men and almost half of the inhabitants of the bigger towns) and for some time past it had been treated as part of France, voting in French elections and sending deputies to the National Assembly in Paris. The guerrilla campaign for independence, which the Arabs began in 1954, was something to which many Frenchmen were determined not to yield. They included not only the French settlers in Algeria itself (many of whose families had been there for several generations), the Army (which was becoming demoralised by so many evacuations), the Right and Centre in France proper, but even many Socialists. Guy Mollet, the leader who became Prime Minister after the Socialist success in the 1956 elections, sent to Algiers as Resident Minister a fellow-Socialist Robert Lacoste who gave full support to the drastic methods which the Army were using against the Arab National Liberation Front (FNL).

Nevertheless the rebels grew steadily more active and by 1958 many people in France were giving up hope of ever overcoming them while the Army and the Right claimed that, though this could still be achieved, even more drastic methods must be employed. The clash of opinion as to whether methods such as torture or imprisonment without trial were justifiable threatened to undermine the Fourth Republic. There was a real danger that the hawks would react to any attempt to clip their wings or negotiate with the Arabs by seizing the Government; neither the regular troops nor the police could be relied on to resist. Of the 569 deputies in the Assembly, 142 Communists were systematically opposed to the Government, which meant that no would-be Prime Minister could obtain a majority without support from enough of the ten remaining parties as to include a proportion of people sympathetic to a strong line in Algeria. Yet the Right were not nearly numerous enough to form a cabinet on their own. Consequently all Governments tended to be divided and their indecision was increased by their fear that, if they tried to be firm, they would precipitate a civil war.

In these circumstances many eyes turned to de Gaulle as the only man strong enough to find a solution. After throwing up the government in 1945 (p. 52), the General had dabbled with forming a political movement of his own – the Rassemblement du Peuple Français –, alienated opinion by carrying his opposition to the verge of Fascism, and in 1955 declared that he was retiring from public life unless a 'rather unusual shock' were to bring him back again. Just such a shock was provided on 13 May 1958 when the news arrived in Algiers that, after an interregnum lasting a month, an undistinguished politician called Pierre Pflimlin had managed to put together a cabinet in Paris. The 'ultras', led by paratroopers, reacted by seizing the government building, setting up a 'Committee of Public Safety', demanding the establishment in France of a Government of National Safety and imploring the General to 'break his silence'. For several weeks previously they had been negotiating with agents of de Gaulle who showed a sympathy towards them which he was said, without real evidence, to share. De Gaulle's reply was to put out a statement that he was ready 'to assume the powers of the Republic'. He was as a result widely expected to lead an armed rising but four days later, while asserting that 'the exclusive regime of parties' could never master the difficulties facing France, and praising the Army for wanting to see Paris at last solving its problems, he suggested that the exceptional powers which he would need for an exceptional task should come to him in an exceptional way, 'an investiture by the Assembly, for instance'. 'Do you think', he asked, 'that at sixty-seven I am going to begin a career as a dictator?' He thus opened the way for negotiations with the party leaders, which he disclosed on 27 May, at the same time as he condemned 'action which would put public order in question' and appealed for strict discipline in the Armed Forces, thereby halting a paratroop plan to seize key points in France. In the next couple of days he was invited by the President to form a Government and agreed to do so on condition that he received plenary powers for six months during which a new constitution would be drawn up and submitted to a referendum.

The new constitution, which in due course won the approval of four-fifths of the voters, embodied de Gaulle's fundamental belief that its predecessors, as a reaction against the strong man who had periodically recurred in French politics and for fear of a Communist dictatorship, had given the legislature too much power over the executive. The President was in future to be elected for seven years by a special body in which representatives of local authorities were mixed with senators and deputies. (In 1962 the method of election was changed on de Gaulle's initiative to universal suffrage.) The President's powers, of nominating Prime Ministers, authorising referendums, ratifying treaties and dissolving Parliament, did not differ much on paper from those of his predecessors. The key change lay in the fact that the Prime Minister and Cabinet could not belong to Parliament (a deputy has to resign if he is made a Minister) and that various changes of procedure limited the ability of Parliament to interfere with and alter the Government's policy. The reduction in the Prime Minister's responsibility to Parliament was accompanied by an increase in his responsibility to the President. In practice it has been the President who has chosen Prime Ministers and Prime Ministers who have resigned when told to do so by the President even though they still possessed a majority in the Assembly. The Assembly retains power to pass votes of no confidence in the Government and to reject bills, including budgets, but has never yet done so; what would happen if the Assembly contained a majority hostile to the President and his Prime Minister still remains to be seen. The Constitution, a sort of hybrid between the British and American systems, has been described as 'tailormade for de Gaulle' and rests on the assumption that the nation will allow itself to be led by the man it has chosen as leader. One effect of the changes has been to strengthen the obstacles to social reform.

Even with the new powers it took de Gaulle four years to carry through the French withdrawal from Algeria. At the start, he probably hoped to keep the country as a self-governing unit inside the French community like the other colonies but he saw that this was not an available option when in 1959 the FNL insisted on their independence. The high value which he attached to national consciousness led him to realise that 'Algerians are Algerians and it's no use expecting them to be Frenchmen'. But to have proceeded to give them their liberty straight away would have precipitated the very situation from which he had saved France in 1958; as it was he had to face two military rebellions in Algiers and several attempts at assassination. That he succeeded was due to the charm which he could exercise when he wanted, to his courage both in personal matters and in refusing to be deterred by threats (as his predecessors had been), to use of the media in projecting his personality, to his ability in devising phrases which could seem to mean several things at the same time and to his skill in exploiting any circumstances favouring him (such as the armed attack on his life in August 1962). He used his military authority to move the more dangerous generals to less vital posts while his ability to win the support of the average Frenchman was particularly valuable in the effect which it had on young conscripts; whereas at the start the question was whether the officers would obey the Government, at the end it was whether the soldiers would obey the officers. What de Gaulle failed however to prevent was a merciless epilogue in which the diehards among the settlers and regular troops fought the Arabs tooth-and-nail and were repaid in kind. The principal victims were the French Algerians, three-quarters of whom fled the country, so that the new regime was deprived of their skills and bitter memories were left behind.

Algeria absorbed so much of the attention of de Gaulle and France that only after 1962 was he able to develop seriously his policies on other matters. As during the war, his method of gaining a position was to act as though he already possessed it. By resorting to these tactics too early, he earned the snub which America and Britain gave him in September 1958 when they turned a deaf ear to his proposal that they should form with France an inner triumvirate for running NATO and the affairs of the West generally. But the shapes which he gave to French policy were ones welcome to many Frenchmen. For there was considerable resentment at the way in which the Americans had thwarted French wishes in the colonies and Germany, while Britain was unpopular because of her claim to a special relationship with America and the climb-down to that country over Suez. And it had been Guy Mollet's Cabinet which decided that France must acquire her own nuclear weapons. De Gaulle wished to see Western Europe acting together under French leadership in politics as well as economics but it was to be a Europe of sovereign national states. He arrived in power to find the Treaty of Rome on the point of coming into force and, instead of insisting on changes, decided to honour France's signature but to work from within to give it the shape he would have demanded had he been involved in its negotiation. Britain he suspected of undue subservience to America, refusing to see how close her ideas about supranationality in the EEC were to his own, and failing to realise that West Germany's dependence on US nuclear weapons for defence against the East made her in the long run just as close as Britain to America. This blindness was largely due to his underestimating the depth, and therefore the permanence, of the antagonism between East and West. He was even less ready than the British to be reconciled to the fact that, in a world of superpowers, his country must drop to the second rank and could only hope for equal treatment by sinking its individuality up to a point with its neighbour. This he was prevented from doing by his insistence on having his own way and by the glorification of nationality which went with it.

4   Britain fails to fit the EEC into the OEEC

By July 1956 the negotiations for the EEC were looking promising enough to make people think seriously about the effect of their success upon the OEEC and accordingly that body set up a working-party to study the question. The step was taken on British prompting and in September British Ministers announced what they thought the answer should be. It was to form the seventeen members of the Organisation into a Free Trade Area, within which the EEC six would count as a single unit. A Free Trade Area is like a Customs Union in so far that in both of them the member states remove all tariffs against each others' goods. But whereas in a Customs Union the members maintain an identical tariff against the rest of the world, each member of a Free Trade Area maintains its own external tariff which it remains free to change without obtaining the agreement of its partners. But one of the arguments which shaped the EEC (p. 161) was that removal of tariffs makes competitive ability dependent on other factors and that for member countries to compete on level terms, these other factors must be harmonised as well. The advocates of a Free Trade Area played down the importance of this point and suggested that it could be adequately met if a member state which felt itself at a disadvantage was allowed to raise the matter in the Council set up to run the Area and get such compensation as its fellow-members might (or might not) think appropriate.

France in particular (whose levies for social services were the highest in the EEC) felt this solution to be inadequate and was further antagonised by the British insistence that the tariffs reduced should not include those on agricultural products (so as to prevent Continental foodstuffs from getting an advantage in the British market over those from the Commonwealth countries). They further argued that as the external tariffs of the members of the Area would differ while trade between the members was free, the protection afforded to one member by high tariffs could be evaded by merchants sending goods into a neighbouring member with low tariffs and thence, without paying any additional duty, into the high-tariff country. The 'rules of origin' which the British suggested to prevent this were dismissed as impractical (although they were to be worked with success from 1960 to 1972).

The French were not the only people among the Six who suspected that the British were seeking to weaken the attractiveness of the EEC by demonstrating that it was possible to get the main advantage of the Community, in the shape of easier access to growing markets, without accepting the obligations, in the shape of commitments over harmonisation, agriculture, etc. A number of enthusiasts for integration, such as Spaak, knew there were prominent figures in Western Europe, notably Dr Erhard, who would be glad to see the scheme embodied in the Rome Treaty replaced throughout the OEEC by the simpler Free Trade Area. There was fear, by no means unjustified, that if the latter was agreed to, the former would never come into being. Accordingly they refused to listen to the British suggestions that the two should be negotiated at the same time and managed to delay progress in the OEEC while the Rome Treaty was first of all signed and then ratified by the French Assembly, so that serious discussion of the Area proposal did not begin until a year after it had been first propounded. When soon afterwards the Community came into existence, the formation of its Commission added an extra body with a vested interest against the rival proposal.

The British Government all along overestimated the desire of the Six to bring the United Kingdom into an integrated Western Europe as well as the readiness of the remaining Five to twist the arms of the French.

They were further handicapped by being overheard on the Continent when they tried to convince a sceptical home public that 'we can't afford to stay out'. As the negotiations went on, they were forced to make one concession after another in the hope of avoiding a breakdown. Had they realised at the outset how serious the obstacles were, and driven their case relentlessly, they might perhaps have secured an agreement. But they would probably have had to accept such far-reaching commitments about agriculture, about alignment of the external tariff, about mutual consultation on commercial policy and about majority voting in the institutions that they might almost as well have joined the Community as normal members.

The Algerian crisis of 1958 (p. 186) not only held up negotiations for a further two months but brought to power in de Gaulle a man who had several scores to settle with Britain. Paradoxically the looser concept of the Free Trade Area might have been expected to appeal to him more than the Community, with its elements of supranationality. But at that juncture he badly needed the votes of French industry and agriculture who, having brought themselves to gamble on the Common Market, were determined to prevent the British from evading the unpalatable choice. He also believed that his talents would in due course enable him to do from inside the Community just what the British were trying to do from outside and gain the advantages (particularly in enlisting the other Five for his own international causes) without accepting obligations which limited his freedom of action. How little importance he attached to acting in concert was shown on 14 November 1958 when, at the very moment that an OEEC Committee was pursuing without much success at its Paris headquarters the question of how a Free Trade Area could be formed, the French Minister of Information announced to the press that the French Government had decided the project was impossible.

Although the British representative at an OEEC Council Meeting in December spoke about 'defensive measures', thereby provoking the French representative into walking out, the London Government had few good ways of hitting back and was reduced to hoping that its friends among the Six would manage to get negotiations restarted. The organisations of industry in the 'Other Six' (Austria, Britain, Denmark, Norway, Sweden and Switzerland – to which Portugal added itself) were less sanguine and more resourceful. They pressed their Governments to form themselves into a rival group and during 1959 on the initiative of Sweden action to that end was gradually authorised. British official hesitations about joining in were overcome by the growing view among EEC members that, if that organisation was to negotiate with anyone, it should be with the rest of the Western world and not just with the rest of Western Europe – a trend encouraged by the United States. The upshot was the signature in November 1959 of the Stockholm Convention setting up the European Free Trade Association (EFTA) which gave the wits the chance to say that the Continent was at sixes and sevens.

By the Convention the seven countries promised to cut their tariffs towards one another as fast as the EEC members were scheduled to do; the EEC reaction was to speed up its own process. Agriculture was excluded though Britain had to make concessions about bacon to bring in the Danes and about frozen fish to do the same with the Norwegians. For the rest the Association followed the lines which Britain had tried to persuade the EEC to accept. A small Secretariat replaced the Brussels Commission but the Council of Ministers was given wide discretion, enabling it to deal with unforeseen emergencies and removing the need for a complex Treaty to anticipate these. The Council was also given the role played in the EEC by the Court of Justice, since it was made the recipient of complaints by members against each other and authorised to suggest remedies by a majority vote; if the offending member refused to act on the suggestion, the others could withdraw the advantages which they had given it. Amendments to the Convention needed unanimous approval and members could withdraw on giving a year's notice.

A natural consequence was that the Convention only had 44 articles compared with the 248 of the Rome Treaty and was administered by a staff proportionately smaller. The chief thing absent from EFTA, particularly as far as the British Government was concerned, was a clear purpose. If intended to bring pressure on the EEC by depriving members of that body of markets valuable to them, it principally pressed those who wanted an association with the rest of OEEC rather than the French who were the obstacle to it. If intended as a consolatory alternative, its markets were not big enough (and most of them easily accessible anyhow). If intended as a foundation for 'bridge-building' or an aid to bargaining, it reinforced Continental belief that British aims were so different as to be irreconcilable and encumbered Britain with six associates whose wishes would have to be catered for if negotiating were to begin again. The best justification for EFTA was as a holding operation. It was a way of encouraging the rump of OEEC not to make a series of individual bargains with the Six and of keeping some European markets at any rate open for British goods until a wider agreement could be worked out.

5   The American and Russian economies compared*

Although much of the impulse towards rapid growth in Europe came from the United States, that country did not share in it. The members of the Common Market, Scandinavia and Britain grew faster between 1948 and 1962 than they had done prior to 1913 and in most cases much faster than they had done between 1913 and 1950 (see Appendix to this chapter). But in the US the average rate during the three periods showed a progressive decline. Particularly after the Korean boom had spent itself, supply outran demand and as a result investment languished. A main explanation of this apparent paradox is simple. In the early years of this century, America had outstripped Britain to become the richest nation in the world (in terms of gross domestic product per head) as well as the greatest manufacturing nation. It had been a major innovator, particularly in methods of standardisation and mass production. In spite of the Depression it had maintained that lead until the Second World War, during which its product per head expanded by 60 per cent, whereas that of Britain only did so by 11 per cent and in most of the German-controlled countries on the Continent output per head actually fell. The US had as a result gone further than any other country to satisfy human needs and were already operating at a high level of efficiency (measured in terms of output per man per hour) so that the known possibilities for increasing output by better methods or better machinery were, in comparison with the rest of the world, smaller. As a result the total annual volume of their output hardly doubled between 1945 and 1965, whereas that of Italy rose fivefold and that of Western Germany fourfold. The only other major country with an equally limited record was Britain but whereas there were only four years during our period when unemployment in Britain was above 2 per cent, there were only four in the US when it was below that figure.

This deceleration of growth, however, largely escaped notice because

---

* Reliable figures are easier to obtain for America than for Russia and it is usually difficult to be sure that the two sets are truly comparable.

America remained the country to which the rest of the world looked as an example in technology and techniques of production. It continued to be the main innovator in the fields of production opened by the latest scientific research, even when the actual invention had been made elsewhere. Chief among these were electronics, heralded by the invention of the transistor in 1948 and of the integrated circuit ten years later. They in turn made possible bigger computers in a smaller compass and the progressive 'automation' of industrial production. The communication of information, pictures and ideas was made simpler and faster, increasing the possibilities of control from a single centre. Television changed from being a luxury into standard household equipment. Other important fields were aeronautics, atomic energy, oil (for which the US was becoming increasingly dependent on external sources, see p. 116), oil-based chemicals, the synthetic materials made from them, synthetic fibres and pharmaceuticals.

At the same time American society led the way into what has been called the 'post-industrial age' in which improved production methods were reducing the proportion of the population needed to work in industry while the attention paid to the consumer was providing increased employment in services. By 1960 the relative figures were 39 and 53 per cent. Manpower was becoming so expensive that costly machinery was often worth while because of the labour saved by it. But the jobs in industry, though fewer, were becoming more responsible, with the consequence that wrong decisions could reach further, so that increasing attention was being paid to the techniques of and aids to management. The concentration of industry into fewer bigger units, though checked in its effects on the consumer by the anti-trust laws, was putting workers in key industries into positions where they could hold the community up to ransom by withholding its vital supplies.

The United States take pride in being a consumer's paradise, with an unprecedented variety of goods on the shelves of self-service supermarkets, giving the purchaser a wide choice for 'discretionary spending'. They have led the way in devising more effective techniques of advertising, packaging and purchase on credit. Since decisions as to what is to be produced have to be taken long before the products go on sale, consumer magazines and other kinds of publicity have been brought in to make the consumer think that what is on the shelves is what he or she has been longing for (even if unconsciously). But competition between chains increases the range of choice and makes it financially risky to offer goods which are less attractive than those in the store across the street. The open door to trade, combined with the desire of other countries to earn dollars, adds to the variety. Relative abundance has encouraged the Americans to use their resources lavishly – and often maybe wastefully, more as 'status symbols' than to satisfy needs. On the other hand they have not been discouraged by scarcity from making innovations on the ground that they could not afford the risk of failure.

Russia did not start on the process of modernisation till some fifty years after America, and even when she did progress was patchy, with some sectors or plants (usually supplied and installed by foreigners) being relatively up-to-date while others remained primitive. After 1914 advance was held up by the devastation of two wars and the dislocation of changing over to a new economic system. In 1929, however, Stalin introduced the first Five-Year Plan which sought above all to develop heavy industry. He imposed on Soviet workers hardships comparable to those endured by the workers of the West in the early days of industrialisation. A growth rate of 3.4 per cent per annum is said to have been achieved between 1937 and 1953, which outdid that in any West European country. Between 1953 and 1958 the overall gross national product rose 6.7 per cent and between 1958 and 1965 5.6 per cent, rates which the Federal Republic and Japan were the only major countries to exceed (significantly they too were war-damaged countries with a special need to catch up). (These figures are for growth in GNP overall whereas those on p. 204 are for growth in GNP per head. The US figures comparable to those here are about 3.5 per cent and 3.2 per cent.) Output quadrupled in the twenty years after 1945, whereas US output did not quite double. But at the end of them the Soviet consumer was still only enjoying a standard of living two-fifths of that of his American counterpart. Moreover a slow-down in Russian growth set in about 1958 which suggested that the easier possibilities of improving output and efficiency were beginning to be exhausted. Whereas in the 1950s the figures gave Khrushchev some justification for talking about overhauling the US, prospects of ever doing this have since then ·dimmed.

Although the Soviet Union is two and a half times the physical size of the US (and is really more comparable with the US and Canada combined), in half its territory the subsoil never thaws, while some of the rest is swamp and considerable areas are virtually uninhabitable. As a result its population is only 18 per cent higher and more widely spread out. The relative apparent inefficiency of Soviet agriculture is not

Problems of the Russian economy, 1962

If we merely appeal to people to grow corn and sugar beet or to introduce mechanical milking but do not organise the production of machines to harvest corn and beetroot, milking machines and other equipment, we shall simply remain babblers. One cannot call for high productivity and cut maize with hatchets.

Khrushchev, at an Agricultural Conference, 5 March 1962

Can we, relying on the material and the degree of mechanisation already reached in the collective farms and state farms, raise agricultural production at once and to an important extent? Yes, comrades, it can be done. ... Let us agree then to talk less about shortages of machines, and to make better and fuller use of the material in the collective and state farms. As the saying goes, it takes no great brains to shout 'Give, give, give'.

Khrushchev, at the same conference four days later.

Our Party constantly pursues the policy of developing heavy industry as the essential base of the material and technological foundation of Communism, of the country's defence and the progressive increase of the people's welfare. Only doctrinaires and revisionist bunglers can oppose heavy industry to the production of consumer goods, or industry to agriculture.

L. F. Ilyichev, one of the Party Secretaries,
at a Presidium meeting 22 April 1962

Our military doctrine is that, however important the role of nuclear armaments and rockets may be, it does not in the least follow that there is no longer any need for other means of armed combat involving mass forces. Victory cannot be secured in modern war without the combined efforts of all types of armed forces.

Marshal Malinovsky, Defence Minister, May 1962

When in the Government we examine the problems of distribution of appropriations ... we are often confronted with agonising problems.

Khrushchev, 28 February 1963

---

therefore surprising. Under Stalin the peasantry were an exploited class, virtually bound to the soil, heavily taxed and with an income only half that of the national average. Khrushchev made the production of more food a top priority and gave aids and incentives to the people involved in producing it. He underrated the time which would be needed to get the new system going and disregarded the limits which climate put upon innovations sensible in themselves (e.g. the need to rotate crops if the virgin lands brought into cultivation in Central Asia were not to become dustbowls; the fact that in many parts of the country summers are apt to be too short or too wet for maize to ripen). He cut down the number of collective farms but increased their size so that it became on average fifty times that of the private American farmstead. Between 1950 and 1963 the area under cultivation rose by 50 per cent, while in the US it fell by 10 per cent. Between 1958 and 1963 16 per cent of total Soviet investment went to agriculture as against 5 per cent in America, but even so the US head-start meant that in 1969 Russian farms still had less than half as many machines as were available in America. This helps to explain why at the end of our period some 30 per cent of the labour force was employed on the land as against a US figure of 6 per cent (and a British one of 3 per cent, only feasible because 40 per cent of consumption is met by imports). Russian grain crops rose remarkably from 81 million tons in 1950 to 171 in 1965, but this was still appreciably less than the crop harvested in the US from a smaller area. Whereas Russian harvests, thanks partly to weather, fluctuate widely and only make the country self-sufficient in good years, America habitually has a surplus. The US produces more meat, the USSR more milk and butter.

In the 1930s Stalin sacrificed present to future comfort by concentrating resources on building up heavy industry as the indispensable foundation for a prosperous economy. Had he not done so, Russia might well have lost the war for lack of weapons. But war damage meant that after 1945 much of his work had to be repeated (though factories which had been evacuated east of the Urals stayed where they were). Over the next twenty years the Soviet Union maintained an investment rate of about 25 per cent of GNP, a figure only exceeded by Japan. (The West German figure (1950–60) was 22 per cent, that for the US 18 per cent, and that for Britain under 17 per cent.) Initially 88 per cent of this went into capital goods but after 1953 consumption per head rose by 5.5 per cent a year although working hours were cut from 48 to 41. Between 1959 and 1964 48 per ce⁻˙ of total investment was going to industry, energy, transport and communications as against an American figure of 34 per cent. Unemployment did not exist officially in Russia whereas in the US the average from 1945 to 1962 was 4.6 per cent. But in practice Soviet workers were often kept on payrolls with nothing to do.

Russian expenditure on defence is hard to estimate with precision but is thought to have amounted between 1953 and 1965 to 12 per cent of GNP, 20-25 per cent higher than in the US and three times as high as the average for Western Europe. This of course does not mean that Russia was spending more, since her total GNP was so much lower; in 1968 the two defence budgets were estimated to be $80 billion for the US and $40 billion for the USSR. But arms and equipment are probably not as costly in Russia.

In 1964 63 per cent of American GNP went on consumption as against 46.5 per cent of Russian. Soviet consumers certainly did not seem to be yet reaping the advantages which might have been expected to result for them from all the investment which had gone on. But this was partly at any rate due to official policy. The Soviet Government, faced as all governments are by the competing claims of investment, defence, welfare and consumption on available resources, was allowing its citizens to live better than hitherto but was providing little of what it regarded as luxuries. Among the things which came into that category were private motorcars; 96 per cent of Russian families were left to depend on public transport which, though crowded, was cheap. The amount of housing available was increasing and rents were kept low but the standards were spartan, if sturdy, and the average Russian had little more than half a room whereas the average American had one and a half. Again, consumption of electricity per household was in the one country a seventh of what it was in the other. Food was reasonably plentiful in Russia but monotonous (the Crimea could not compete with Florida as a source of fresh fruit in winter!) and the average family spent half its income on food and drink, compared with a quarter in America. Fashions were only allowed to change slowly and there was no attempt to keep up demand by 'built-in obsolescence'. On the contrary, equipment tended to be kept in use till it was worn out. Whereas in the US it was often cheaper to buy a replacement than to get a worn or damaged article repaired, in Russia the difficulty was to obtain spare parts.

Less importance was attached to providing the consumer with a varied choice; exactly similar goods tended to appear in all stores. The chance was thus virtually eliminated of competing manufacturers laying down duplicate capacity and the market being satiated as a result though, as supplies became more ample, customers began to disconcert the planners by leaving on the shelves goods which were found unattractive or faulty. The chief function of such little advertisement as there was seemed to be to brighten the streets! Whereas in America an excess of demand over supply was likely to result in higher prices, in Russia it manifested itself in queues, wire-pulling and bribery. Officially, inflation did not exist any more than unemployment. Prices were rigidly controlled and often kept unaltered for years, the assumption being that the amount paid out as wages would be kept in line with the supplies being provided under the plan. The phenomenon of 'wage drift' was not however unknown.

To be ill in the US is notoriously expensive but Russia has an elaborate if bureaucratic health service and is said to have half as many doctors again in proportion to the population. In 1966 radio sets were three times and television sets six times more plentiful in America but the difference may well have resulted from a time-lag which will in due course be made up, for the regime is well aware of the utility of broadcasting as a means of indoctrination. Russian newspapers were only one-third as expensive, while twice as many books were produced. Admittedly the US product in both fields was probably a good deal more varied, interesting and amusing, but a high proportion of the Russian output was technical. Culture (music, theatre, films) and sport were plentifully available at subsidised (i.e. non-economic) prices. The Soviet educational system is said to turn out fewer first-degree graduates than the American (though more than most other European ones) but the proportion in science, engineering and economics is noticeably higher.

In 1962 only 27 per cent of the Russian labour force was employed in 'services' so that the country had some way to go before it could be said to enter the 'post-industrial age'. It seemed unlikely to move in that direction as fast as the industrialised economies of the free world had done. This was not simply because Russia was still a poorer country with a lower GNP per head. It was also because the country's rulers had different priorities to those in the West and their political system, coupled with their command economy, enabled them to enforce those priorities. The first aim of the Soviet regime was not to make their people affluent in the present but to provide for security in the future. Preference was therefore given to industrial investment and defence over welfare and private consumption. As a result the Soviet regime might be expected to gain in relative strength as time goes by. Against this however must be set the possibilities that

(a)   the initial American lead was too great for catching up to be possible.

(b)   the waste inherent in a command economy is higher than the waste of a different kind inherent in a free economy.

(c)   the known innovations in products or methods of production which bring quick increases in GNP have all been already introduced in Russia, leaving for introduction only those bringing smaller increases, so that henceforward the growth rate will slow up.

(d)   the relative disregard of the consumer (along with the suppression of free speech and movement) will lead either to a political upheaval or to mounting inefficiency bred of disaffection.

How Communists criticise

During the 1950s and 1960s criticism of the Government was expressed in Russia by the invention of an imaginary Radio Armenia, broadcasting stories and question-and-answer programmes. Typical items were:

Q: What would happen if the Soviet Union took over the Sahara desert?
A: For fifty years, nothing. Then there would be a shortage of sand.

Q: What should I do if warning is given of a nuclear attack?
A: Cover yourself with brown paper and walk – but do not run – to the nearest shelter.
Q: Why should I not run?
A: Because running might start a panic.

Q: Is it true that the cosmonaut Gagarin won a Zis limousine in a tombola in Moscow?
A: In principle, yes. Only it wasn't the cosmonaut Gagarin but a schoolteacher of the same name. And it wasn't a tombola in Moscow but a dancing competition in Kiev. And what he won was a bicycle, not a Zis limousine. And he didn't win it, it was stolen from him.

An Armenian who was going to Moscow for the first time arranged that he would send a postcard to tell his friends at home what the city was really like. If he wrote in red ink, all that he said was to be believed. If in green, they were to believe the opposite.
 In due course the postcard arrived. It was written in red ink. 'Moscow is a wonderful city. All you have heard about it is true. Everything you desire can be bought in its shops – except green ink.'

---

6   Half the American dream comes true

The first cuts in tariffs under the Rome Treaty occurred on 1 January 1959. Where trade between the member countries was restricted quantitatively by quotas, these too were considerably eased. There had been some doubt as to whether France would be prepared to fulfil this obligation but at the last moment she devalued the franc by 17 per cent and thus gained a trading advantage which made her willing to take the risk. Some of the tariff cuts were extended to other members of GATT and some of the quota ones to OEEC. These concessions silenced the British accusation, flung about after the scheme for an OEEC-wide Free Trade Area had collapsed (see p. 191), that France, by implementing the tariff cuts only towards her EEC partners, would be breaking promises not to discriminate against other OEEC members.

The British matched the French devaluation by declaring that current payments in sterling by and to non-residents in the sterling area would henceforward be freely convertible into all other currencies, including dollars. The Federal Republic at once followed suit. Thirteen other members of OEEC and fifteen countries closely related to them in monetary matters took equivalent steps. Though Britain had already gone further in the direction of convertibility than was generally recognised, the events at the end of 1958 constituted a mile-post in post-war recovery; most of the non-Communist world had at last succeeded in re-establishing a system of free monetary exchange. The relaxations removed the need for the European Payments Union (p. 87), which had been set up to make possible free exchange between the countries of Western Europe at a time when they were not prepared to risk the strain of such exchange on a wider basis. The Union was accordingly brought to an end; countries which had accumulated a debt (chiefly France and Britain) were required to pay up, to the benefit of those which had accumulated a credit (chiefly West Germany).

The extension of convertibility for West European countries outside Europe weakened their case for maintaining quotas on imports from outside the OEEC area of goods which had been freed from quotas inside that area. For that case rested on the protection which EPU gave against the risk of unwieldy surpluses or deficits between individual member countries. But the extension of convertibility to a wider area meant that most currencies used in trade could be freely exchanged into most other currencies so that there was little danger of piling up a surplus which could not be converted; the need for the quotas was thus largely removed. Accordingly the next few years saw their progressive removal, which also lessened the distinction between Western Europe and the rest of the free world.

This disappearance of quotas left OEEC with little to do since the distribution of US aid had ended some time before. To the chagrin of de Gaulle, the creation of the EEC had made Brussels rather than Paris into the city where the economic policies of Western Europe would henceforward be discussed, even when it was a question of the relations between the Six and the Seven, so that OEEC was in something of a backwater. Moreover the French disliked the OEEC as an organisation in which the Americans and British had too much influence. Even the Americans had come to dislike it as an institution which seemed to them an unsatisfactory halfway house between a closely integrated Economic Community and co-operation on a free-world scale. On their initiative but after a considerable amount of hesitation, OEEC was wound up at the end of 1960 and replaced by the Organisation for Economic Co-operation and Development (OECD); the US and Canada became full members. The tasks of the new body were to collect statistics and other information on a comparable basis about the economies of the members, and to produce reports about their prospects, in the hope that discussion of these at Ministerial level would lead to co-ordination of aims and activities. OECD has also served as a meeting-place of the industrialised nations of the free world (particularly since Japan became a member in 1964) at which they can consider their relationship with the less developed areas.

GATT negotiations for reducing tariffs held in 1956 had been disappointing, largely because the US delegates had already taken advantage of almost all the scope allowed them by Congress for bargaining. The GATT secretariat however had been unwilling to accept defeat and in a Ministerial session in November 1957 had managed to get a review of the international trade situation put in hand, which a year later resulted in a decision to start another set of negotiations (the 'Dillon Round') in 1960; some such action would have been needed anyhow because the new EEC tariff in some cases meant countries departing from undertakings given in previous negotiations and for this the non-EEC members of GATT were entitled to demand compensation. Indeed the whole question as to whether the EEC, and still more EFTA, were compatible with GATT caused some heart-burning. These new arrangements however did more to remove existing barriers to trade (even if only over a limited area) than to add new ones and this consideration, reinforced by doubts as to how much attention the Six and Seven would pay to GATT protests, won the day in favour of approval. But what perhaps did more than anything else to give GATT fresh impetus, besides enabling President Kennedy to get from Congress authority to negotiate more widely, was the emerging concern of the US about their exports.

For, by the end of the 1950s, the 'dollar gap', so prominent a problem at their outset, had disappeared. Partly this was due to the successful efforts which a reconstructed Europe had made to sell to North America; here the devaluations of 1949 had helped. Partly it was due to the re-establishment of multilateral trade, by which US exports to Europe could be paid for by European exports to Asia and Africa, and thus by exports of raw materials from those areas to the US. Partly it was due to the growing ability of Western Europe to supply its own needs for sophisticated goods rather than obtain them from America. Partly again it resulted from extensive investments by American 'multinational' firms in Western Europe. The net result was deficits in the US balance of payments of $3.5 billion and $3.7 billion in 1958 and 1959, rising to $3.9 billion in 1960. Many of the developments which have been described, and in particular the re-establishment of convertibility, were only made possible by the change. Although US gold reserves were still so big that the deficits were more a problem for the future than the present, they marked the end of an era.

Thus by 1959–60 a point can be seen in the economic history of the free world at which the eighteenth-century ideas revived in the US during the war had, despite a number of setbacks, gone an appreciable way towards being achieved – perhaps as far as in this imperfect world it is ever reasonable to expect. The dominating economic feature of the period was, as the table at the end of this chapter shows, a faster and more continuous growth in the main industrialised nations of the world than at any previous period in history. The average rate of investment was half as high again as it had ever been on a sustained basis, yet the saving which this involved was not being done at the cost of private consumption. The industrial worker in particular had never been so well off. The gross inequality caused by industrialisation had been mitigated. The 'trade cycle' (i.e. the regular recurrence of boom and slump) seemed to have been got under control, since the recessions which did occur in 1951–2 and 1957–8 were shallow. Private enterprise, widely considered during the Depression of the 1930s to be on the point of collapse, had been restored to health and vigour. Moreover the foreign trade of European nations grew faster than their gross national products and at a faster rate than had ever been achieved before. The fact that much of the growth in trade occurred between the developed countries suggested that they did not depend for their prosperity on markets or openings for investment in undeveloped ones. The conclusion is hard to escape that there was a connection between these unprecedented results and the policies of free trade and payments which were pursued at American instigation. It remained to be seen whether the path in future would continue upwards more or less steeply, move onto a plateau or start to go down again.

A climacteric can also be discerned in international political relations and in defence. In these fields the attempts of the US to impose their conceptions on the world had not merely been less successful but actually counter-productive. Those countries inspired by a different ideal and organised on a different principle had refused to be either persuaded or coerced. Their efforts to make their preparations for defence look convincing made them look threatening as well and, even after the need for co-existence had been recognised, the process of working out a basis for it took time. Consequently the break between periods here came a little later than in economics and the final episodes remain to be described.

Appendix: Average annual rates of growth of output per head of population

Country	1870–1913	1913–50	1948–62
Belgium	1.7	0.7	2.2
Denmark	2.1	1.1	2.8
France	1.4	0.7	3.4
Germany/W. Germany	1.8	0.4	6.8
Italy	0.7	0.6	5.6
Norway	1.4	1.9	2.9
Sweden	2.3	1.6	2.6
UK	1.3	1.3	2.4
US	2.2	1.7	1.6

Sources
Columns 1 and 2: A. Maddison, *Economic Growth in the West.*
Column 3: M. M. Postan, *An Economic History of Western Europe 1945–1964.*

CHAPTER 7

1961-2

1 The building of the Berlin Wall

In February 1961, three weeks after John F. Kennedy had taken office as President, he sent a message to Khrushchev saying that he would welcome a meeting. But the Russian leader played hard to get and only in May did he reply, suggesting Vienna as a suitable site. The talks on 3 and 4 June toured the horizon as a whole and Berlin was not mentioned till the second day. In keeping with his general tactics of trying to frighten the younger man, the First Secretary (his confidence strengthened by having just put the first man successfully into space) repeated the threat that, unless the West offered concessions, Russia would sign a Peace Treaty with the DDR. This state would thereafter be responsible for controlling access to a demilitarised city of West Berlin; the end of 1961 was mentioned as a new deadline. The President, who emerged from the encounter disillusioned rather than intimidated, made clear at the time and afterwards his country's determination both to resist unilateral action and to pursue quadrilateral agreement. 'We do not want to fight – but we have fought before.' American reservists were called up, defence expenditure raised, troop strengths in Germany increased and a decision announced to restore 500,000 as the target figure for the *Bundeswehr* (p. 153). The Russians were left guessing as to what form would be taken by the Western reply to any move against West Berlin but in no doubt that there would be one. The combination had its intended effect of making Khrushchev opt for, and induce his more hawkish colleagues to be content with, the least risky solution. The reduction in numbers in the armed forces announced by Khrushchev in 1960 was however cancelled and the defence budget increased.

In pursuance of Ulbricht's policy of making the DDR into a model socialist state (p. 146), the amount of land in communal hands was raised in 1960 from 45 to 85 per cent while the pressure to produce more was relentlessly maintained. As a result the flow of migrants to the West (p. 147) was also maintained and Khrushchev's mention of a time limit showed all who were thinking of leaving that they could not afford to wait; during the summer of 1961 the stream swelled to a flood. Ulbricht insisted that, unless something was done to stop it, his regime faced collapse. Now in May the NATO Council had defined the West's essential requirements as regards the city: the right to keep troops in the Western Sectors, the right of free access to those Sectors from Western Europe and the continued viability of their economy. Nothing explicit was said about access from the East and voices were heard in America suggesting that the Communists had the power, if not the right, to close this down. The course thereby indicated, midway between nuclear war and political humiliation, was put into effect on 13 August, though preparations for it had been made beforehand. A barbed-wire fence, later developed into a wall, was set up through the middle of Berlin along the boundary between the Russian and the remaining Sectors; only four crossing-points were left and at them passage was closely controlled, though America, Britain and France successfully maintained their right to send their official vehicles into all parts of the city. Reaction did not otherwise go beyond indignant protests: Kennedy was told that 'he had talked like Churchill and acted like Chamberlain' while Bonn students sent him an umbrella as a symbol of appeasement. But Ulbricht later admitted that the Wall was his greatest propaganda defeat and, although there were some anxious days while the East hinted at and the West waited for further measures, the passage of time showed that a situation tolerable to each side had been established. Monstrous as the Wall may appear, especially when actually seen, it was preferable to the practical alternatives (remembering that solutions which would have involved a Western climb-down or an Eastern breakdown did not come into that category). Ten years' experience of the new arrangements was to show that they could provide the basis for an agreed settlement.

The building of the Wall was not however without consequences. It is true that about 6,000 people a year still managed to get out of East Germany (including some sent by the Communists for their own purposes). But the majority of the population resigned themselves to staying where they were and as a result set out to make their conditions of life better; they can hardly be blamed for taking pride in the considerable progress which they achieved. Over the next fifteen years, the Democratic Republic was to be as successful among the command economies as the Federal Republic among the free ones. It inherited not only the military traditions of Prussia but also the virtues of efficiency, discipline, method and hard work. The Russians found themselves having to pay more attention than ever to the most loyal of the satellites and to value the contributions to their system which could be made by the world's ninth largest industrial state. Perhaps they have even reflected that a Germany which was both united and Communist might put them in the shade.

West Germany by contrast lost its most valuable source of extra manpower and West Berlin much of its function as an exchange-point between East and West. People and business tended to leave rather than come to or pass through it. There were fewer visitors to look at its shop windows while the contrast between them and those over the Wall grew less impressive. The proportion of pensioners in its population rose and its most remarkable feature became its freedom from congestion. Its decline would have been even more marked but for the considerable subsidies poured into it by the Federal Republic. The beleaguered bastion of liberty showed signs of degenerating into a dead end. It also illustrated the proverb that nothing lasts as long as the provisional.

The Western discussions about meeting the Russian challenge over Berlin had refocused attention on the extent to which the West was still relying on 'tactical' nuclear weapons (p. 154) to withstand a conventional Communist attack. There was every sign that only a short interval would elapse between the start of such an attack and resort to 'nukes'. But doubt was spreading as to whether the enemy would be willing, or indeed even able, to distinguish between an atomic shell fired from a gun and a short- or even medium-range missile with a nuclear warhead, and whether as a result resort on the battlefield to the former might not quickly escalate into full-scale nuclear war. Moreover the Federal Republic, on whose territory the initial battles in a future war were likely to be fought, showed no enthusiasm for having that territory devastated by such powerful weapons. These considerations led on Kennedy's initiative to fresh thought about Western strategy. The solution which in due course found most favour was that of the 'graduated response'; any attack on NATO would be met by a series of measures, each involving more extensive retaliation than its predecessor while the enemy was left guessing as to the point at which he would by his own actions bring on the next step. A main aim of this course was to provide time both for mediation and for discovering precisely what the aims of the enemy were (so as to avoid misunderstanding or even accident leading to a major clash). At the same time NATO did do more to strengthen its conventional forces, though not to the extent which the US urged. Although they were still barely sufficient to withstand the probable weight of attack, they might, in the light of the theory that the aggressor needs for success half as many troops again as the defender, just be sufficient by themselves to deter the Russians from gambling on the belief that a conventional attack could safely be made because public opinion in the West would prevent nuclear weapons from ever being brought into use.

2   Adenauer in decline

Before the Wall went up, 17 September had already been set as the date for the *Bundestag* elections due in 1961. At the previous elections in 1957, the Christian Democrats and their Christian Social allies had obtained an absolute majority of seats. Now however their failure to reply actively to the Communist challenge had its effect, especially when contrasted with the spirited behaviour of the young Socialist Lord Mayor of West Berlin, Willy Brandt, who had been chosen by the SPD as their candidate for the Chancellorship. Adenauer was eighty-five, had been becoming more high-handed than ever in his methods and in 1959 had incurred criticism by first announcing his intention of standing as a candidate for the Presidency and then drawing back. He had not merely failed to groom any younger man as his successor but was at odds with his party as to who should succeed him. Erhard's record as Minister of Economics and sponsor of the 'Miracle' made him the obvious man but Adenauer considered (as events between 1963 and 1966 were to show, rightly) that Erhard had an exaggerated reputation inside his own field and few qualifications outside it. The old gentleman's change of mind over the Presidency had been due to his discovery that, if he ceased to be Chancellor, the Party would insist on Erhard following him and that, under the *Grundgesetz*, the President could do little to control the Chancellor.

Foreign and defence policy were the spheres in which Adenauer was beginning to seem most obviously out of date. This was not entirely justified. He was not quite as inflexible as he appeared. He did not in practice give German reunification overriding priority; in secret he showed himself ready for talks with the Russians. But Khrushchev was more interested in seeking a direct arrangement with the Americans and left the West German approaches unanswered. Adenauer and his colleagues were not however prepared to volunteer a readiness to make concessions, since they regarded these as bargaining counters which should only be given up in return for counter-concessions. Consequently they gave the impression of clinging rigidly to the position of the 1950s: no recognition of the Democratic Republic or the Oder–Neisse line; insistence on the Federal Republic's claim to be the only state legally entitled to speak internationally for Germans; undeviating membership of NATO.

What Kennedy's firmness in the summer of 1961 did to reassure Adenauer was counteracted by his part in evolving the new doctrine of 'graduated response' and by the readiness which he showed to negotiate. The Germans, like the French, suspected that the Americans were capable of making a deal with the Russians at the expense of Western Europe and without consulting its inhabitants. With Dulles the Chancellor had known where he was, with Kennedy he did not. The resulting coolness helps to explain the warmth acquired by his relations with de Gaulle in spite of the General's anti-German attitude after the war, his hostility to the Common Market and his statement in 1959 that existing frontiers (including presumably the Oder–Neisse line) must be maintained.

The events of 1961 suggested that neither East nor West were prepared to risk resorting to force in order to upset the settlement reached in practice rather than by design in 1945; the desire of the German people for reunification was therefore unlikely to produce a nuclear war. But for many non-Germans (and even for some liberal Germans) that danger had been the only reason for seeking to reunite the two republics; partition otherwise provided an effective answer to the problem posed between 1870 and 1945 of an over-powerful state dominating the rest of the Continent from its centre. As a Frenchman put it, '*J'aime tellement l'Allemagne que je suis heureux qu'il y en a deux.*' But if the Democratic Republic and the Oder–Neisse line had come to stay for the foreseeable future, a refusal to recognise these facts was unlikely to be a recipe for success. The various undeniable inducements which the Federal Republic could hold out to get concessions from the East only became counters if there was bargaining. But not only had Adenauer become too old for new ideas and new methods, the CDU and CSU had been formed as political parties in order to support a government policy instead of, in the usual way, formulating a policy as parties in order to become a government. They had remained primarily machines for collecting votes; when the reasons for voting for them ceased to be acceptable, they were ill-adapted for devising new ones. Thus a change in policy was unlikely to be made without a change not only in the man but also in the party providing the government.

The Social Democrats had already surmounted a comparable problem. After their failure in the 1957 election, their younger leaders had decided that, to have any hope of ever succeeding, they must jettison the traditional dogmas which they had inherited from the nineteenth century, abandon what had become little more than lip-service to Marxism, revise their programme to take account of the Welfare State and the Communist threat, and set out to win from the middle classes the marginal votes needed to give them a majority. Such a transition was made all the easier by the effect of prosperity in assimilating many of the workers into those classes. They voted in favour of entry into the Common Market in 1957, declared their support for rearmament and coined the slogan 'Competition as far as possible, planning so far as necessary'. These new attitudes found expression in the Bad Godesberg programme of 1958 on which they fought the 1961 election.

In that election they gained twenty-one additional seats, whereas the CDU/CSU lost twenty-eight. These changes meant that neither of the two major parties had a clear majority and (as the German Party which had hitherto been Adenauer's coalition partner lost all its seats) the Free Democrats who had gained twenty-six found themselves in a key position. The difference between the CDU and SPD had been sufficiently reduced to make no longer absurd the idea of a coalition between them. But the opponents in both camps, and particularly in the CSU, were still strong enough to prevent this from coming about. The FDP thus became essential to any government and they still preferred to work with the CDU. Adenauer, after seven weeks of bargaining, in which he was made to promise that he would retire in 1963, succeeded in forming his last cabinet. But as events were to prove, the first step had been taken towards ending the predominance of the right which had until then characterised West German politics.

3 Britain fails to enter the EEC

On 31 July 1961 Macmillan, as Prime Minister, announced his Government's decision to open negotiations with the Six for British entry into the EEC. In view of the number of occasions during the preceding ten years on which senior British Ministers had said that it was out of the question for Britain to do any such thing, the probable reasons for it merit description. In the first place, the 1950s had put

---

This parliament and this country could not accept ... that an executive body in Europe ... can arrive at decisions which, by means of a simple majority, can be imposed upon a state.

Bevin in the House of Commons, 28 March 1950

In our view, participation in a political federation, limited to Western Europe, is not compatible either with our Commonwealth ties, or obligations as a member of the wider Atlantic community or as a world power.

Cripps in the House of Commons, 26 June 1950

With our position as the centre of the British Empire and Commonwealth and with our fraternal association with the United States in the English-speaking world, we could not accept full membership of a federal system of Europe.

Churchill in the House of Commons, 27 June 1950

One thing is certain and we may as well face it. Our people are not going to hand to any supranational authority the right to close down our pits or steelworks. We will allow no supranational authority to put large masses of our people out of work in Durham, in the Midlands, in South Wales or in Scotland.

Macmillan at Strasbourg, August 1950

---

paid to the idea of keeping the Empire intact by labelling it a Commonwealth. India, having obtained independence in 1947, became a republic in 1950; Pakistan followed suit. More of a departure was the granting of independence to the African colonies, Ghana in 1957, Nigeria in 1960, Sierra Leone, Uganda and Tanganyika in 1961. In 1960 South Africa became a Republic and left the Commonwealth, after the other Asian and African members had made clear that, in the light of the Sharpeville massacre in March 1960, an application to remain in it would be rejected. The realisation among some Conservatives that this was a process which could not be arrested had been shown in 1959 when Macmillan, on a visit to Cape Town, spoke about the winds of change. States which had as colonies been closely tied to the British market took advantage of their independence to shop around, while others gave their infant industries protection against British competition. Increasingly Britain seemed about to relapse into its pre-seventeenth-century role of being an offshore European state.

In any case the Commonwealth as a whole could not compare with Western Europe for prosperity. Macmillan, surveying the results of growth in Britain, said sardonically of his countrymen: 'They've never had it so good.' But paradoxically, although this was true, it was at about this very same period that Britain was overtaken, in annual gross domestic product per head, by several European states including France and West Germany. In 1961 British exports to Western Europe for the first time exceeded those to the entire Commonwealth. But if the Common Market were to achieve its aim of becoming a single entity, it might prove largely self-sufficient, so that a continued rise in British exports to it could not be taken for granted; EFTA was an inadequate substitute, seeing that its six other members put together only had a population equal to Britain's. There seemed to be something wrong with British industry and there was a belief that integration into the fastest-growing area of the free world might provide a remedy, even if of the 'kill-or-cure' variety. The Suez affair had demonstrated Britain's dependence on the United States and the Americans were all for her joining the EEC since they were worried that a Continent divided economically might not be able to remain united for defence or prove prosperous enough to take over a bigger share of the cost.

But although the past could be broken with, it could not be obliterated and proved a two-fold impediment to Britain's candidature. For one thing, the grassroots of the Conservative Party remained dubious about the need to change and, in order to avoid a split, they had to be given reassurances. Britain's application was represented as indicating not a decision to join but a decision to find out the terms for joining. Satisfactory arrangements were said to be essential on imports from the Commonwealth, on agriculture and on EFTA. The hope was held out that many Commonwealth goods would continue to enter free of duty and that Britain would act as a link between the Community and the outside world. The British would have liked to go on with their system of importing food at world prices and paying subsidies to make farming a viable occupation in European conditions; they failed to realise that such a system was unacceptably expensive to countries like

France which grow nearly all their own food. Finally, although the Six had refused to negotiate as a whole with EFTA as a whole, the British had only won the consent of their EFTA partners to negotiations by promising that they would not themselves enter unless acceptable terms could be found for all the other EFTA countries which wished to do so.

Though the enthusiasts for Europe welcomed Macmillan's decision, the Governments of the Six could hardly be blamed if, in the light of the past, they doubted how genuine Britain's conversion was. The political skill with which the Prime Minister outflanked his domestic opponents exacerbated his difficulties with his external ones. What concerned them was not so much the belief that the change of view had been caused by re-calculations of self-interest, since states are seldom motivated by anything else. They suspected that the British had not really changed their views on what was ideally desirable and would use membership, if not the entry negotiations themselves, to reshape the Community to their own liking. They knew that the Labour Party, under Hugh Gaitskell, had declared against British membership, might easily win the election due by 1964 and would then be almost bound to precipitate a crisis of one sort or another. Accordingly their general view was that, if Britain did join, she must do so on their terms rather than hers.

From the start, they rejected all idea of reaching an overall agreement about the Commonwealth. The British negotiators, led by Heath, were thus driven to expend time and goodwill on bargaining about each item separately. Much of their effort was spent on protecting the interests of others, such as the New Zealanders, dependent on the British market for disposing of their mutton and cheese, and the West Indians, similarly dependent over sugar. Debate gradually degenerated into details, among which tinned kangaroo meat won a derisive notoriety. Five of the Six wanted to see Britain a member and if matters had rested with them alone, agreement could probably have been reached – at the price of considerable British concessions. But their benevolence was not strong enough for them to put the continuation of the Community at risk and only by doing so could they have overborne the opposition of France – which is to say of de Gaulle.

There were three main reasons for the General's antagonism, apart from resentments harboured since the war which are unlikely to have been decisive. As a condition to agreeing to talks with Britain at all, he had driven his partners to accept the basic principle of what later became the Common Agricultural Policy. By this the farmers of the

De Gaulle on European integration

What are the pillars on which Europe can be built? In truth, they are the States, States that are, certainly, very different from one another, each having its own soul, its history and language, its glories and its ambitions. But States are the only entities with the right to give orders and the power to be obeyed.

5 September 1960

I do not believe that Europe can ever be a living reality if it does not include France with its Frenchmen, Germany with its Germans, Italy with its Italians etc. Dante, Goethe, Chateaubriand belong to all Europe to the extent that they are, respectively and eminently, Italian, German and French. They would not have served Europe if they had been countryless, or if they had thought and written in some integrated Esperanto or Volapük ....

There have been those who say 'Let us group the six States into a supranational entity, that would be very simple and practical'. But it is impossible to create such an entity unless there is in Europe a federator with the strength, the resources, the skill to do so. That is why one falls back on a type of hybrid, in which these six States would undertake to comply with what will be decided by a certain majority. ... These are ideas which may perhaps beguile certain minds but I do not see how they could be carried out in practice, even if there were six signatures on the dotted line. Would the French people, the German people, the Italian people submit to laws voted by foreign deputies – laws which would perhaps run counter to the deepest feelings of the peoples concerned? No, there are at present no means of forcing unwilling nations to accept the decisions of a foreign majority. ... But then perhaps the world would follow the lead of some outsider who did have a policy. There would perhaps be a federator but the federator would not be European [would he be American?] and it would not be an integrated Europe but something quite different. ... In great matters it is often pleasant to dream of Aladdin's wonderful lamp which it was sufficient to rub in order to give substance to unreality. But there is no magic formula which will enable us to carry out such a difficult task as the building of United Europe.

15 May 1962

Community were to be given guarantees as to the prices which their products, regardless of quantity, would fetch throughout its markets, while levies were to be placed on imports so as to bring cheaper food from elsewhere up to the same price. Such a scheme was incompatible with the British system and involved an increase in the price of food for the British consumer (though relieving the taxpayer of the need to pay subsidies). French farmers clearly stood to benefit but details still had to be worked out and prices named; de Gaulle was determined that the small print should be drafted in a way which strengthened rather than weakened the principle.

Second came his conception of the Community as a whole. Its founders, such as Monnet, had sought an economic unity which would gradually develop into a political federation. De Gaulle sought an alliance between states which would enable them to act together in international affairs and deal on equal terms with the superpowers; he was prepared to accept the Community in so far as he could use it as a tool to this end. He pressed his partners to accept a political Council of Heads of Governments which would work independently of the Community; the Belgians and Dutch, suspecting that it was intended to do so at the Community's expense, blocked the idea. His admiration for the nation-state as a unique social unit made him disdain attempts to transcend it as futile, but in doing so he had to minimise the difficulty of getting sovereign states to act together. Yet he was aware of the difficulty and aware that each extra state which joined the Community would be an extra obstacle to making his conception of it work. As long as its members were limited to six, he saw some prospect of dominating it and of making it suit the interests of France. He distrusted additions and in particular the addition of Britain because, although she might share his objections to supranationalism, she obviously had different approaches to many other matters and in particular was unlikely to let the Community be used as an anti-American league.

As negotiations went forward, Macmillan's Government gradually staked more and more of its prestige on being successful and accordingly made so many concessions that by the autumn of 1962 de Gaulle seems to have begun regarding Britain's entry as inevitable. What made him decide to employ 'diplomacy by thunderbolt' as a means of keeping her out was political or even strategic rather than economic in character. To satisfy his own aspirations, to appease his army still smarting over the Algerian surrender, and to give France the international status to which he considered her entitled, de Gaulle had to have his own nuclear weapons. But to acquire both the know-how and the equipment without any help from outside was difficult and expensive, especially after the arrival of the missile era. Neither the United States nor Britain showed readiness to help. The British however had difficulties of their own. In 1960 they decided to cancel their missile, Blue Streak, as being too vulnerable, expensive and erratic, and to rely instead on Skybolt, a missile which the Americans were developing. But Skybolt proved a failure and in November 1962 was scrapped. Britain was then faced with a choice. Either she could ask the Americans to supply her with Polaris, a missile fired from nuclear submarines (which she would then have to build). Or she could join forces with the French to develop a European missile.

The second course would obviously have suited de Gaulle and he seems to have been led to hope that it would be the one preferred; the available evidence does not yet enable us to tell whether he was unjustified, whether the British were merely keeping the French option open in case the American one fell through or whether they were putting round the idea of combining with France in order to make the Americans more ready to supply Polaris. By striking a bargain with France, Macmillan might have removed her opposition to British membership of the EEC. He however preferred the American option and at Nassau just before Christmas obtained a promise from Kennedy that Britain would receive Polaris missiles, provided she agreed to make them and their launcher-submarines part of a multinational NATO force and use them only for the purpose of the Western Alliance, 'except where the British Government may decide that supreme national interests are at stake'.

A similar arrangement was offered to de Gaulle who rejected it without hesitation. He did not wish to become dependent on America for his missiles (as the British were doing) and his conception of international co-operation ruled out the idea of putting France's vital weapons under the command of any non-Frenchman – he had already withdrawn all French warships from NATO. He was confirmed by Macmillan's decision in his belief that Britain, if forced to choose, would always go with America rather than Europe and that therefore his opposition to her joining the EEC was fully justified. He called a Press Conference in Paris on 14 January 1963 and, without a word in consultation with anyone, made clear that he did not consider Britain yet qualified for membership. The question, in his view, was whether

> Great Britain can at present place herself, with the Continent and like it, within a tariff that is truly common, give up all preference with regard to the Commonwealth, cease to claim that her agriculture be privileged and, even more, consider as null and void the commitments she has made with the countries which are part of her free trade area. That question is the one at issue and I cannot say that at present it has been resolved.

In fact the negotiations at Brussels had gone a considerable way towards resolving it and were still continuing when de Gaulle spoke. The inference is clear, and is supported by other remarks of his, that the issues in debate at Brussels were not the real objection so much as symptoms of it. A fortnight later, to the indignation of everyone else in the EEC including the Commission, the French insisted on negotiations being broken off. Whether anybody could by that time have influenced the French is doubtful but Adenauer had missed a chance of doing so a week earlier when he had come to Paris to sign a Franco-German Treaty of Friendship, without making the visit conditional on a change in de Gaulle's attitude. The *Bundestag* was acutely conscious that West Germany depended on the US for atomic defence and, in ratifying the Treaty, insisted on adding a preamble which reaffirmed West Germany's loyalty to the Atlantic Alliance and her desire to strengthen the Community by the inclusion of Britain, thus ruling out the use of the document to support Gaullist policies.

The story did not of course end at that point. But it is all the same a good place to break off. A pause – and a change of Government – ensued while the British collected their thoughts after the rebuff. The integration of Western Europe was destined to be a long-drawn-out process, so that the circumstances in which it approached completion would be very different from those in which it was begun. Some would put the blame for this on an elderly and obstinate man, some on over-optimistic idealists who tried to do too much too quickly. But a share must certainly fall on an island whose people were deeply divided about their future role in the world.

4   The Cuban crisis

Slightly longer though considerably narrower than Britain, with a population of under eight million, Cuba stretches east and west like an immense breakwater ninety miles from the southern tip of Florida. For long its prosperity depended on how much the world was prepared to pay for its sugar – its income from cigars being more limited though more stable. The island had belonged to Spain till her defeat by the US in 1898 and had thereafter been nominally independent; America preferred indirect control through pliable rulers, bolstered by a pledge to buy sugar above the world price. Fulgencio Batista, who had taken part in a revolt against a corrupt and arbitrary regime in 1933, turned himself in 1952 into a corrupt and arbitrary dictator.

In 1953 the twenty-five-year-old illegitimate son of a businessman, Fidel Castro, attempted a revolt; it failed ignominiously and he went to prison, followed by exile. In 1956 however he managed to establish a band of guerrillas in the mountains. He started as a nationalist with peasant support, since the relatively few industrial workers in Cuba had been seduced by Batista, who established relations of mutual tolerance with the Communist party. The dictator's fall was due as much as anything to a decision by the Eisenhower Administration in March 1958 that he was doing more harm than good to America's interests. (In view of this, it was a trifle ungrateful of Castro to say to the Non-aligned Conference in 1979, 'I wonder whether the US has ever helped a single liberation movement anywhere in the world?') When both they and the army deserted him, he fled, whereupon Castro, as the most active rebel leader, was allowed to take power. But though the new regime was anti-American it did not include Communists and drew much support from the lower middle classes who had no desire to see free enterprise abolished. The general expectation was that Castro would follow the example of many other Latin-American new brooms and in due course come to terms with the existing order, including the US. His has been described as 'a revolution in search of an ideology'.

Cuban conundrums

We are against all kinds of dictators, whether of a man or of a country or a class or an oligarchy or by the military. That is why we are against Communism. We don't agree with Communism but democracy has many faults. And the people should get something besides theoretical democracy.

Fidel Castro in Washington, April 1959

Neither bread without liberties nor liberties without bread; neither dictatorships of men nor of classes; the government of the people without oligarchies; liberty with bread and without terror, that is humanism.

Castro in New York, April 1959

We cannot do everything at once. ... We cannot undertake at the same speed industrialisation, public works, health, education and day nurseries. ... If we want to do everything at once, we will not succeed in the fundamental task, which is to transform the economy. As long as Cuba does not industrialise itself, as long as it does not augment its agriculture, it will not be able to have all the hospitals and housing it needs.

Carlos Rafael Rodríguez, Cuban Communist leader, 2 June 1960

In practice however he moved left rather than right, in response partly to his own inclination and partly to his treatment by other people. To satisfy his peasant followers he introduced a land reform, which turned some of the officers and middle classes against him; as a result his need for Communist support increased. Early in 1960 he signed a trade agreement with the USSR, though neither side was keen at that stage to endanger its relations with the US by too close an embrace. In the following summer an American-owned oil company on the island refused to refine oil supplied by the Russians and was punished by expropriation; Eisenhower retaliated by a 95 per cent cut in American purchases of sugar. This sanction however lost much of its sting when the Soviet Government, which had already bought a little sugar, promised to buy a lot more. Khrushchev into the bargain told the Americans not to forget that 'Soviet artillerymen, in case of need, can support the Cuban people with missile fire if the aggressive forces of Washington dare begin intervention. ... As recent tests have shown, we have missiles capable of striking accurately at a distance of 13,000 kilometres.' Although the commitment to action, if examined carefully, was less than categoric, it led Castro to decide that, having burnt his boats with the Americans, his best course was to make himself too socialist for the Russians to dare desert him.

The Americans thereupon set about organising a force of Cuban exiles to invade the island and overthrow Castro. Kennedy, on taking office in January 1961, found the plans far advanced and allowed the operation to go ahead; he later blamed himself for not having examined the planning more closely since, if he had, its gaps and inadequacies must have come to light. When 1,400 exiles landed on 18 April at the Bay of Pigs, they found themselves faced by over 20,000 of Castro's men and had to surrender within twenty-four hours. Kennedy, realising that the only way of saving the situation would be to commit US forces to what might prove a long campaign, refused to let them become engaged. Khrushchev, on learning of this decision, attributed it to the threats which he himself had repeated after the failure of the landing had become obvious. He drew the conclusion that the US, realising how the balance of world power was shifting against them, would always be deterred by similar threats of nuclear war on all issues outside their own territory. He was rash enough to boast that the Monroe Doctrine was dead.

During the hubbub occasioned by the Bay of Pigs, Khrushchev denied having any intention of making Cuba into a Russian base. But in the course of the following year he and his colleagues would seem to have thought worse of this restraint; if the Americans had missiles based in Turkey, why should the Russians not have some based in Cuba? By installing short- and medium-range ones there, they would immediately increase the fire-power which they could direct at the US and achieve a balance of weapons for which they would otherwise have to wait until in some ten years' time they had accumulated enough long-range missiles for them to offer a serious threat from their own territory (p. 179). Such a balance would enable them to extort concessions from America in other parts of the world, such as Berlin (over which Ulbricht was still being importunate), or a promise that the Federal Republic would never be allowed nuclear arms. Russia would be shown capable of protecting from interference any state which embarked on a Communist revolution and would acquire an answer to Chinese reproaches that she had lost her revolutionary fervour.

To be successful however the project depended on two suppositions. One was that the Americans would not find out about it until the missiles were in position; the other that, even if they did, fear of bombardment by long-range missiles from Russia (and possibly also fears for Western Europe) would inhibit them from interrupting the installation. The second was more vital than the first because the Russians probably reckoned that, even if Kennedy did discover what was going on, he would keep quiet about it because he would be reluctant to face the pressure of his hawks for action (pressure to which on the second supposition he was not going to yield) until after the mid-term elections to Congress were over on 6 November and the danger of losing votes by failing to act had disappeared.

Neither supposition proved valid. The Americans found out in August that missiles of some kind were going into Cuba and openly taxed the Russians about it. But at first the evidence available to them supported the Russian assurances that only ground-to-air defensive missiles were involved. On 4 September Kennedy announced that there was no evidence of a Russian combat force in Cuba or of any offensive ground-to-ground missiles. He added: 'Were this to be otherwise, the gravest issues would arise.' On 15 October however he was brought pictures, taken by a U2 reconnaissance plane, giving clear evidence of forty short- and medium-range ground-to-ground missiles being within about a fortnight of becoming ready for action.

Fortunately this information was known only to very few and even rumours took time to leak out. This enabled the President and his aides to consider the situation coolly, without having to take decisions on the spur of the moment, a fact which helped to avoid disaster. They saw six possibilities. The first was to do nothing. Some have since argued that this was too lightly dismissed. It is claimed that the US were already under threat from long-range missiles in Russia and that Khrushchev would only have fired the missiles in Cuba if the Americans had fired first, so that nothing vital in the situation was being changed. But if Kennedy had nothing to lose by leaving the missiles in Cuba, Khrushchev would have had nothing to gain by putting them there, and gain he undoubtedly hoped to do. Moreover American views about the Communist threat were such that inaction by Kennedy might well have led to his impeachment, as he himself recognised. The second course, diplomatic action in the UN and elsewhere, was dismissed as time-consuming and of doubtful efficiency; the third, pressure on Castro, met the same treatment because Castro was not the person primarily responsible. Three courses were left — blockade of the ships bringing the missiles, an air-strike at the launching sites, and invasion. The last two had strong supporters to begin with but lost favour on closer consideration because, in the light of experience at the Bay of Pigs and elsewhere, their instant success could not be guaranteed and, if action became prolonged, the risk of it escalating to a nuclear exchange was too great. Blockade (or, as it was euphemistically termed, 'quarantine') was easier to apply and had the great advantage that it offered the enemy a chance of withdrawing without excessive humiliation.

Accordingly Kennedy set going on the evening of 22 October an operation mounted with great care and thoroughness, by making a broadcast in which he told the world what was happening, announced that Russian ships approaching Cuba would be boarded and, if found to carry missiles, forced to stop, and gave a warning that, unless the missiles already in Cuba were removed, American forces would land on the island. When the first Russian reply sounded as though they believed the President to be bluffing, he sent a further message to disabuse them of the idea. On 25 October Russian ships bound for Cuba began to turn round and next day a message arrived from Khrushchev saying that he would comply with the American demands if they in return would recognise Castro and promise not to invade Cuba. A parallel message, which seems likely to have been the work of the Presidium rather than the First Secretary, sought to include the removal of missiles from Turkey in the package but, although the weapons were becoming obsolete and were in fact removed in 1963, for the moment this demand was disregarded. The main Russian requests were granted and the crisis ended.

It is to Kennedy that mankind should have and on the whole has been grateful for their escape from nuclear catastrophe. But although the crisis might never have arisen if Khrushchev had understood more clearly how the Americans would react, he did, once his mistake was clear, have enough good sense to cut his losses. Nor were they confined to Cuba; on 16 January 1963 he told the SED Party Congress in the DDR that the conclusion of a German Peace Treaty was no longer as urgent as it had been before the building of the Berlin Wall, thereby in effect relaxing the tension in Central Europe. Those of his colleagues who did not think that he had been weak thought that he had been rash; the Chinese said the 'capitulationism' had followed 'adventurism'. Though his fall in the autumn of 1964 was chiefly due to internal problems, the humiliation in which he had involved Russia seems to have counted against him. The experience of that humiliation may well have incited his successors to embark on a programme of arms expansion, particularly at sea, which would safeguard them against ever having to beat a similar retreat again.

The lesson of the episode was however clear. Equality of terror, even if it was achieved more indisputably than it had been in 1962, would not automatically make nuclear war impossible. There were certain actions by each side which the other would not tolerate; arrangements were essential to ensure that each knew where the other's limit lay. The installation of a 'hot line' between White House and Kremlin symbolised the paradoxical situation in which the leaders of the two sides, while remaining adversaries, became intimates.

CHAPTER 8

Concluding reflections

1 Adjusting to change

The staircase of history has been said to resound with the clatter of clogs going up and the tinkle of tiaras coming down. What is true of families is also true of societies – and perhaps even of continents. The winds of change are always blowing.

Changes in climate bring economic and social change in their wake, as do discoveries of new resources (like North Sea oil), the exhaustion of old ones (like Derbyshire lead) and technological innovations which make old resources (like uranium) more or (like jute) less important. But the principal cause of change is human mortality. Individuals grow old, die and are succeeded by others who are fewer or more numerous, cleverer or more stupid, better or worse informed, lazier or more industrious, healthier or frailer, more enterprising or more sluggish, honester and kinder or more ruthless. Each generation has its own favoured ideas and distinctive outlook. All these variations constitute significant changes in the 'resource endowment' of individual countries which will be reflected in the growth rate of their economies as well as in the degree of satisfaction which they provide for their members, and hence in their ability to compete both economically and militarily. Inside states, competition may be deprecated and restrained but between states an effective method of limiting it has yet to be discovered.

Primitive man feared change because his imperfect understanding of his environment made him nervous lest the unknown should bring disaster. Human progress has however depended on people innovating and hence being eager to make changes. But though men today may have got into the habit of taking change for granted and expecting steady improvement, there are many to whom change threatens discomfort or loss, at any rate in the short term, and who therefore resist having it imposed upon them. They are usually the people whose relative ability to compete is waning. But most people's loss is someone else's gain and those whose ability to compete is growing expect to see the gain reflected in increased status, prosperity and influence. If the normal institutions of society do not in due course produce these increases, the gainers will hardly be human if they do not exert their power to seize what they consider themselves entitled to enjoy – in other words, to make institutions and the national and international distribution of wealth correspond to the real relativities of power. This is the main ultimate cause of wars, civil wars and revolutions. The longer that an adjustment in status is resisted, the bigger may become the adjustment which is appropriate and the greater the reluctance of those going downhill to make it. Yet the longer it is delayed, the greater the danger of violence being used to bring it about. Those who are losing ground often fail to realise what is happening and think themselves stronger than they are; violence is most likely to occur between groups which have discrepant estimates of what its outcome will be. Few countries fight a war which they know they are bound to lose.

One of the major advantages claimed by advocates of a free world is that, by giving scope to individual initiative, it facilitates change (see p. 19). Yet by making changes on a small scale more frequent, it tends to make the process as a whole gradual so that individuals can adjust with less discomfort. Another advantage claimed for the system is that the prosperity which freedom brings enables change to be achieved by levelling up rather than by cutting down; if individuals and societies are getting richer, they are less likely to notice or resent the fact that others are getting richer faster. Loss of employment in declining industries is easier to absorb if plenty of alternative jobs are being created. One man's gain is not necessarily another man's loss. A third advantage is that by decentralising decisions about change and taking them so far as possible out of the hands of organisations, resistance to them is weakened; scattered individuals are less likely to succeed in erecting effective obstacles than associations, unions and above all governments.

The main justification for allowing free movement of men, money and materials is that economic resources are thereby drawn to the places where they can be used most efficiently. The interdependent world created by modern transport and communications allows specialisation and division of labour on a far larger scale than ever before. But this freedom undoubtedly increases the advantages of those enjoying higher productivity, lower costs, economies of scale or better resource endowment. Those disadvantaged in these respects find their imports rising and their exports dwindling, to the detriment of employment and standards of life. If they are not prepared to meet the competition by working harder, earning less or saving more, if the scale of adjustment needed in these directions is socially unacceptable, the theoretical remedy is to shift resources into new activities where the disadvantages are less. But such activities are not necessarily easy to find; they too may favour producers who have cheap labour available (transistors) or may require massive amounts of capital expenditure without quick prospects of profit (aeronautics). Moreover the new industries, if left uncontrolled, are unlikely to develop in the same places as the declining ones so that the shift means moving population and leaving behind derelict areas – or even derelict countries.

As a result the free world inevitably produces pressures for its own limitation. In a country which is losing power those who are disadvantaged organise themselves into pressure groups and lobbies which demand government action to protect them from the normal operation of market forces. Much the same argument is heard in countries which, although developing, are not growing as fast as they wish and resent the terms of business imposed on them by the strong, often in the shape of foreign-owned companies. It is argued that economics should be made to fit human beings instead of human beings having to be sacrificed on the altars of economic law. The onus on governments to act is strengthened by the prevalent belief that they should and can sustain demand; state-controlled industries in particular are expected to be run in the general interest even if this means making a loss. Protection takes many forms of which tariffs and quotas are the most obvious, along with subsidies to save uncompetitive industries from the need to shed workers. Some of the protective schemes proposed are initially justified as interim measures designed merely to slow down the impact of change and make the process of adjustment gentler. But the adjustment is seldom completed within the time-span proposed and the temporary is apt to become permanent. Moreover government action to stimulate a flagging economy may easily lure workers into patterns of employment and wages which are not sustainable in the long run, thus aggravating the ultimate problem. The overall net effect is to increase rigidity and make change harder to bring about.

But no country is self-sufficient in every respect; the Soviet Union may possess almost all the raw materials needed in modern society, but it is anxious to speed up its growth by importing knowledge. The most vulnerable are those which cannot feed themselves. Countries which refuse to buy in the cheapest market, where resources are being used most effectively, not merely impoverish themselves. If they bar or impede cheap imports in order to avoid social disruption, they deprive the producers of those cheaper goods of a market and hence of an opportunity to earn money for buying the other goods which such producers desire to have. Any official interference with the free flow of commerce tends to breed resentment and invite official interference by other governments in retaliation. International trade becomes a matter of inter-governmental bargaining (and recrimination!) in which countries most dependent on external supplies are at a disadvantage. Many of the opportunities for doing business which private entrepreneurs would have found if left to themselves, go undeveloped and the total amount of wealth-creating activity is less than it might have been. These developments need not of themselves end in war but states which confess their weakness by obstinately impeding change create a risk that stronger states which stand to gain from change will challenge them with violence. Yet prophecies of ultimate doom are not likely to have much inhibiting effect once unemployment and idle resources prove persistent or are on the increase. The individuals concerned seldom understand the underlying causes of their misfortunes and, even if they do, prefer quick, easy and superficial palliatives to less comfortable but more permanent cures. Politicians may know better but if they are anxious for popularity will be under great temptation to prefer the short term to the long. Even authoritarian rulers nowadays have to produce results if they are to keep power.

There are two situations in which these restrictive forces can more easily be held in check. One occurs when the world or a substantial part of it is dominated by a powerful state which throws its weight on the side of free movement, as Britain did in the nineteenth century and the United States during the period covered by this book – the situation described by those whom it disadvantages as 'imperialism'. By making theories of free movement orthodox and by offering advantages to other states which engage in it, such a state can encourage its spread and maintenance, even if it does not actually compel its neighbours by force to open their doors. The other situation, already mentioned, occurs when growth is both fast and widespread, bringing full employment and expanding demand, thereby reducing the attraction of restrictions. That is what makes so important the question whether sustained growth is practicable.

2 The prospects for growth

For twenty or more years after the Second World War, the free economies appeared to have escaped from the traditional trade cycle of the industrialised world, with its alternation of booms and depressions. As has been seen (p. 203) growth was both faster and steadier than at any previous period. Was this merely due to the time needed to catch up with the demand which had had to go unfilled since 1939 (and to some extent since 1929)? If so, why did it continue so much longer than it had done after 1919? How far was it affected by the new recognition on the part of governments that they could and should sustain demand by intervention? Did the rate of technological innovation speed up or was it merely that an unusually large number of such innovations which had already been pioneered, mainly in the US, had still to be brought into use elsewhere? What was the effect of the spread of state capitalism in mixed economies? In 1962 the answer was still uncertain. Today it looks more and more as though a combination of all these (and maybe other) factors made the boom more sustained than any of its predecessors without however making it permanent. The urgent question for the present, though one to which the answer can only become clear in the future, is what caused growth to slow down and how it can be restarted. Anyone who could provide the answer might seem to have his success assured – unless of course that answer required too many people to act too much against the grain.

The problem of how to increase the rate of growth (i.e. the rate at which output is increasing per head of population) is the problem of how to bring about an increase in real demand which will justify bringing back into operation existing though unused resources of labour and equipment or installing new capacity. If the increased demand were such as to be capable of satisfaction from the resources standing idle, the problem would be much simpler, but of course the forces making for change mean that it never is. For the most part the need is to instal new machinery, to bring fresh land into cultivation and to train or retrain workers in new techniques. If the demand is created without this being done, the result is an increase in the amount of money (credit, etc.) available without a corresponding increase in the quantity of goods available to meet it and/or imports of the goods which are in demand but cannot be supplied from home resources. The attempt to create growth simply by stimulating demand is therefore apt to result in either inflation or a balance of payments crisis or both.

The evidence in this book strongly suggests that healthy growth occurs where it is led by investment. A number of reservations have however to be made.

(a)   Only a relatively small part of what is usually described as 'investment' consists in the installation of new productive capacity. Over 50 per cent consists in non-industrial building. How much the latter does to stimulate output and efficiency is arguable – and variable. The effect of new and better schools is easy to see. The same would be true of hospitals if most of the patients in them belonged to the active working force. It is hard to say whether new and better houses cause their inmates to work better. Of course, building means employing contractors and labourers and as a result stimulating demand generally; in the past, growth has often gone hand in hand with building booms.

(b)   Though investment appears at first sight to be an alternative to consumption, one is soon translated into the other. For much of the cost of providing the new equipment turns at the second if not the first remove into the salaries and wages of the people involved in making or installing it, or obtaining the raw materials for it, or into the dividends received by those who have lent money to pay for all the steps connected with its installation. Thus all kinds of investment stimulate demand while 'productive' investment also provides the means for satisfying increased demand more efficiently than before. If the phasing of the two processes gets out of line, investment can be inflationary. The same is true of investment on a scale which demands more from the sectors of industry making capital goods than they are capable of producing. The higher the rate of investment, the higher the rate of saving needed to go with it.

(c)   Productive investment does not automatically result in growth. There is certainly no fixed ratio between the two; one cannot say that a certain amount of investment will result in a certain amount of growth or even (as rash speculators have often found to their cost) in any growth at all. The purpose of the investment must be to make at competitive prices goods for which there is or will be a demand. This prescription is reminiscent of the advice to tourists: 'Never see more than half the things which the guide-book says you should but make sure it is the right half.' Judgment, knowledge and luck are needed in deciding what comes into the right category – and all three are seldom present together.

(d)   Growth can result just as well from better use of existing equipment as from the installation of new. Indeed in an economic and social climate in which existing equipment is being used wastefully, new equipment, if installed, is unlikely to be used to capacity and this prospect will of course discourage investors from installing it. Lack of success in investment is often due to faulty use of installed equipment by either management or labour or both. This undoubted fact has led to the view that investment is not a primary cause of growth and even to the view that investment is a consequence rather than a cause. Undoubtedly the most favourable climate for investment is a 'virtuous spiral' such as the Federal Republic enjoyed in the 1950s (p. 129) or else a situation in which a number of external economies (and particularly the US) are booming, so that exports are easy and profitable. If the climate does not encourage efficiency, it is unlikely to encourage investment, and vice versa. This makes it hard to believe that much growth is likely without productive investment and even if a high investment rate is not bound to result in a high rate of growth, such a rate is unlikely to develop where productive investment is low.

If investment is so closely connected with growth, one might expect that all eyes would be focused on and every incentive given to it. Yet comparison between countries and periods shows that the proportion of resources devoted to it vary widely and it is hard to believe that the lower figures always represent the maximum which is desirable. What holds investment back?

In free economies investment generally occurs because the people responsible for deciding on it judge that there will in the foreseeable future be enough demand to take up the extra output resulting from it. Nobody in his senses would lay out money in investment if he thought that the products of it would remain unused, or could only be disposed of at a price which did not bring an adequate return on the cost of production (adequacy being judged chiefly by the return available on the money if laid out in alternative ways). There are therefore several possible reasons why investment does not occur.

(a) The potential investors may fail to see where promising openings for investment exist or, if they see them, may judge the potential profitability wrongly. Britain after 1870 is a notable example. She was investing a smaller proportion of her net GNP than Germany and the US and in addition placing abroad a much higher proportion of what she did invest. As a result she gained a large invisible income but failed to keep abreast of competitors in such industries as chemicals, electric equipment and the internal combustion engine. Some British businessmen may have seen the potentialities but have been sufficiently well off already to make unattractive the effort and risk involved in innovating.

(b) Growth is ultimately inseparable from technical innovation, the introduction of new products and new methods of production. Such innovation depends on research and discovery (inadequate expenditure on research before 1914 may partly explain the British failure just described). There is no reason why discoveries should be made at a regular rate. The faster they come, the greater the chances for growth (provided that the money and other resources needed to introduce them can be made available). The problem however for most countries is not to discover new products and techniques but to introduce ones already discovered and applied elsewhere. All the same investment may flag and growth slow down in a particular country, in proportion as the available stock of innovations has been applied.

(c) Innovating is often less profitable than continuing to sell products for which the demand has been established. In recent years few firms have made big profits by developing new designs for airliners, nuclear power plants or computers. Yet any design has to be innovated before it can become established, so that, although in the short term innovation may be risky for the individual firm, failure to innovate is likely in the long term to mean loss of sales for a country's industry. Yet once the yardstick of profitability is discarded, it is hard to find another reliable means of telling how to use resources wisely.

(d) The claims of investment on resources have always had to compete with the claims of other things. Today, as in the past, there are three main rival claims; private consumption, public consumption (including particularly all the welfare services) and defence. Our epoch is notable for the growth in the second of the three. Even authoritarian states cannot altogether disregard the expectations of their population, while in the free world the view has become established that every human being is entitled as of right to a minimum level of welfare and comfort which the State should provide if other sources are inadequate or non-existent. Trade unions and professional associations regard it as their duty to protect by organised pressure the living standards of their members regardless of what is happening to the competitive position of the country in the world. Defence is more expensive than ever, though this book has shown how reluctant most peoples are to spare for it the amounts thought necessary by the strategists. The net result is a continuous battle for the allocation of inadequate resources, in which the advocates of consumption (both public and private) tend to come off best. The future is sacrificed to the present. This is particularly the case if for any reason growth slows up or a higher proportion of resources has to be devoted to a particular sector like oil, so that there is relatively less to distribute elsewhere; cutting defence or investment is much easier to effect than cutting consumption.

Not only does this mean that, in the trade-off, investment receives less than might, on a long-term view, be wise. The total pressure of demand for resources exceeds the supply and governments lack the authority and firmness of purpose needed to bring the two into line. We have got into the habit of thinking that, because some proposed activity looks rational or pleasurable or humane, it should be embarked on, and do not stop to make sure that the necessary resources are there to be made available. The argument that they are not there (or can only be made available by transfer from some other use which it has not been decided to abandon) seldom admits of demonstrable proof and the would-be spenders get the benefit of the doubt.

This does something to explain the chronic inflation which has plagued the free world since the war. But policies of deflation and monetary restraint, with which governments seek to restrain inflation, are inimical to investment, since they not only involve high rates of interest but create the impression that demand is going to fall, or at least only expand slowly. Yet investors can only afford to borrow money at such rates if they see a prospect of demand expanding to absorb the additional output at the high prices they will need to charge in order to break even. Instead there is agitation in the opposite direction for statutory limitation of prices in order to prevent the cost of living from rising further. Moreover profits are regarded with suspicion, regardless of the fact that it is out of them that many firms find the funds for investment.

For a country faced with runaway inflation, deflation and monetary restraint may provide the best short-term way of escaping disaster. But as a long-term policy, deflation is itself a recipe for disaster because it is bound to cut down severely the extent to which the country's productive equipment is renovated and extended. Yet without an adequate level of renewal and extension, a country cannot hope to keep abreast of its competitors. Its growth will slow down, its exports decline, its currency depreciate in value, its imports become more expensive, its living standards fall and internal strife sharpen as each section of the population struggles to shift the pain of that fall on to the other sections. The correct remedy in such a situation is of course to attack the roots of inflation by cutting consumption, both public and private. Societies which have been living beyond their means must reduce their standards, not simply to make these match their means but to make possible an expansion of those means. In such a situation living standards are bound to fall, no matter what option is chosen, as the mistakes which have already been made proceed to take effect. But if the fall is induced deliberately and if the resources thereby saved are transferred to investment, there is more prospect of the fall proving temporary rather than permanent.

When in a mixed economy investment flags in the private sector, the demand is often heard that the state should step in and make good the shortfall so as to ensure that adequate provision is made for the future. But such a step, if taken in isolation, would only increase the total demand on resources and stoke inflation. Other forms of demand need to be cut by as much and more, so as to get an adequate level of investment and at the same time reduce the total call on resources. The crucial question is whether a government in a free society can prove strong enough to carry through such a shift of resources. The size of it should not be exaggerated, since, as has been said, the part of investment which is directly productive and needs to be increased is relatively small. On the other hand experience suggests that it is not something which can in a free society be successfully imposed by law on a public unconvinced of the need for it. The ultimate question is whether a society which refuses to accept the consequences of freedom in the economic sphere can remain free in the political one – or at any rate do so and hope to prosper.

Transferring resources from demand to investment of course means cutting demand, yet the expectation that demand will increase is what induces private-sector entrepreneurs to invest. Is there not then a danger that, although resources are set free for investment, they will not be used, or else used for other purposes than to improve productive efficiency? This is a tricky problem, though perhaps less so in practice than in theory. The ideal way of resolving it is for the extra production to be absorbed in exports. Moreover, as has been said, investors should be able to rely on the money which they lay out turning in due course into demand. There is certainly a danger that excessive investment will turn into excessive home demand which in due course will have to be curbed ('Stop' and 'Go' policies). As always, much depends on the balance between saving and spending. And when interference with the laws of the market has gone as far as it has in most 'free' economies, the process of reversing engines may well itself involve a certain temporary disregard of those laws and hence action by the government (e.g. in investment) since, being in less immediate danger of bankruptcy, it can afford to do so in a way in which private concerns cannot.

Note

Only after this section had been written did I read *Financing Industrial Investment*, by John C. Carrington and George T. Edwards (Macmillan, 1979). They argue, with impressive statistical backing, that a major reason for the more rapid growth of Japan, West Germany and France in recent years, as compared with the USA and Britain, lies in the different methods used in the two groups of countries for transforming savings into investment. In the Anglo-Saxon ones, the raising of funds for productive investment is largely left to industry itself; the banks do not regard it as their function to provide long-term capital. Much of the saving is done by households, and the resulting funds go to building societies, insurance companies and pension funds, whence it is largely returned to individuals for spending on consumption. Investment and unit trusts buy stock in the market but do not make loans to industry. In so far as private savings are deposited with banks, they are largely passed (through the purchase of government stock) to the public sector, where again they are largely used through welfare benefits in consumption.

In the other three countries, by contrast, the banks are a major focus of savings which they hand on in the form of long-term fixed-interest loans to industry. As a result, such savings are more likely to reach enterprises which can invest them with profit. Moreover companies know that their chances of obtaining further finance from outside depends on their satisfying the close scrutiny of the banks. Short- and even medium-term loans are inadequate for financing re-equipment or expansion because enterprises do not feel able to use such loans in acquiring fresh plant which will not generate profits quickly enough to repay the loans by the time these fall due.

This involves two practices which are regarded with traditional misgiving in Britain. One is that the banks are borrowing short and lending long. The other is that companies commit themselves to paying the interest on a higher proportion of their total borrowings at fixed rates, thus leaving themselves with less scope for adjusting payments in bad years. But it can be argued that the proof of the pudding is in the eating; it is the economies which have engaged in such practices which have prospered, not those which have fought shy of them (but this may be because in an economy which is for other reasons successful such practices lose their dangers).

I am convinced that the diagnosis contains an element of truth and that British arrangements for making savings available more easily as long-term finance for productive investment (and less easily available for consumption) need to be improved. Past experience in my opinion shows that private enterprise has failed over a long period to invest on a large enough scale to keep the country up to date and one reason for this has been the lack of adequate pressure for investment outlets from holders of unemployed money.

On the other hand:

(a)   A major reason for lack of investment in Britain is the number of factors eroding profit – high taxation and social service contributions, wage claims made without regard to their effect on ability to sell in international competition, low productivity, high government expenditure leading to inflation and so to high rates of interest and to attempts to hold down profit margins.

(b)   The relatively low level of profit aggravates the fact that the essential work of pioneering new products and processes is for a number of reasons apt to be expensive and to result in low profits or none at all. Consequently it is only in specially favourable economic climates that private enterprise can be relied on to engage in the investment needed if the society is to prosper in future years. (c)   Experience in both mixed and controlled economies suggests that a great deal of waste will result if decision-making about innovative investment is put into the hands of officials who take decisions on rational (which means largely theoretical) criteria without having to risk their own money or careers on being right. Of course the waste which occurs when private enterprise does the innovating escapes notice because individuals going bankrupt attract less publicity – and stigma!

Even if bankers and financiers in Britain were to copy their fellows in West Germany and Japan and play an active part in deciding where to invest, their previous lack of experience might well prevent them (initially at any rate) from achieving an equal degree of success.

3   Is growth desirable?

In the 1950s people were so exhilarated by the experience of fast and continuing growth that their chief concern was whether it would continue. But with the 1960s a reaction set in. Voices began to be heard questioning the possibility and indeed the desirability of unlimited growth, stressing its threat to the world's resources, none of which are infinite, as well as the damage which might result to the environment. Congestion and pollution became painfully familiar. There was mounting concern about the harm which might be done by bringing new products and processes into use before the dangers and side-effects had been investigated adequately. For some, conservation became the watchword rather than progress, while others argued that it was more important to spread existing resources equally than to increase them. These warning voices have been reinforced since it became obvious that mankind had taken its future supplies of energy far too much for granted.

A society should certainly seek to be humane as well as efficient. If the pursuit of growth and the free movement of men, money and goods means giving overriding priority to profit-making, there is plenty of evidence that competition is an inadequate safeguard against exploitation. The poor, the old, the weak, the ignorant, even the feckless all need protection. 'Let the buyer beware' is only a justifiable maxim if he knows what to beware of and can afford the alternatives. Again, there can be a case for conducting activities at a loss if they serve desirable social purposes (provided other enterprises can supply enough profits to offset that loss). It is only a small step to say that uncompetitive industries should be kept in operation to provide employment for their workers and save the latter from having to shift. The doctrine of 'each according to his needs' can be used to justify gearing wages to the cost of living rather than to the recipients' performance or the employers' ability to pay. Just as it is thought justifiable to counterbalance by taxation above-average ability to earn, so there is a case for limiting the free use of land if it produces conurbations here and derelictions there.

Conservation and planning both seek to make man use his resources more rationally and look before he leaps. No sensible person will quarrel with this broad aim. They do however involve interfering with human initiative and creativity. They imply an appeal to reason and better nature against the lust to acquire. Not all the persons appealed to will comply voluntarily, so that they can only be effective if backed by sanctions and compulsion which usually need to be undertaken by the state or by a state-authorised body. Conservationists and planners, to get their way, must either have state power at their command or be able to influence those who do. More regulation undoubtedly means more regulators while the drive to achieve equality of treatment must continually tend to increase the size of the area over which comparisons are drawn in the process of seeing whether treatment is equal. For the public or their representatives to have any say over what happens complicates procedures and slows up action. Thus both planning and social justice mean an increase in bureaucracy and in the gap between 'them' and 'us'. Moreover conservation implies a lack of confidence in our ability to do better than our ancestors, a fear of the future instead of a faith in it, and can easily degenerate into mere opposition to change as such.

To make growth more rational and circumspect is one thing; it is another to argue against growth altogether. There can be no denying that, if growth were to continue at its present rates indefinitely, a time would come when it would exhaust resources and lead to conflict over scarce valuables. But in most fields the danger is still some way in the future. Projections of population sizes and of demands for food or energy are notoriously liable to error, while human ingenuity in finding substitutes for scarce resources (especially when there is a strong incentive to do so) should not be underrated. Even the most fervent opponent of growth would hardly advocate halting it if doing so would mean leaving large sections of the world's population below 'subsistence level' – whatever that essentially relative term may mean. The rich can only afford to buy more from the poor if they themselves are getting richer and not poorer. As the prevalence of inflation indicates, mankind, whether in free, mixed or command economies, has little inclination to stop making demands which can only be satisfied if growth continues. Even the relative minority who are content with what they themselves have desire to see more money spent on 'good causes' and culture. Not to expect improvement means abandoning hope of progress and it is asking a lot of the average man to expect him to be satisfied with improvements confined exclusively to the quality of life and involving no increase in the total quantity of available material resources.

Any economy in which all units operated at a loss would soon find inflation racing out of hand, with exports falling and imports rising as its currency steadily lost value. If some parts are to operate at a loss and others not to engage in gainful activity at all, the remaining parts have to make all the greater gain and operate all the more efficiently. Resources for humanitarian and cultural and other non-gainful activities can only be provided if the productive sectors of the economy have become efficient enough to satisfy the basic needs not only of the persons who work in them but of all the rest of the community as well. More resources for non-gainful activities can only be made available if the productive sectors become more efficient still. Theoretically this need not involve growth in total GNP; exactly the same amount could be provided by fewer people. But in practice an increase in the total would make it infinitely easier to transfer extra resources to the non-gainful sector.

If the aim should be to concentrate on redistributing wealth rather than on producing it, then (apart from the question whether this will not result in swelling consumption and demand rather than investment and supply — if a rich man gives a penny to a beggar, the chances of it being saved rather than spent go down) the problem arises of what international body is going to do the redistribution and how it will acquire the authority to impose sacrifices on nations which do not feel a compulsive moral obligation to restrict themselves for the benefit of others. Power and wealth are close companions and people who possess power are under a constant corrupting temptation to do as they like; codes of morality and prudence may restrain them up to a point but justifications for evading these are notoriously easy to find. The problems of a society with slow or zero growth (whether demographically or materially) are formidable and a single country which took a deliberate decision to move towards such rates might well find that it could not do so without losing political status or halt the process at a point of its own choosing. And if the human appetite for acquisition is to be curbed in any particular area or respect, how can this be achieved without serious inroads on personal freedom and initiative? The attack on growth comes close to being an attack on the human condition (or, as earlier generations would have put it, 'original sin'). History suggests that, although this is an attack which needs continual renewing, success in it can never be more than relative.

4 The days of horse and candle are over

In November 1834 Sir Robert Peel, travelling 'post-haste', took thirteen days to get from Rome to London. Agricola, the Roman governor of Britain in AD 66, probably took little longer. Fifty years later the time had been cut to a day and a half, while now it could be two hours. A missile could reach America from Russia in twenty minutes. For the world's political organisation still to be much as it was in Peel's era is anomalous; the days of horse and candle are over. For many modern industries most single countries offer too small a market. Few individual states can afford to protect themselves on their own. An increase in international organisation is inevitable, which is one reason why the enthusiasts for smallness find themselves fighting an uphill battle.

Many international organisations of course already exist. But the majority of them, in deference to the legal sovereignty of each member state, require unanimity before any substantial decision can become valid. Experience has by now demonstrated that in such circumstances achievement will be slow. But sovereignty has, to a much greater extent than is generally admitted, been eroded by technology and lost much of its practical importance. For the right of a state to take its own decisions matters less than its ability to carry out those decisions, and that ability is more and more dependent on the co-operation of its neighbours. If states want to take advantage of the possibilities afforded by modern communications, they have in fact two choices. One is to preserve the right of veto in international bodies but with increasing frequency to refrain from exercising it, on the ground that, if everyone insists on having his own way all the time, an organisation whose overall objectives are worth while (and if they are not, it should not exist) will be rendered impotent or moribund. The other is to accept agreed rules by which valid decisions can be taken without formal unanimity (such as the EEC's 'qualified majority'). There is not really much difference between the two.

The EEC method of advance seems more promising than that of following the American example and seeking straight away to set up a political Federation. De Gaulle may have gone too far when he said that for such a development a federator would be essential with enough strength, resources and skill to bring the constituent units together. The thirteen colonies were not induced to accept the Federal Constitution of 1787 by the power, influence or skill of any dominating individual or state but by fear of what might happen to them, particularly at the hand of foreign enemies, if they did not accept some closer bonds than those involved in the original Confederation. 'We must all hang together or, most assuredly, we shall all hang separately.' But in Western Europe not only is a single dominating individual or state lacking. Fears of domination by both the US and the Soviet Union exist, but neither have proved acute enough to enable the advocates of unity to surmount differences distinctly greater than those which faced the Founding Fathers.

The basic obstacle to integration is that voiced by de Gaulle (with whom Enoch Powell no doubt sympathises). It is that a group of men can only form an effective community if they have more than geography and government to unite them. One barrier in particular which modern communications have done little to surmount is that set up at the Tower of Babel, and along with language go history, culture and institutions. All combine in varying ways to produce a sense of common interest which inclines individuals to accept the subordination of private to public advantage within their own community in a way they will not do between communities (see p. 114). It also inclines individuals to react spontaneously on similar lines to the problems facing the community, thus increasing substantially the chances of an effective response. (One does not automatically qualify to be described as a 'racist' by fearing that this sense of common interest will be weakened, the spontaneous reaction diluted and effective responses impeded, if too many people with different backgrounds are allowed to enter the community too fast.) The coercive power of a government has to rest upon a shared loyalty of this kind. Such a loyalty hardly exists (and some would say cannot exist) between states, so that international co-operation may be thought destined to remain co-operation between individual sovereign governments and attempts to transcend this level to be doomed to failure.

Existing states and governments are undeniably greedy of loyalty. The task of getting agreement on common policies and putting them into practice, of persuading minorities to accept majority decisions, is not easy and politicians naturally fear that the development of competing loyalties to supranational causes may make it harder. How much easier to win loyalty by arousing fear and xenophobia! Ministers – and indeed all leaders of pressure groups – are in the position of trustees whose duty it is to be selfish on behalf of the people for whose advantage they hold their positions. To expect states to surrender powers eagerly to a supranational body is to invite disappointment. Even where some system of decision by qualified majority has been accepted, the other members of a supranational organisation would be wise to think twice before insisting on compliance from a recalcitrant one which considered that 'very important issues' were at stake. For they might find themselves faced with a choice between accepting the objector's resignation and, like the US in 1861, using violence to prevent it. Even a national government has difficulty in enforcing the law against any large organised body of its subjects who are resolute against compliance.

All the same, governments and citizens alike have to realise that they cannot expect to enjoy the undoubted benefits obtainable from international co-operation unless they are ready to make considerable compromises with the views of others. Moreover loyalties and a sense of community are not immutable. Governments have done as much and more to create nations as nations have to create governments. It is for example governments (and the state-wide educational and administrative systems organised by them) which are responsible for everyone in a country speaking the same language (where they do). A sense of loyalty to humanity at large and to regional units like Western Europe certainly exists though it is weaker than loyalties to individual states and does not exert the attraction of Christianity or Marxism. The existence of an organisation can help to develop it, particularly if that organisation can be shown to bring advantages. Yet the organisation's effectiveness partly depends on the loyalty it can inspire. This is the hen-and-egg problem of international relations and, like most such problems, is not susceptible of a clearcut solution. The organisation and the loyalty must develop side by side and the process is bound to be gradual.

There can be no doubt that Western Europe is growing in uniformity (e.g. styles of life and dress), interdependence and awareness of common interests. Equally undoubtedly the early successes of the EEC gave a misleading impression of the speed with which common supranational institutions could develop. The reluctance of member States to surrender the right to take their own decisions, particularly in such matters as the management of their economies, has become more patent; the Council of Ministers has gained power at the expense of the Commission. The slowing down of growth and the rise in unemployment has made it harder to adopt policies which offer long-term benefits at the cost of short-term dislocation. The danger is that the Community, unable to agree on major matters, will fill up its time with minor ones, become entangled in its own procedures and move so slowly as to excite impatience and derision, thereby giving ammunition to its enemies. Yet the reasons which originally brought it into being are still valid and are unlikely to lose their force. We would do well to stop arguing about the wisdom of membership and concentrate on making the organisation work effectively.

Integration into larger units undeniably increases the chances of disputes between members being settled peacefully; war between France and (West) Germany is often said to have become unthinkable. This progress of course may seem to have its danger. The Cordell Hull school of thought believed that the best way of getting change effected was by small but continual instalments. In much the same way disputes were less likely to be dangerous if they remained small-scale; even if they ended in violence, the damage would be limited. But if the antagonists are integrated into a big state and can mobilise the support of its government for their cause, may not a small dispute end as a big one? Such a development is not however inevitable. The rulers of a big state may well hesitate to put the whole country at risk for the sake of a small section. The time when small disputes become dangerous is when two major states are on collision courses and tend as a result to treat all minor quarrels as symptoms of the underlying clash of interests, with the result that compromises which could easily in a better atmosphere have been reached are rejected for fear that they will not end the antagonism but merely leave the compromiser weaker in future encounters.

Short of a threat from outer space or a World Conqueror (whose Empire would probably be as transient as Alexander's) there is no prospect of creating a worldwide state. A worldwide machinery for peaceful change depends therefore on agreement between the superpowers, which as often as not is lacking. It has been argued that war has not thus far 'shown any discernable long-term trend towards greater costliness', measured in terms of the proportion of the gross national product of the combatants which it diverts from productive to destructive uses. But it is highly questionable whether such a conclusion is valid for the age of nuclear weapons, with their radioactive consequences. Mankind, having failed over so many millennia to eliminate the use of violence in its affairs, may be unlikely to succeed altogether in doing so from now on. But our continued existence depends on reducing the scale on which it is used. What are the prospects of avoiding major collisions between superpowers?

5 The limits of co-existence

A major theme of this book has been the process by which the two superpowers came to realise that they must co-exist. 'Co-existence' denotes the recognition that, with nuclear missiles, force has become an unprofitable means of effecting major change (though still held in reserve as a means of last resort for resisting such change). That does not of course imply that there is no longer going to be any change or that force will never be involved in bringing it about. The Communist states confidently expect the world to change to their advantage, as the contradictions which they believe to be inherent in capitalism develop. It is part of their creed that the inevitable is to be accelerated by judicious action. They argue that struggle can be maintained without necessarily leading to large-scale war and that, if such war breaks out, the blame will lie with their opponents.

As has been said (p. 60), their ideal is 'salami tactics' – a series of encroachments, none quite important enough to justify resorting to war for its prevention, yet adding up in the long run to a significant shift in power. Their own preponderance in 'conventional' weapons makes this strategy all the more attractive, as does the fact that guerrilla warfare is more easily practised by those who seek to undermine the *status quo* than by those who seek to uphold it. No doubt they also consider that the power of public opinion militates against the governments of the free world embarking on action which might lead to nuclear war and consider this a weakness which invites exploitation by pacifist movements and similar methods aptly called 'the Trojan Dove'. Moreover the advocates of allowing a people to decide freely for themselves on their form of government can find the ground cut from under their feet if that people decides, in apparent freedom, in favour of an authoritarian system.

The crucial question is therefore whether the nations of the free world can afford to let this strategy run its course without at some stage turning what appears to be a minor issue into a major one and whether they can devise any way of halting it without using nuclear weapons. Otherwise they may find – as some of their inhabitants are already afraid of finding – that they have allowed the balance of power to tip so far against them as to make war a forlorn hope and leave them merely with the choice of becoming red or dead.

The leaders of the Communist world are well aware of what a nuclear war would be like and are as anxious to avoid it as the leaders of the

West. But, as with Germany before 1939, the problem is to convince them that there is a point at which the West will fight rather than give way. There are two obstacles to carrying conviction. The first is that, unless the West is to get the worst of every negotiation, it must often give the impression that it is ready to fight when in fact it is not. Dulles's remarks about going to the brink without getting into war may sound foolhardy but are only an extreme way of expressing a tactic which often has much to recommend it. The second obstacle is the doubt as to whether there *is* any point (short of resistance to an actual attack on their own territory) at which the peoples of the West would be ready to fight, at any rate until they had been given a practical demonstration of dire consequences flowing from a refusal to fight.

The problem of the free world at present is that its ideas and ideals seem to have lost their appeal, so that the people brought to power by change, particularly in the Third World, are seldom prepared to support it. This is partly a by-product of the decolonising process and might therefore be expected to be temporary, were it not for the fact that that process is increasingly seen by the Third World as one which must extend beyond politics into economics. In the North–South debate the less developed countries are demanding a reform of the world economic system at the expense of the rich whom the leaders of the East gleefully portray as being identical with the West. Consequently Communism seems to the newcomers a more natural ally than Liberalism, even though the countries which have become free from the domination of London, Paris, Brussels and Lisbon are quite alive to the danger of falling under the domination of Moscow or Peking.

What is more, free institutions depend for their success on a fairly high level of public spirit, honesty, mutual respect and self-restraint in the societies which are trying to operate them. Such conditions cannot be produced to order, or at short notice. It is hard to deny that, where they are absent, authoritarian methods of rule and command economies are more likely to produce order and prosperity than are parliamentary or presidential democracy. In a way this is a paradox because the defects in Stalinist Communism are becoming widely recognised and the respect which the rulers of Communist states profess for Marxism is degenerating into lip-service, so that free institutions might be expected to regain popularity by contrast. But as free institutions have failed to produce complete freedom for everyone everywhere, their advocates are treated as hypocrites and there is a persistent belief that Socialism, by bringing greater equality, will lead to greater freedom. Its failure to do so thus far is regarded as an aberration rather than a congenital defect. In any case many people, if given the choice, would prefer prosperity to freedom.

Moreover the struggle against inflation and the erosion of living standards which deflation brings are undermining the consensus on which free societies are founded and, if prolonged, could easily result in a chaos to which authoritarian rule would seem preferable. This tendency will be exacerbated if more suppliers of essential raw materials manage to follow the examples of the producers of oil and coffee and demand substantially higher prices for their wares. For by reducing the amount of money available in the free economies for spending on other things, this will intensify the efforts of individuals and groups to make sure that the cuts in living standards are made by others rather than themselves. The Soviet Union, being more self-sufficient, is less vulnerable.

This process might easily produce civil war in one or more Western countries. In the Communist world also internal violence, though less likely, cannot be entirely ruled out; it could be sparked off by frustration over the denial of liberties or disappointment at failure to fulfil hopes of rising living standards, or struggles over the succession to the top places. The superpowers would find it harder to keep out of such conflicts than they have done in the Middle East and South-East Asia. The confrontation need not escalate into nuclear war but could obviously do so, especially if more countries acquire nuclear weapons. The danger about local feuds is that fears for personal security and desires for revenge cause passions to rise. Compromises then become unacceptable so that there is no solution except the subjugation, expulsion or extirpation of the weaker side. Participants in such quarrels would sooner destroy the world than let the enemy win. It is a humiliating thought that, despite all the efforts put into the study of psychology, sociology and crisis management, mankind is still unable to 'defuse' such situations.

To live in peace and prosperity people only need to exercise reason and self-restraint both as individuals and as members of organisations. But history shows how hard they find it to do this. That makes all the more remarkable the cases described in this book where at least an approximation to such behaviour has been achieved.

Books for further reading

This list of books is designed to help readers who want more information about subjects mentioned in preceding pages. It is confined to books in English.

1   Documents

It is often instructive to read official documents about a particular subject under study. Such documents can be found in:

Documents on International Affairs – published annually for the years 1947–63 by the Royal Institute of International Affairs, London.

Foreign Relations of the United States – published at regular intervals about twenty-five years after the events dealt with in them, by the US State Department, Washington. Those for a single year often occupy several volumes. At present the series goes to 1951.

European Community Treaties – a convenient collection published by Sweet & Maxwell, London, 3rd edn, 1977.

Two documents of particular interest for this period are:

Report of the Committee on European Economic Co-operation (the Franks Committee) (Paris and London, 1947).

Some Factors in the Economic Growth in Europe during the 1950s (Part II of Survey for 1961 by UN Economic Commission for Europe) (UN New York and Geneva, 1962).

2   Memoirs

Illuminating memoirs include:

D. Acheson, *Present at the Creation* (New York, 1970).

K. Adenauer, *Memoirs*, vols I and II (the remaining volumes of the

German edition have not been translated into English) (London, 1966–8).

C. Bohlen, *Witness to History 1929–1969* (New York, 1973).

A. Cadogan (ed. D. Dilks), *Diaries 1938–1945* (London, 1971).

W. Churchill, *The Second World War*, 6 vols (London, 1948–54).

L. D. Clay, *Decision in Germany* (New York, 1950).

P. Dixon, *Double Diploma* (London, 1968).

M. Djilas, *Conversations with Stalin* (London, 1969).

A. Eden, *Full Circle* (London, 1960).

A. Eden, *The Reckoning* (London, 1965).

C. Hull, *Memoirs*, 2 vols (New York, 1948).

G. Kennan, *Memoirs 1925–1950* (New York, 1969). This first contains the text of the 'Long Telegram'.

G. Kennan, *Memoirs 1950–1963* (Boston, 1972).

N. Khrushchev, *Khrushchev Remembers* (London, 1970). This contains the text of the 'Secret Speech'.

W. Leonhardt, *Child of the Revolution* (London, 1957).

H. Macmillan, *Tides of Fortune 1945–1955* (London, 1969).

H. Macmillan, *Riding the Storm 1955–59* (London, 1971).

H. Macmillan, *Pointing the Way 1959–61* (London, 1972).

H. Macmillan, *At the End of the Road 1961–3* (London, 1973).

V. Mićunović, *Moscow Years* (London, 1980).

R. Sherwood, *Roosevelt and Hopkins*, 2 vols (New York, 1949) (originally entitled *The White House Papers*).

H. Truman, *Years of Decisions* (New York, 1955).

H. Truman, *Years of Trial and Hope* (New York, 1956).

3 General books

Useful overall accounts are:

Royal Institute of International Affairs, *Survey of International Affairs*. Several volumes on different subjects cover the period 1939–1946. Thereafter there is a separate volume for each year down to 1963.

P. Calvocoressi, *World Politics since 1945* (3rd edn, London, 1977).

R. Morgan, *West European Politics since 1945* (2nd edn, London, 1980).

D. K. Urwin, *Western Europe since 1945* (London, 1968).

The handiest way of checking individual events and dates is to consult *Keesing's Contemporary Archives*.

4 US foreign policy

The 'orthodox' version of Anglo–American–Russian relations over the years 1941–50 is contained in four books by H. Feis, who had access to the State Department's unpublished archives: *Churchill, Roosevelt, Stalin* (Princeton, 1957); *Between War and Peace, The Potsdam Conference* (Princeton, 1960); *The Atomic Bomb and the End of World War II* (Princeton, 1966); *From Trust to Terror* (New York, 1970).

'Revisionist' views are to be found in W. A. Williams, *The Tragedy of American Diplomacy* (New York, 1962); G. Alperowitz, *Atomic Diplomacy; Hiroshima and Potsdam* (New York, 1967); G. Kolko, *The Politics of War* (London, 1968); D. S. Clemens, *Yalta* (New York, 1970); B. Kuklick, *American Policy and the Division of Germany* (Ithaca, 1972).

These are criticised in R. J. Maddox, *The New Left and the Origins of the Cold War* (Princeton, 1973).

Other books which try to steer a middle course are L. J. Halle, *The Cold War as History* (New York, 1967); J. L. Gaddis, *The US and the Origins of the Cold War* (New York, 1972); L. E. Davis, *The Cold War Begins* (Princeton, 1974); D. Yergin, *Shattered Peace* (London, 1977); J. L. Gaddis, *Russia, the Soviet Union and the United States, an Interpretative History* (New York, 1978). The two last contain useful bibliographies.

The signing of the Atlantic Charter is described in T. A. Wilson, *The First Summit* (Boston, 1969). The text of the Charter can conveniently be found in Churchill, *op. cit.*, III, p. 393. For US aid to Russia, see G. C. Herring, *Aid to Russia 1941–1946* (New York, 1973).

5 Great Britain

E. Barker, *Britain in a Divided Europe* (London, 1972).

V. Bogdanor and R. Skidelsky, *The Age of Affluence 1951–1964* (London, 1970).

J. C. D. Dow, *The Management of the Economy 1945–1960* (London, 1968).

F. S. Northedge, *Descent From Power: British Foreign Policy 1945–73* (London, 1974).

Books for further reading

A. Shonfield, *British Economic Policy Since the War* (Harmondsworth, 1958).

A. Sked and C. Cooke, *Post-war Britain* (Harmondsworth, 1979).

G. D. N. Worswick and P. H. Ady (eds), *The British Economy 1945–50* (Oxford, 1952).

G. D. N. Worswick and P. H. Ady (eds), *The British Economy in the 1950s* (Oxford, 1962).

6 France

J. J. Carré, P. Dubois and E. Malinvaud (tr.), *French Economic Growth* (Stanford, 1976).

A. Horne, *A Savage War of Peace, Algeria 1954–1962* (London, 1977).

D. Pickles, *France, the Fourth Republic* (London, 1955).

D. Pickles, *The Fifth Republic, Institutions and Politics* (London, 2nd edn, 1965).

A. Werth, *De Gaulle* (Harmondsworth, 1960).

P. N. Williams, *Crisis and Compromise, Politics in the Fourth Republic* (London, 1964).

G. Wright, *France in Modern Times* (London, 1960).

7 Italy

M. Grindrod, *Italy* (London, 1968).

F. Willis, *Italy Chooses Europe* (New York, 1971).

E. Wiskemann, *Italy since 1945* (London, 1971).

8 Germany

M. Balfour, *Four-Power Control in Germany 1945–6* (Volume in Survey of International Affairs 1939–1946, ed. A. J. Toynbee, London, 1956).

M. Balfour, *West Germany* (London, 1968, 2nd edn, 1981).

D. Childs, *East Germany* (London, 1969).

D. Childs, *Germany Since 1918* (London, 1971).

L. Edinger, *Kurt Schumacher* (Oxford, 1955).

J. Gimbel, *The American Occupation of Germany, Politics and the Military 1945–1949* (Stanford, 1968).

J. F. Golay, *The Founding of the Federal Republic of Germany* (Chicago, 1958).

A. J. Heidenheimer, *Adenauer and the CDU* (The Hague, 1960).

A. J. Heidenheimer, *The Governments of Germany* (London, 1966).

R. Hiscocks, *Germany Revived* (London, 1966).

N. Johnson, *Government in the Federal Republic of Germany, the Executive at Work* (Oxford, 1973).

J. P. Nettl, *The Eastern Zone and Soviet Policy in Germany* (Oxford, 1951).

G. Pridham, *Christian Democracy in Western Germany* (London, 1977).

T. Prittie, *Adenauer* (London, 1972).

A. Sharp, *The Western Alliance and the Zonal Division of Germany* (London, 1975).

J. Snell, *The Origins of the East–West Dilemma over Germany* (New Orleans, 1959).

K. Sontheimer, *The Government and Politics of West Germany* (London, 1972).

J. Steele, *Socialism With a German Face* (London, 1977).

C. Stern, *Ulbricht* (London, 1965).

H. C. Wallich, *Mainsprings of the German Revival* (New Haven, 1955).

9 The USSR

Z. Brzezinski, *The Soviet Bloc, Unity and Conflict* (2nd edn, London, 1967).

E. Crankshaw, *Khrushchev's Russia* (Harmondsworth, 2nd edn, 1963).

E. Crankshaw, *Khrushchev, a Biography* (London, 1966).

S. Deutscher, *Stalin* (Oxford, 1966).

M. Kaser, *COMECON, Integration Problems of the Planned Economies* (London, 2nd edn, 1967).

A. Maddison, *Economic Growth in Japan and the USSR* (London, 1969).

R. and Z. Medvedev, *Khrushchev, the Years in Power* (London, 1976).

A. Nove, *An Economic History of the USSR* (London, 1969).
A. Nove, *The Soviet Economic System* (London, 1977).
R. W. Pethybridge, *A History of Post-war Russia* (London, 1966).
R. M. Slusser, *The Berlin Crisis of 1961* (Baltimore, 1973).
M. Tatu, *Power and the Kremlin* (London, 1968).
A. Ulam, *Expansion and Co-existence* (London, 1968).

10   Yugoslavia

S. Clissold, *Yugoslavia and the Soviet Union, a Documentary Survey* (Cambridge, 1975).
D. Rusinow, *The Yugoslav Experiment 1948–1974* (London, 1977).
F. Singleton, *Twentieth-century Yugoslavia* (London, 1976).
A. D. Wilson, *Tito's Yugoslavia* (Cambridge, 1979).

11   International economic affairs

R. N. Gardner, *Sterling-Dollar Diplomacy* (Oxford, 2nd edn, 1969).
R. Harrod, *The Life of John Maynard Keynes* (London, 1951).
R. E. Hudec, *The GATT Legal System and World Trade Diplomacy* (New York, 1976).
K. Kock, *International Trade Policy and the GATT 1947–1967* (Stockholm, 1969).
A. Maddison, *Economic Growth in the West* (New York, 1964).
W. H. Parker, *The Super-Powers* (London, 1971).
E. F. Penrose, *Economic Planning for the Peace* (Princeton, 1953).
M. Postan, *An Economic History of Western Europe 1945–1964* (London, 1967).
A. Shonfield, *Modern Capitalism* (London, 1965).
B. Tew, *International Monetary Co-operation 1945–65* (London, 8th edn, 1965).
A. van Dormael, *Bretton Woods, the Birth of a Monetary System* (London, 1978).
The absence of a good book about US economic history since 1945 is remarkable.

12   The Marshall Plan

W. Diebold, *Trade and Payments in Western Europe* (New York, 1952).

J. Gimbel, *The Origins of the Marshall Plan* (Stanford, 1976).

J. M. Jones, *The Fifteen Weeks* (New York, 1964).

H. B. Price, *The Marshall Plan and its Meaning* (Ithaca, 1955).

13   European institutions

N. Beloff, *The General Says No* (Harmondsworth, 1963).

M. Camps, *Britain and the European Community 1955–1963* (Princeton, 1964).

C. Cosgrove, *A Reader's Guide to Britain and the Economic Community* (Bibliography. London, 1970).

V. Curzon, *The Essentials of Economic Integration: Lessons of EFTA Experience* (London, 1974).

W. Diebold, *The Schuman Plan* (New York, 1959).

L. Lister, *Europe's Coal and Steel Community* (New York, 1960).

M. Palmer and J. Lambert, *European Unity, a Study of the European Organizations* (London, 1968).

A. H. Robertson, *European Institutions* (London, 2nd edn, 1966).

A. H. Robertson, *The Council of Europe* (London, 1961).

F. Willis, *France, Germany and the New Europe* (London, 2nd edn, 1968).

14   Strategic questions

C. Bell, *Negotiation from Strength* (London, 1962).

G. Kennan, *Russia, the Atom and the West* (London, 1958).

H. Kissinger, *Nuclear Weapons and Foreign Policy* (New York, 1955).

H. Kissinger, *The Necessity for Choice: Prospects of American Foreign Policy* (London, 1960).

R. E. Osgood, *NATO, The Entangling Alliance* (Chicago, 1962).

15   The Nuremberg Trial

F. Bradley Smith, *Reaching Judgment at Nuremberg* (London, 1977).
W. Maser, *Nuremberg, A Nation on Trial* (London, 1979).

16   Anti-communism in the US

D. Caute, *The Great Fear* (London, 1978).
A. Cooke, *A Generation on Trial: USA v. Alger Hiss* (London, 1950).

17   Suez

S. Lloyd, *Suez 1956: A Personal Account* (London, 1978).
A. Nutting, *No End of a Lesson* (London, 1967).
H. Thomas, *The Suez Affair* (London, 1966).

18   The Cuban crisis

G. Allison, *The Essence of Decision* (Boston, 1971).
S. Dinerstein, *The Making of a Missile Crisis* (Baltimore, 1976).
T. Sorensen, *Kennedy* (London, 1965).
H. Thomas, *Cuba, or The Pursuit of Freedom* (London, 1971).

Material has also been used from the following:
M. Balfour, *Propaganda in War* (London, 1979).
T. Barman, *Diplomatic Correspondent* (London, 1968).
J. Harvey, *The War Diaries of Oliver Harvey* (London, 1978).
D. Healey, 'When Shrimps Learn to Whistle', *International Affairs*, vol. 32, no. 1 (January 1956).
Sir Arthur Lewis, *Growth and Fluctuation 1870–1914* (London, 1978).
A. Milward, *War, Economy and Society 1939–1945* (London, 1977).
R. G. Opie, 'West Germany's Economic Miracle', *Three Banks Review*, March 1962.
Lord Strang, 'Prelude to Potsdam: Reflections on War and Foreign Policy', *International Affairs*, vol. 46, no. 3 (July 1970).
G. Warner, 'From Teheran to Yalta: Reflections on F.D.R.'s Foreign Policy', *International Affairs*, vol. 43, no. 3 (July 1967).

Index

People (e.g. Eden) have been given the style to which they were entitled during the period of the book. Biographical details have been confined to ones relevant to the same period.

Index

Index

Index